TASTING THE WORLD

...ONE COUNTRY AT A TIME

NICOLE J. O'DONNELL

Fathead & Edmund, LLC
Birmingham, AL

Printed in the United States of America

Third Printing, November 2021

ISBN 9798764892528

Front cover photograph by Natalia Lisovskaya
Back cover photographs by (left to right) Tatiana Bralnina,
Konstantin Kopachinsky, and Natalia Lisovskaya
Book design by Nicole O'Donnell
Edited by Patrick O'Donnell
Typography: Mango Tango and Avenir Next Condensed

Fathead & Edmund, LLC
5260 Goldmar Drive
Irondale, AL 35210

www.fatheadandedmund.com

TABLE OF CONTENTS

INTRODUCTION
SECOND EDITION

In January of 2017, I made my first trip to Ho Chi Minh City. (As of writing it's also my only trip, but I hope it won't be my last. The thought of my next meal at Secret Garden on Pasteur Street sometimes keeps me awake at night.) Like most places I have been abroad, you can learn a lot about it in the first few minutes after leaving the airport. During the thirty-minute taxi drive to my Airbnb in District 1, I made three observations about Vietnam's largest city:

- It's very crowded. (But then again, it's one of the most densely-populated cities in the world. What would you expect?)
- There are at least fifty motorbikes on the roads for every one car, and the roads are designed for them. (In such a crowded city, this is a great idea. I can think of a few American cities that could take a page from this book.)
- There is at least one KFC on every single block. (KFC has only 68 locations in Ho Chi Minh City as of writing, but that's hard to believe.)

When it comes to fast-food chicken, the Vietnamese aren't limited to KFC. Popeyes, Texas Chicken (a re-brand of Church's), and a few non-American chains are well-represented. Google "Vietnamese fried chicken" and you'll get results for recipes that include fish sauce, brown sugar, cilantro, and chili sauce (wow that sounds delicious!). But with the exception of a few Korean- and Taiwanese-style variants, the people of Vietnam prefer the same greasy, salty, buttermilk-breaded variety that's so familiar on this side of the pond.

The predilection that Vietnamese people seem to have for American fried chicken reminded me of a sign I saw on my first trip to London two decades earlier, which advertised KFC as having "America's Favorite Fried Chicken!" (Most Americans I know like Chick-Fil-A better, but I'm no expert on the matter.) The major takeaway is that while Americans love their Chinese, Mexican, Italian, and other international cuisines, the affection goes both ways. But we rarely see foreign chains popping up on American soil. Their ubiquity elsewhere in the world is viewed by some as a form of capitalist colonialism.

From my general observations, however, fried chicken is not the favorite food of most Vietnamese people. That honor would go to a more expected contender, pho. People in Vietnam eat pho for breakfast, lunch, dinner, and frequently as a snack. It's not all that uncommon to see a person walking down the sidewalk with a bowl of hot noodle soup the size of a basketball in one hand and a set of chopsticks in the other. That's not surprising. After all, anyone who's ever been to a Vietnamese restaurant in the United States will tell you that pho is a quintessential Vietnamese food. Right?

What *is* a bit surprising is that pho isn't a purely indigenous Vietnamese dish at all. It could be called the fried chicken of the nineteenth century. When the French colonized Vietnam, they brought with them many of their own customs and traditions—recipes included. Among these was pot-au-feu, a French stew made from a rich beef broth and whichever other ingredients were available. And in Vietnam, that included cilantro, spring onion, basil, and red pepper. Pho as we know it today was invented in Hanoi in the 1880s. Hanoi's proximity to the Chinese border allowed rice noodles (a Chinese ingredient) to make their way into it as well.

Does the fact that the people of ancient Vietnam did not eat pho make it any less authentic a national dish? No; it represents the people of this nation and the food that they enjoy. Many other Asian, African, and Latin American national dishes are based upon European counterparts. The reverse is even true; pierogi developed from the dumplings of the Far East that made their way to Poland via the Mongols, and Spanish paella (whose influence on other world cuisines cannot be overstated) was first brought to Spain from the Arab world.

When I released my first edition of this cookbook in 2020, it was met with a flattering amount of praise and a little controversy. The latter included suggestions by many that it was too Eurocentric. This concerned me, as it was something that I actively tried to avoid. But since so many world dishes are based on European standards, I don't think Eurocentrism can be avoided in its entirety. Instead, we can look at a cookbook such as this as a celebration of what the world is today—a seamless and inseparable global community.

For this second edition, I have made an effort to include nutritional information for every recipe. (This isn't designed to be a healthy cookbook, but for those who are health-conscious there are many excellent choices that can be made.) I have also expanded the content to include a total of 200 recipes; those newly included in this edition are Hong Kong, Kashmir, Kosovo, Macau, Micronesia, Palestine, Tajikistan, and Tibet.

Once again, I would like to extend my gratitude to the people involved in the production of this cookbook: Marques Andrews, Harry David, Ildie David, Leah Dueffer, Danny Gray, Rosa Johnson, Rachael Jones, Kathy LaChine, Johnny Lee, Aimee Love, Beth Martin, Elaine Martin, Patrick O'Donnell, Kristey Stoisor, Cliff Tercenio, and Bradford Watson. I also invite anyone reading to contact me at www.fatheadandedmund.com with any input they may have.

As a final word, this cookbook is intended as a living document. As the world changes, and the world's cuisine changes, further editions will reflect their life cycles.

Cook, eat, and enjoy!

HOW TO USE THIS COOKBOOK

Overall, this cookbook resembles most others that you have on your kitchen shelf. I have tried to organize it so that it's as easy to read as possible. For those features that may be a little difficult to understand, here's a brief explanation.

THE THREE NUMBERS NEXT TO THE RECIPE'S NAME

Each recipe is rated based on three parameters: how easy (or difficult) it is to make, how easy (or difficult) it will be to find the ingredients you'll need to make it, and how unusual or exotic the recipe is to the typical American palate. Here's a breakdown:

FIRST NUMBER: DIFFICULTY TO MAKE

1. No special skills are needed.
2. May take a long time or involve a lot of work.
3. A great way to test your ability as a cook!

SECOND NUMBER: AVAILABILITY OF INGREDIENTS

1. You'll be able to find everything you need at your local supermarket.
2. You may need to make a trip to a specialty store.
3. You might have trouble finding what you need to make this.

THIRD NUMBER: EXOTIC LEVEL

1. Something you're likely to be familiar with, or similar to a dish that is.
2. Not something the average American eats every day.
3. For most Americans, it will not be familiar.

SERVING SUGGESTIONS, VARIATIONS, AND TIPS

You will also notice that most of the recipes in this book have sidebars with additional information. Reading these might answer a few questions that you have.

SERVING SUGGESTIONS:

All of the recipes in this cookbook are main dishes. But not all of them are one-pot meals. If you're wondering whether to serve a dish with rice, noodles, potatoes, or something else, this section will help.

VARIATIONS:

National dishes tend to be controversial. Some, according to the people they represent, must be made in a prescribed manner without any deviation. Most, on the other hand, can be prepared using a wider array of ingredients and methods. If there are others, they will be listed here.

TIPS:

I have made an effort to make this a user-friendly cookbook. But there are a few recipes that require a little extra guidance regarding substitutions, cooking methods, or other conventions. Read this section for advice on how a complex recipe can be made simpler.

EUROPE

ALBANIA
FËRGESË TIRANE

Bordered by greece to the south and the balkans to the north and east, Albania's distinctive cuisine is characterized by fresh vegetables and rich cheeses, olive oil and butter, seafood and red meat. Peppers are one Albanian staple found in the country's national dish, Fërgesë Tirane (or "fried cheese of Tirana," Albania's capital city).

1 lb. sirloin steak or other lean cut of beef, cut into small slices
1 small onion, diced
Olive oil, for sautéing
2-3 large tomatoes, peeled, seeded, and chopped
1 large green bell pepper, seeded and sliced
2 Tbsp. butter
½ lb. cheese curds, or a mixture of curds and feta cheese
1-½ tsp. all-purpose flour
Salt and pepper, to taste

In a heavy skillet, heat olive oil over medium-high heat. Add onions and sauté until translucent, about 5 minutes. Add steak, tomatoes, and peppers and cook 5 minutes longer or until steak is medium-rare. Set aside to cool.

Meanwhile, melt butter in another saucepan over medium heat. Add cheese and flour, and season with salt and pepper. Cook slowly until cheese is fully melted, about 3-5 minutes.

Preheat oven to 350 degrees. Combine meat and vegetables with cheese sauce in a covered baking dish. Bake for 15 minutes. Serve immediately.

Per serving: 535 calories, 34 g fat, 18 g saturated fat, 594 mg sodium, 10 g carbohydrates, 49 g protein.

SERVING SUGGESTIONS:

Serve with crusty white bread to sop up cheese sauce.

VARIATIONS:

Albanians traditionally use beef or veal liver in this recipe.

ANDORRA
TRINXAT

2 / 1 / 2
COOK TIME: 1 HOUR
ACTIVE PREP TIME: 5 MINUTES
MAKES 6 SERVINGS

ANDORRA IS A TINY COUNTRY SITUATED IN THE CATALAN REGION ON

the French and Spanish border. The name of its best-known dish, trinxat, translates to "chopped" or "shredded" in Catalan. Traditionally eaten during the cold winter months, this savory cake of shredded cabbage and potatoes seasoned with bacon is an ideal comfort food.

1 head Savoy or other green cabbage, roughly chopped
Salted water, for boiling
3 large potatoes, peeled and chopped
1 head garlic, peeled and thinly sliced
6 slices thick-cut bacon, chopped
Oil, for frying

Bring a large pot of salted water to a boil. Add cabbage and boil for 10 minutes. Add potatoes and continue to boil until potatoes are tender, about 25-30 minutes.

As cabbage and potatoes boil, heat a small amount of oil in a skillet. Fry bacon until crisp on both sides, about 5-10 minutes. Remove bacon from pan, reserving fat, and drain on paper towels.

Carefully drain the water from the cabbage and potatoes. Place cabbage and potatoes in a large bowl, add garlic, and mash until smooth. Form mixture into either one single cake or several smaller ones. Fry mashed cabbage and potato cake in reserved bacon fat until golden brown on both sides, about 2-3 minutes. Remove from pan, drain any excess fat on a paper towel, and slice. Top with fried bacon and serve.

Per serving: 268 calories, 11 g fat, 3 g saturated fat, 263 mg sodium, 36 g carbohydrates, 8 g protein.

VARIATIONS:

Cheese, chopped parsley, peppers, onion, thyme, or nutmeg can all be added to trinxat to enhance its flavor. Other greens may be used in place of cabbage, including spinach, kale, chard, or Brussels sprouts. Adjust boiling time accordingly.

AUSTRIA
WIENER SCHNITZEL

2 / 1 / 1
COOK TIME: 10 MINUTES
ACTIVE PREP TIME: 15 MINUTES
MAKES 4 SERVINGS

AUSTRIAN CUISINE IS OFTEN COMPARED TO THAT OF ITS NEIGHBOR, GERMANY. But many other countries that border Austria or have claimed its territory throughout history have left their mark on its food, including Italy, Hungary, the Czech Republic, and the Balkan states. The small nation has many regional cuisines, with that of its capital city Vienna being the best known. Viennese dishes include desserts such as apfelstrudel (apple strudel) and main courses like wiener schnitzel, whose name translates to "Viennese veal."

4 veal cutlets (about 5 oz. each)
¼ c. all-purpose flour
¼ tsp. salt
½ c. breadcrumbs
2 eggs, beaten
Oil, for frying

Place cutlets between two pieces of plastic wrap. Pound with a meat mallet until cutlets are as thin as possible (no thicker than ¼ inch). Dredge cutlets in flour until completely coated. Coat in egg, drain excess, and roll in breadcrumbs. Be careful not to press the breadcrumbs into the meat; they should form a shell.

Heat a layer of oil in a heavy skillet over medium-high heat. The oil should be deep enough so that the cutlets will float and not touch the bottom of the pan. Fry until both sides are golden brown, about 3 minutes per side. Drain cutlets on paper towels and serve while hot.

Per serving: 977 calories, 46 g fat, 14 g saturated fat, 685 mg sodium, 16 g carbohydrates, 117 g protein.

SERVING SUGGESTIONS:

Serve with lemon slices and spaetzle (German egg noodles), potato salad, or French fries.

VARIATIONS:

Chicken or pork cutlets can be used instead of veal. It is traditional to use lard instead of oil for frying wiener schnitzel.

BELARUS MOCHANKA WITH DRANIKI

2 / 1 / 2
COOK TIME: 1 HOUR, 4 MINUTES
ACTIVE PREP TIME: 15 MINUTES
MAKES 4-6 SERVINGS

THE PEOPLE OF BELARUS SHARE A CULINARY CULTURE VERY SIMILAR TO THAT of their larger neighbor, Russia, but there are a few distinctly Belarussian dishes. One is mochanka, a thick, meaty soup with mushrooms and onions. Mochanka is traditionally served with draniki, thin potato pancakes that are rolled up and dipped in the soup.

For mochanka:
1 lb. pork (shoulder or other cut), cut into small pieces
1 lb. sausage (such as kielbasa), sliced in 1-inch pieces and with casings removed
Oil, for frying
2 c. water, divided
1-½ c. beef broth
1 onion, chopped
8 oz. white mushrooms, stems removed
2 bay leaves
1 Tbsp. whole peppercorns
1 tsp. salt
½ c. white flour

Heat oil in a heavy skillet over medium-high heat. Fry pork until browned, about 5-10 minutes. Boil 1-½ c. water and broth in a large saucepan. Add pork, cover, and simmer for 1 hour. In the meanwhile, heat more oil in skillet. Fry sausage slices in oil until fully cooked, about 15-20 minutes. Remove from pan and add onion. Sauté onion until translucent, about 5 minutes. Add mushrooms and continue to cook until mushrooms are soft, about 3 minutes.

After pork has finished simmering, add sausage, onion, mushrooms, bay leaves, peppercorns, and salt to the pot. Continue to simmer until the sausage pieces begin to float on top, about 10 minutes.

Combine flour with remaining water in a small bowl. Stir vigorously with a fork or whisk until all lumps are gone. Add flour mixture to the pot and stir until flour is dissolved. Bring to a boil and immediately remove from heat.

Per serving: 557 calories, 35 g fat, 10 g saturated fat, 1356 mg sodium, 13 g carbohydrates, 45 g protein.

For draniki:
20 small- to medium-sized potatoes
¼ c. all-purpose flour
1 tsp. salt
2 Tbsp. lard

Peel potatoes and grate by hand or with a food processor or potato ricer. Add just enough flour to achieve a batter-like texture. Grease a small frying pan with lard. Pour enough potato batter into the pan to make a pancake 6 inches in diameter. Fry until just brown on both sides (about 1 minute per side) and carefully lift from pan. Repeat with remaining batter. Serve draniki with mochanka.

Per serving: 176 calories, 5 g fat, 2 g saturated fat, 946 mg sodium, 28 g carbohydrates, 3 g protein.

VARIATIONS:

Olive oil may be used for frying draniki. Add garlic, parsley, thyme, or other seasonings to mochanka and/or draniki while cooking.

BELGIUM
MOULES-FRITES

1 / 1 / 2
COOK TIME: 25 MINUTES
ACTIVE PREP TIME: 20 MINUTES
INACTIVE PREP TIME: 30 MINUTES
MAKES 4 SERVINGS

BELGIUM LIES BETWEEN FRANCE, GERMANY, AND THE NETHERLANDS, AND its cuisine reflects those of these three neighbors. *Moules-frites* is one of the few dishes originating in Belgium. Mussels, commonly found along Belgium's coast, and potatoes are two staples of Belgian cooking.

For mussels:
4 lbs. mussels, in shells
Olive oil, for sautéing
3 large shallots, diced
1 carrot, diced
3 cloves garlic, minced
1 sprig thyme
1 sprig rosemary
1 sprig parsley

1 c. dry white wine or Belgian-style beer
1-½ Tbsp. butter

Rinse mussels in cold water; discard any opened mussels and remove beards. Heat olive oil in a large stockpot over medium-high heat. Sauté shallots, carrot, and garlic until soft, about 5 minutes. Add mussels, herbs, and wine or beer to pot, shaking the pot so that the mussels form an even layer. Steam about 5 minutes or until mussels have opened.

Remove mussels from the pot. Add butter and stir until melted. Pour sauce over mussels before serving.

Per serving: 504 calories, 17 g fat, 4 g saturated fat, 1332 mg sodium, 21 g carbohydrates, 54 g protein.

For French fries:
2 lb. Yukon Gold potatoes
Olive or canola oil, for frying
Salt, to taste

Cut potatoes into ¼-inch thick sticks. Heat oil in a large frying pan and fry potatoes until tender, about 5-10 minutes. Remove from pan, place on baking sheet, and refrigerate until chilled, at least 30 minutes.

Before serving, reheat oil and continue frying chilled potatoes until brown and crisp, about 2-3 minutes longer. Season generously with salt and serve with mussels.

Per serving: 185 calories, 14 g fat, 1 g saturated fat, 47 mg sodium, 15 g carbohydrates, 2 g protein.

SERVING SUGGESTIONS:

Moules-frites are typically served with mayonnaise. For a traditional homemade Belgian-style mayonnaise, whisk together 1 egg yolk with 1 tsp. of Dijon mustard, then add 2 tsp. each white wine vinegar and lemon juice.

BOSNIA
BOSANSKI LONAC
(BOSNIAN POT)

1 / 1 / 1
COOK TIME: 2 HOURS, 10 MINUTES
ACTIVE PREP TIME: 15 MINUTES
MAKES 6-8 SERVINGS

LIKE MOST MEAT AND VEGETABLE STEWS, THE NATIONAL DISH OF BOSNIA and Herzegovina does not have a definitive recipe. Over the centuries, Bosanski Lonac has been widely eaten by people of all economic classes, in all regions, and during all seasons. While most cooks prepare the stew on the stove today, it can be made the traditional way as well—over a fireplace or open fire.

2-3 lbs. beef, cut into bite-sized pieces
2 Tbsp. oil
1 head cabbage, coarsely chopped
3 carrots, peeled and chopped
3 large tomatoes, seeded and chopped
3 large potatoes, peeled and chopped
2 onions, chopped
4 stalks celery, chopped
½ c. parsley, finely chopped
3 bay leaves
2 c. water
½ c. white wine
½ tsp. smoked paprika

Heat olive oil in a large stockpot. Cook beef until browned, about 5-10 minutes, and remove from heat.On top of beef, layer cabbage, carrots, tomatoes, potatoes, onions, celery, and parsley. Add bay leaves, water, wine, and paprika. Season with salt and pepper.

Bring to a boil over high heat. Reduce heat to medium-low, cover and simmer for 2 hours or until cabbage and potatoes are fully cooked, stirring every 30 minutes.

Per serving: 465 calories, 13 g fat, 4 g saturated fat, 149 mg sodium, 40 g carbohydrates, 45 g protein.

VARIATIONS:

This stew can be made with lamb or pork instead of beef. Vegetables such as peas, bell pepper, or green beans can all be added to this stew (in addition to or in place of the vegetables listed in the recipe).

BULGARIA
GYUVETCH

1 / 1 / 2
COOK TIME: 50 MINUTES
ACTIVE PREP TIME: 10 MINUTES
MAKES 6-8 SERVINGS

BORDERING GREECE AND TURKEY TO THE NORTH, BULGARIA'S CUISINE incorporates many standard Mediterranean ingredients, such as cheese, yogurt, and olives. But as a Slavic nation, hearty meat and vegetable stews form its backbone. One example is gyuvetch, which shares its name with that of the earthenware casserole dish in which it is traditionally prepared.

1 lb. beef stew meat, cut into small pieces
Olive oil, for frying
1 large white onion, chopped
3 Tbsp. paprika
1-½ tsp. red pepper flakes
3 large tomatoes, chopped
½ c. red wine
Water, to cover
4 oz. mushrooms, chopped
1 c. white rice, uncooked
1 red bell pepper, seeded and chopped

1 green bell pepper, seeded and chopped
4 oz. black olives, pitted and chopped
Chopped fresh parsley, for serving

Heat olive oil in a Dutch oven over medium-high heat. Fry beef in oil until very brown, about 10 minutes. Add onion, paprika, and red pepper flakes and continue to cook until onion has softened, about 3 minutes longer. Add tomatoes, wine, and enough water to cover ingredients and bring to a boil. Add mushrooms and rice and reduce heat to medium-low. Simmer for 10 minutes, add red and green bell peppers, and simmer for 10 minutes longer.

Preheat oven to 375 degrees. Pour the beef and vegetables into a large oven-safe baking dish and place olives on top. Finish cooking in oven for 20 minutes. Garnish with parsley and serve.

Per serving: 330 calories, 11 g fat, 3 g saturated fat, 194 mg sodium, 33 g carbohydrates, 24 g protein.

SERVING SUGGESTION:

Serve with a roasted eggplant and pepper salad.

VARIATIONS:

Other vegetables can be added, such as green beans or eggplant. Add garlic with the onion and spices. Add bacon to the pan when browning the beef. Gyuvetch be made with or without meat.

CROATIA
PASTICADA

3 / 2 / 3
COOK TIME: 2 HOURS, 50 MINUTES
ACTIVE PREP TIME: 20 MINUTES
INACTIVE PREP TIME: 12 HOURS
MAKES 8 SERVINGS

PASTICADA IS A SPECIALTY OF DALMATIA, A SMALL STRIP OF LAND IN THE southern region of Croatia along the Adriatic coast. A quintessential Mediterranean dish, it synthesizes several dishes of ancient Greek, Roman, and southern French origin. Since it requires so much work and attention to prepare, it is traditionally reserved for weddings and other special occasions.

One 3-4 lb. beef roast (top round or rump)
2 tsp. salt
2 oz. thick smoked bacon, cut into 1-inch pieces
5 cloves garlic, sliced
1 large onion, sliced
1 Tbsp. fresh rosemary
2 tsp. peppercorns
1 tsp. juniper berries
2 c. balsamic vinegar
Olive oil, for frying
2 Tbsp. all-purpose flour
3 carrots, coarsely chopped
½ c. prunes
½ c. beef broth
2 c. dry red wine
1 c. Prošek, Marsala, or other sweet dessert wine
1 tsp. ground nutmeg
½ tsp. whole cloves
1 Tbsp. sugar
1 Tbsp. water
Chopped fresh parsley, for serving
Sliced cucumbers, for serving

Season the meat with salt. With a knife, cut small pockets throughout the surface of the meat and insert a slice of garlic and a piece of bacon in each pocket. Place roast in a large bowl with onion, rosemary, peppercorns, and juniper berries. Cover with balsamic vinegar. The roast should be completely submerged; if it is not, add enough water to the marinade so that it is. Cover and refrigerate for at least 12 hours.

Discard marinade, reserving onions and spices. Remove the garlic slices and bacon pieces from the roast and set aside.

Heat olive oil in a large stockpot over medium-high heat. Dust meat with flour. Fry roast until browned on all sides, about 7-10 minutes. Remove from pan and set aside.

Add reserved onions, garlic, and bacon from marinade to pot, along with carrot and prunes. Sauté until onions are soft and bacon is brown, about 5 to 10 minutes. Add broth to the pot and cook over medium heat until about half the broth has evaporated.

Return roast to the pot and add red wine, dessert wine, nutmeg, cloves, and reserved spices. Cook over low heat for 2 hours. If the liquid begins to evaporate, add a small amount of water to the pot.

Remove roast from pot and cut into several small pieces. Remove bay leaves and juniper berries. Use an immersion blender to puree vegetables and spices in the pot, and then return meat to pot.

In a small saucepan, combine water and sugar. Cook over medium heat until a thick, slightly dark mixture develops. Add syrup to the stockpot and simmer for another 30 minutes, stirring frequently. Garnish with chopped parsley and sliced cucumbers and serve.

Per serving: 1082 calories, 35 g fat, 12 g saturated fat, 1134 mg sodium, 23 g carbohydrates, 140 g protein.

SERVING SUGGESTIONS:
Serve with gnocchi or homemade pasta.

CYPRUS AFELIA

2 / 1 / 2
COOK TIME: 1 HOUR, 5 MINUTES
ACTIVE PREP TIME: 10 MINUTES
INACTIVE PREP TIME: 6 HOURS, 30 MINUTES
MAKES 6 SERVINGS

THE WORD AFELIA COMES FROM THE GREEK WORD OVELIAS, WHICH MEANS "cooked meat." This dish is eaten in Greece, but it is more often associated with the island of Cyprus. Traditional Cypriot afelia is made from pork marinated in red wine, seasoned with crushed coriander seeds, and roasted in an earthenware dish called a tava.

2 lbs. pork roast (shoulder or loin), cut into large pieces
½ c. olive oil
3 Tbsp. coriander seeds
2 bay leaves
3 c. dry red wine
2 lbs. baby potatoes
1 onion, chopped
Chopped parsley, for serving

Crush 2 Tbsp. of coriander seeds with a mortar and pestle. Sprinkle meat with crushed coriander and add bay leaves and red wine. Cover with plastic wrap and marinate in refrigerator for 6 hours or overnight. Remove meat from refrigerator and allow it to sit at room temperature for 30 minutes, reserving marinade.

Preheat oven to 325 degrees. With a mallet, hit each potato softly so that its skin splits.

Heat olive oil in a heavy skillet over medium-high heat. Fry meat until brown on all sides, about 5-6 minutes. Remove meat from pan and place in baking dish. Add potatoes to skillet and sauté until golden, about 5 minutes. Crush remaining 1 Tbsp. coriander seeds and sprinkle onto potatoes. Add potatoes to dish with meat. Add onions to skillet and sauté until soft and translucent, about 5 minutes. Add marinade to skillet and continue to cook until liquid is reduced by half.

Add onions to dish and pour marinade over meat and potatoes. Cover dish with lid or aluminum foil and cook for 45 minutes. Garnish with parsley and serve.

Per serving: 650 calories, 31 g fat, 8 g saturated fat, 107 mg sodium, 24 g carbohydrates, 47 g protein.

SERVING SUGGESTION:

In addition to potatoes, afelia is traditionally served with bulgur and yogurt.

VARIATION:

Sliced button mushrooms (8 oz.) may be used in place of potatoes.

CZECH REPUBLIC
SVÍCKOVÁ

3 / 1 / 3
COOK TIME: 2 HOURS, 10 MINUTES
ACTIVE PREP TIME: 20 MINUTES
INACTIVE PREP TIME: 6 HOURS, 30 MINUTES
MAKES 6 SERVINGS

THE FULL NAME OF THE CZECH NATIONAL DISH, SVÍCKOVÁ NA SMETANE, translates to "tenderloin in sour cream sauce." While this description may sound simple, svíčková is among the most complex dishes in this cookbook. The meat is marinated with flavorful vegetables and heavily spiced, and a delicate cream sauce is made from its gravy. Many different versions of this dish exist throughout the Czech Republic, as well as among Czech immigrant communities in the United States.

1-½ lb. beef tenderloin
2 tsp. salt
2 oz. thick smoked bacon, cut into 1-inch pieces
1 lb. vegetables, chopped (e.g., onion, celery, turnips, carrots, or leeks)
1 tsp. dried thyme
½ tsp. allspice berries
1 tsp. ground black pepper
2 bay leaves
1 c. red wine vinegar
2 Tbsp. olive oil, plus more for frying
½ c. water
2 Tbsp. butter
Juice of 1 lemon
¾ c. sour cream

Season the meat with salt. With a knife, cut small pockets throughout the surface of the meat. Insert a piece of bacon in each pocket. Place the meat in a large glass or ceramic dish and surround with vegetables. Season with thyme, allspice, and pepper. Add bay leaves, red wine vinegar, and olive oil.

Cover and marinate in the refrigerator for at least 6 hours or up to 24 hours. Remove meat from refrigerator and allow it to sit at room temperature for 30 minutes.

Preheat oven to 350 degrees. Heat olive oil in a Dutch oven over medium-high heat and sear meat on all sides until brown, about 5-10 minutes. Place meat and vegetables in a large baking dish.

Add water to Dutch oven and bring to a boil, scraping the bottom of the pot. Add marinade and pour over meat and vegetables. Pat meat with butter. Cover and roast for 1-½ to 2 hours, basting occasionally.

Remove vegetables and puree in a blender or food processor. Strain the mixture through a sieve to remove large pieces. Heat vegetable puree and lemon juice in a medium-sized saucepan over medium heat. Just before serving, add sour cream and heat until warm (do not allow sauce to boil).

Per serving: 934 calories, 50 g fat, 20 g saturated fat, 1269 mg sodium, 9 g carbohydrates, 104 g protein.

For dumplings (knedliky):
2 c. all-purpose flour
½ tsp. baking powder
½ tsp. salt
½ tsp. sugar
2 eggs
1 c. whole milk
3 slices white bread, cubed
Salted water, for boiling

Sift flour, baking powder, salt, and sugar together in a mixing bowl. Add eggs and milk and stir vigorously for about 10 minutes. Add bread cubes gradually to make a thick dough. Place dough on a floured board and divide into three portions. Knead each portion into a small loaf.

Bring a large pot of salted water to a boil. Carefully add loaves to pot and boil gently for 25 minutes, turning once. Remove from pot and set aside to cool.

Once dumplings have cooled, slice very carefully with a serrated knife or a piece of sewing thread. Slice meat and serve with sauce and dumplings.

Per serving: 211 calories, 3 g fat, 1 g saturated fat, 266 mg sodium, 37 g carbohydrates, 8 g protein.

SERVING SUGGESTIONS:

Serve with cranberry sauce or jam.

VARIATION:

Add 2 tsp. mustard or 2 oz. mustard seeds to the sauce before stirring in the sour cream, if desired.

DENMARK FRIKADELLER

1 / 1 / 2
COOK TIME: 20 MINUTES
ACTIVE PREP TIME: 15 MINUTES
INACTIVE PREP TIME: 30 MINUTES
MAKES 6-8 SERVINGS

THE CENTERPIECE OF DANISH CUISINE IS THE "COLD BUFFET" (DET Kolde Bord), a banquet-style feast usually reserved for special occasions. As its name suggests, the cold buffet includes mostly uncooked or room temperature foods, such as smoked fish and shellfish, fruit salads, cheeses, raw vegetables, and chilled sauces. But a few hot dishes are usually included as well. These almost always include frikadeller, or Danish meatballs, which can be served either hot or cold.

1 lb. ground veal or lean beef
1 lb. ground pork
1 large onion, finely grated
2 eggs, beaten
½ c. white breadcrumbs

½ c. rolled oats
2 Tbsp. fresh thyme
2 tsp. salt
2 tsp. ground black pepper
½ tsp. ground allspice
Oil, for frying

Combine meat, onion, eggs, breadcrumbs, oats, thyme, salt, pepper, and allspice. Chill in refrigerator for at least 30 minutes. Roll meat mixture into medium-sized balls. Use about 2 Tbsp. of meat mixture to form each meatball.

Heat oil in a large skillet over medium-high heat. Fry meatballs in batches for about 10 minutes per side, or until brown and no longer pink in the center. As you cook the meatballs, flatten them slightly with a spatula so that they are more oval-shaped than perfectly round.

Per serving: 322 calories, 13 g fat, 4 g saturated fat, 830 mg sodium, 13 g carbohydrates, 37 g protein.

SERVING SUGGESTIONS:

Serve warm with potatoes and cabbage or egg noodles and gravy, or cold with mayonnaise on bread as an open-faced sandwich.

TIP:

To make a gravy for the frikadeller, add 3 Tbsp. flour and 1 tsp. butter to drippings after frying meatballs. Stirring constantly with a fork, gradually add 1 c. milk or cream and 1 Tbsp. beef bouillon until desired consistency is reached.

ENGLAND
ROAST BEEF WITH YORKSHIRE PUDDING

IN BRITISH CULTURE, THE TERM "PUDDING" IS OFTEN USED INTERCHANGEABLY with "dessert." But not all English puddings are sweet. By definition, a pudding is any dish that is boiled or steamed in a cloth or dish. Some English puddings would be referred to as custards, cakes, or even sausages by Americans. The most famous pudding recipe of all, Yorkshire pudding, was first recorded in a 1737 cookbook under the name "Dripping Pudding." Interestingly, it is not boiled or steamed, but roasted with meat in an extremely hot oven. Along with roast beef, it forms the cornerstone of the English Sunday meal.

One 4-lb. beef rib roast
¼ c. olive oil
2 Tbsp. fresh rosemary, finely chopped
2 Tbsp. fresh thyme, finely chopped
4 cloves garlic, finely chopped
1-¼ c. whole milk
1 c. all-purpose flour
3 eggs
1 tsp. salt

Place roast on a rack in a roasting pan. Combine oil, rosemary, thyme, and garlic and rub surface of roast. Cover with plastic wrap and refrigerate for at least 8 hours.

Remove roast from refrigerator and allow to stand at room temperature for at least 2 hours. Unwrap and insert meat thermometer in thickest part of roast (do not allow it to touch bone or fat).

Preheat oven to 350 degrees. Roast meat until thermometer reaches desired temperature. For medium-rare, remove roast from oven when temperature reaches 130 degrees; for medium, 140 degrees. (Roast will continue to cook while standing.)

While roast is cooking, mix batter for pudding. Combine milk, flour, eggs, and salt and allow to stand at room temperature for 1 hour.

Increase oven temperature to 450 degrees. Transfer roast to cutting board to rest and collect drippings from pan. There should be at least ¼ c. of drippings; if there is less, add a small amount of oil.

Spoon ½ tsp. of pan drippings into each cup of a 12-cup muffin pan. Place in oven for 15 minutes. Add remaining pan drippings to pudding batter. Divide batter evenly among cups in muffin pan. Bake for 20 minutes or until brown on top. Reduce oven temperature to 350 degrees and cook 10 minutes longer. Slice roast and serve immediately with pudding.

Per serving: 1256 calories, 101 g fat, 40 g saturated fat, 600 mg sodium, 20 g carbohydrates, 63 g protein.

VARIATION:

Use bacon drippings in place of pan drippings for a considerably different flavor.

ESTONIA HAKKLIHAKOTLET WITH CABBAGE

1 / 1 / 2
COOK TIME: 55 MINUTES
ACTIVE PREP TIME: 15 MINUTES
MAKES 4 SERVINGS

AS A SMALL COASTAL COUNTRY WITH A FRIGID CLIMATE, ESTONIA'S TRADITIONAL cuisine includes few fresh vegetables and lots of meat, fish, and potatoes—especially in the winter. In past centuries, Estonians preserved vegetables such as cabbage by blanching them and then leaving them outside in the snow to freeze. Pickling and fermenting are other ways that Estonians preserve the summer's harvest during the cold months. But meat dishes, such as hakklihakotlet ("minced meat cutlets"), form their cold-weather diet's backbone.

For hakklihakotlet:
½ lb. very lean ground beef
½ lb. ground veal
½ lb. ground pork
1 small onion, finely chopped
2 eggs
1 tsp. salt
¼ tsp. ground black pepper
1 c. breadcrumbs, divided
Oil, for frying

Combine meat, onion, eggs, salt, and pepper in a bowl. Add ½ c. of breadcrumbs and knead until smooth. Divide the mixture into 8 portions. Shape each portion into a ball and flatten slightly to form a patty. Dredge patties in remaining breadcrumbs.

Heat oil in a heavy skillet over medium-high heat. Fry patties in batches for 5 minutes on each side or until brown and cooked throughout.

Per serving: 493 calories, 21 g fat, 6 g saturated fat, 938 mg sodium, 21 g carbohydrates, 52 g protein.

For cabbage:
1 head red cabbage, thinly sliced
Butter, for sautéing
1 onion, thinly sliced
¼ c. water
3 Tbsp. apple cider vinegar
3 Tbsp. sugar
½ tsp. salt
1 apple, thinly sliced
1 Tbsp. caraway seed

Heat butter in Dutch oven over medium-high heat. Add onions and sauté until translucent, about 5 minutes. Add water, vinegar, sugar, and salt to pot and stir thoroughly. Add cabbage, apple, and caraway seed. Reduce heat to low, cover, and simmer for 30 minutes, stirring occasionally and adding water if necessary.

Per serving: 177 calories, 6 g fat, 4 g saturated fat, 367 mg sodium, 31 g carbohydrates, 3 g protein.

SERVING SUGGESTIONS:
Serve with potatoes, rye bread, sour cream or yogurt, and cranberry jam.

FINLAND
KARJALANPAISTI WITH PERUNASOSELAATIKKO

1 / 1 / 1
COOK TIME: 2 HOURS, 45 MINUTES
ACTIVE PREP TIME: 15 MINUTES
MAKES 6 SERVINGS

THE REGION OF KARELIA, WHICH LIES NEAR THE BORDER OF FINLAND AND Russia, has been a disputed territory for centuries. In 1939-1940 Finland and the Soviet Union fought the Winter War, which ended with the Soviet Union occupying most of Karelia and its population being relocated throughout Finland. These refugees never returned to their homeland, but they went on to make a considerable mark on the nation's culinary culture. Karjalanpaisti (Karelian hot pot) is a stew that is today among the country's most popular dishes. In this recipe it is served with perunasoselaatikko (oven-baked mashed potatoes).

For karjalanpaisti:
1 lb. beef chuck roast, cubed
1 lb. pork shoulder, cubed
2 onions, chopped
Oil, for frying

1 qt. beef stock
2 carrots, peeled and chopped
1 Tbsp. allspice berries
2 tsp. ground allspice
2 bay leaves
Salt and pepper, to taste

Heat oil in a heavy Dutch oven over medium-high heat. Cook meat and onions until brown, about 10 minutes.

Preheat oven to 300 degrees. Add stock, carrots, allspice, and bay leaves to pot. Cover and bake in oven for 2 hours, 15 minutes. Raise heat to 375 degrees. Add potatoes to oven and cook for an additional 20 minutes. Serve with potatoes.

Per serving: 551 calories, 40 g fat, 15 g saturated fat, 536 mg sodium, 7 g carbohydrates, 39 g protein.

For perunasoselaatikko:
6 Russet potatoes, peeled and chopped
Water, for boiling
2 eggs, beaten
1 c. whole milk
Salt and pepper, to taste
¼ c. butter, softened (plus more for baking)
½ c. breadcrumbs

Bring a large pot of water to a boil. Boil potatoes until tender, about 20 minutes. Drain water and mash with a potato masher. Transfer hot potatoes to a separate bowl, stir in eggs and milk, and season with salt and pepper.

With an electric mixer, fold butter into potato mixture 1 Tbsp. at a time. Continue to beat potato mixture until fluffy. Spread potatoes into a medium-sized casserole dish. Coat surface with breadcrumbs and dot with butter. Cook potatoes at 375 degrees (along with stew) for 20 minutes.

Per serving: 296 calories, 11 g fat, 6 g saturated fat, 170 mg sodium, 42 g carbohydrates, 8 g protein.

FRANCE
POT-AU-FEU

2 / 1 / 1
COOK TIME: 4 HOURS, 50 MINUTES
ACTIVE PREP TIME: 10 MINUTES
INACTIVE PREP TIME: 8 HOURS
MAKES 6 SERVINGS

GIVEN THAT FRANCE HAS ONE OF THE MOST CELEBRATED CUISINES IN THE world, the task of choosing a single dish to represent the French people may appear daunting. But in this case, the clear choice is one that is relatively simple, enjoyed by people from all walks of life, and truly speaks to the nation's diverse culture and rich history. Pot-au-feu, or "pot on the fire," has been a staple of French cuisine since the seventeenth century. Kings and peasants alike enjoyed this rich stew, which could be made with whatever vegetables were available and whichever cuts of meat one could afford (with a small adjustment in cooking time). It remains the centerpiece of the French Sunday dinner today.

For broth:
1 large beef bone, with marrow
3 c. water
2 stalks celery
1 small onion
1 carrot
2 whole cloves
2 Tbsp. fresh parsley
1 tsp. fresh thyme
1 head garlic

Place all ingredients in a large stockpot. Make sure that ingredients are completely submerged (add more water if necessary). Bring to a boil, cover, reduce heat to low, and simmer for 3 hours. Strain broth and refrigerate for 8 hours or overnight. Remove from refrigerator and skim any fat that has risen to the surface.

For pot-au-feu:
3 lbs. beef round roast or brisket
1 large onion, diced
4 cloves garlic, minced
Olive oil, for sautéing
1-½ tsp. salt
½ tsp. ground black pepper
4 carrots, cut into 1-inch pieces
2 bay leaves
2 small potatoes, cut into 1-inch pieces

Heat oil in a large Dutch oven over medium-high heat. Sauté onions until translucent, about 5 minutes. Add garlic and cook until fragrant, about 2 minutes. Add beef to the pot along with broth (add water if necessary to cover beef), salt, and pepper. Bring to a boil, cover, and reduce heat to medium-low. Simmer for 30 minutes.

Add carrots and bay leaves to pot and cook for 1 hour longer or until beef is fork-tender. Add potatoes and cook for 20 minutes longer, or until potatoes are fully cooked. Remove bay leaves and serve.

Per serving: 528 calories, 19 g fat, 6 g saturated fat, 585 mg sodium, 15 g carbohydrates, 70 g protein.

GERMANY
SAUERBRATEN
WITH SEMMELKNÖDEL

3 / 2 / 2
COOK TIME: 3 HOURS
ACTIVE PREP TIME: 30 MINUTES
INACTIVE PREP TIME: 3 DAYS, 10 MINUTES
MAKES 8 SERVINGS

EVEN THOUGH AMERICANS HAVE THEIR OWN IDEAS ABOUT GERMAN FOOD in general, it is a very diverse cuisine that varies depending on region of the country. Germany is made up of dozens of territorial states, each having its own distinct culinary traditions. Germans eat far more meat than most cultures; it is not completely surprising that the country is home to over 1,500 different varieties of wurst (sausage). Braised meats are also common, including those made from tougher, less choice cuts of meat that are tenderized by marinating for long periods of time. Sauerbraten, or "sour meat," is traditionally made from horsemeat, venison, or mutton. But today, beef is the most common choice for this roast.

For sauerbraten:
One 4-lb. boneless bottom-round beef roast
1 c. dry red wine
½ c. red wine vinegar
½ c. apple cider vinegar
2-½ c. water
3 onions, sliced, divided
2 bay leaves
1 Tbsp. black peppercorns, crushed
1 Tbsp. juniper berries, crushed
1-½ tsp. whole cloves
1 tsp. mustard seed
1 tsp. salt
3 Tbsp. butter
6 large carrots, chopped
4 stalks celery, chopped
2 Tbsp. all-purpose flour
¾ c. gingersnap cookies, crushed

Combine, wine, vinegars, 2 c. water, 1 onion, bay leaves, peppercorns, juniper berries, cloves, mustard seed, and salt in a medium saucepan. Bring to a boil, and then remove from heat and cool to room temperature.

Place roast in a large non-reactive dish and cover with marinade. Allow roast to marinate in refrigerator, tightly covered, for at least 3 days (or as long as 10 days), turning roast once a day so that its entire surface has contact with marinade. After at least 3 days, remove from marinade and pat dry. Strain marinade and reserve liquid.

Heat butter in a large Dutch oven over medium-high heat. Cook roast in butter until evenly browned on all sides, about 10-15 minutes. Remove from pot and set aside. Add remaining onions, carrots, and celery to pot and sauté until softened, about 5 minutes. Add flour and cook for 2-3 minutes longer, stirring constantly. Add 2 c. of reserved marinade and ½ c. water to pot. Bring to a boil, then reduce heat to medium-low and return roast to pot. Cover and simmer for 2 hours or until meat is tender.

Transfer roast to a serving platter and slice. Pour liquid from pot into a large bowl and skim any fat that collects on top. Measure 2-½ cups of liquid, including vegetables, and combine with gingersnaps in a small saucepan. Cook for 10 minutes or until gingersnaps are completely dissolved and sauce is thick. Strain sauce through a sieve and serve with roast.

Per serving: 918 calories, 30 g fat, 12 g saturated fat, 763 mg sodium, 29 g carbohydrates, 119 g protein.

For semmelknödel:
1 lb. stale white bread, torn into pieces
1 small onion, finely chopped
3 Tbsp. fresh parsley, finely chopped
2 tsp. butter
1 c. whole milk
3 eggs, beaten
Salt and pepper, to taste
Breadcrumbs, as needed
Salted water, for boiling
Chopped fresh parsley, to serve

Heat butter in a small skillet over medium-high heat. Sauté onion and parsley until onion is softened but not until parsley has lost its color, about 3 minutes. Add milk to skillet and heat just until milk is warm. Combine milk and onion mixture with bread pieces and allow to sit for 10 minutes.

Add eggs to mixture and season with salt and pepper. Mix until a soft dough is formed. If necessary, add more breadcrumbs to thicken the dough.

Bring a large pot of salted water to a boil. Form dough into 1-½-inch balls and lower into boiling water with a slotted spoon. Reduce heat to medium and boil for about 20 minutes or until dough balls rise to the surface. Drain dumplings and serve with sauerbraten sauce and chopped parsley.

Per serving: 205 calories, 6 g fat, 2 g saturated fat, 429 mg sodium, 31 g carbohydrates, 8 g protein.

SERVING SUGGESTION:
Serve with cooked red cabbage.

TIP:
Instead of simmering on the stove, roast can be baked in oven at 350 degrees for 2 hours.

GREECE
MOUSSAKA

3 / 1 / 2
COOK TIME: 1 HOUR, 20 MINUTES
ACTIVE PREP TIME: 15 MINUTES
INACTIVE PREP TIME: 15 MINUTES
MAKES 8 SERVINGS

LIKE MANY MEDITERRANEAN DISHES, MOUSSAKA IS THE PRODUCT OF THE divergence of many cultures over many centuries. The first recipes for this dish have been traced to the thirteenth-century Islamic world. But today, even Arabs recognize moussaka as a uniquely Greek dish (which happens to be popular throughout the Middle East as well). It is the thick, creamy béchamel sauce that tops this casserole that distinguishes it from similar lamb and eggplant dishes.

1 lb. lean ground beef or lamb
2 zucchini, sliced into circles
2 small eggplant, sliced into circles
Olive oil, for sautéing

1 onion, chopped
3 cloves garlic, minced
1 Tbsp. fresh thyme
1 tsp. sugar
1 Tbsp. tomato paste
One 15-oz. can diced tomatoes
¼ c. fresh parsley, chopped
¼ c. fresh basil, chopped
½ c. butter
½ c. all-purpose flour, sifted
3 c. whole milk
¾ c. Parmesan cheese, grated
3 egg yolks
¼ tsp. ground nutmeg
3 potatoes, peeled and thinly sliced

Heat oil in a heavy skillet over medium-high heat. Sauté zucchini and eggplant until soft and brown, about 5-10 minutes. Remove from pan and drain on paper towels.

Add more oil to pan. Sauté onion until translucent, about 5 minutes. Add garlic, thyme, and sugar to pan and cook until caramelized, about 2-3 minutes. Add ground meat to skillet and cook until brown, about 5-6 minutes. Add tomato paste and diced tomatoes. Reduce heat to medium-low and simmer for 5-10 minutes or until most of the liquid has evaporated. Remove from heat and stir in parsley and basil.

Heat butter in a medium-sized saucepan over medium heat. Once melted, add flour and whisk until a light-brown roux is formed. Pour the milk into the pan a little at a time, whisking constantly. Once the sauce begins to bubble, remove from heat and stir in ½ c. Parmesan cheese, egg yolks, and nutmeg.

Preheat oven to 350 degrees. Cover the bottom of a medium-sized baking dish with potato slices and season with salt and pepper. Cover potato layer with a layer of eggplant and zucchini.

Add ¼ c. of cream sauce to ground meat mixture and stir. Spread the ground meat mixture in a layer on top of the eggplant and zucchini layer. Cover ground meat layer with remaining cream sauce and top with remaining Parmesan cheese. Bake for 35-40 minutes or until top layer is golden brown. Allow to cool for 15 minutes before slicing.

Per serving: 504 calories, 27 g fat, 14 g saturated fat, 432 mg sodium, 36 g carbohydrates, 32 g protein.

HUNGARY
GOULASCH

2 / 1 / 2
COOK TIME: 1 HOUR, 45 MINUTES
ACTIVE PREP TIME: 20 MINUTES
INACTIVE PREP TIME: 10 MINUTES
MAKES 4 SERVINGS

GOULASCH, ONE OF EUROPE'S OLDEST AND MOST BELOVED NATIONAL DISHES, has very humble origins. Shepherds and cowherds ate goulash in its earliest form in the ninth century, cooking stews of dried meat, millet, onions, and salt in cauldrons over fires on the open plains. They would add black pepper when available, and over time red chilies were introduced to Hungary. Finely ground red pepper soon became the trademark ingredient of the dish, and as it was elevated to the tables of the Hungarian aristocracy in the nineteenth century the demand for paprika rose to the point that farmers could not produce enough to meet the demand of the hungry market. Today, Hungarian goulasch is a favorite among tourists as well as citizens.

1-½ lb. beef chuck or round roast, cut into small cubes
Lard or oil, for sautéing
2 onions, one large (chopped) and one small (whole)
¼ c. plus 2 Tbsp. sweet paprika
1-½ qt. beef broth or water
4 cloves garlic
2 tomatoes, seeded and chopped
2 stalks celery, finely chopped, stems and leaves separated
1 green bell pepper, chopped

2 Tbsp. caraway seed
1 tsp. crushed red pepper flakes
1 lb. carrots, peeled and sliced
1 lb. parsnips, peeled and sliced
3 large potatoes, peeled and cut into small cubes
½ c. fresh parsley, finely chopped
Salt and pepper, to taste
Chopped parsley, for serving

Heat lard or oil over medium-high heat in a Dutch oven. Add chopped onions and sauté until transparent, about 5 minutes. Remove from heat and stir in paprika. Return to heat, add beef to pot, and cook until browned on all sides, about 10 minutes, stirring frequently. Add broth or water, whole onion, garlic, tomatoes, celery stems, bell pepper, caraway seed, and red pepper flakes and reduce heat to low. Cover and simmer for 1 hour.

Add celery leaves, carrots, parsnips, potatoes, and parsley to pot and bring to a boil. Recover and simmer for 30 minutes longer. Season with salt and pepper and garnish with chopped parsley. Serve with dumplings.

Per serving: 627 calories, 12 g fat, 4 g saturated fat, 200 mg sodium, 89 g carbohydrates, 44 g protein.

For dumplings:
2 eggs
½ tsp. salt
2 c. all-purpose flour
Salted water, for boiling

Beat eggs in a small bowl and add salt. Slowly add flour, stirring constantly, until a soft, solid dough forms. Cover with a damp paper towel and allow to rest for 10 minutes.

Bring a large pot of water to a boil. Using a small spoon, scoop one spoonful of dough at a time and drop into boiling water, dipping spoon into water after each spoonful. Work quickly until all dough is boiling.

Cook dumplings until they rise to the water's surface. Lift each cooked dumpling from the water with a slotted spoon and drain in a colander. Rinse dumplings with cold water to stop cooking and serve with goulasch.

Per serving: 259 calories, 3 g fat, 1 g saturated fat, 323 mg sodium, 48 g carbohydrates, 9 g protein.

SERVING SUGGESTION:

Serve with sour cream.

VARIATION:

American goulash is much different from its Hungarian counterpart. For an American version, use ground beef instead of chuck roast, replace broth with two 15-oz. cans each of diced tomatoes and tomato sauce, and add 2 c. of uncooked elbow macaroni to pot 20 minutes before cooking is finished.

ICELAND SUNNUDAGS- LAMBASTEIK

3 / 2 / 1
COOK TIME: 4 HOURS
ACTIVE PREP TIME: 15 MINUTES
INACTIVE PREP TIME: 15 MINUTES
MAKES 6 SERVINGS

SINCE ICELAND IS SURROUNDED BY OCEAN AND HAS A RATHER HARSH CLIMATE, fish, rustic game dishes, and preserved meats and vegetables have dominated its cuisine since Medieval times. But every Sunday, the typical Icelandic family enjoys its own version of a meal familiar to people throughout the world: roasted lamb (or "Sunday lamb," as this dish's name translates) with potatoes.

One 3-4 lb. leg of lamb, including bone
1 onion, quartered
5 cloves garlic, halved

1 Tbsp. ground coriander
Salt and pepper, to taste
2 c. water (plus more if needed)
1 Tbsp. all-purpose flour, sifted
¼ c. heavy cream (optional)

Preheat oven to 400 degrees. Rinse leg of lamb under cold water and pat dry. Rub surface of lamb with onion and garlic and season generously with coriander, salt, and pepper. Set lamb on a rack in a large roasting pan and place onions and garlic in the bottom of the pan. Insert a meat thermometer in thickest part of meat (do not allow it to touch bone or fat).

Once oven is preheated, place pan in oven and immediately reduce temperature to 250 degrees. Allow to roast for about 20 minutes, and then add water to pan and roast for 1 hour longer. Raise oven temperature to 300 degrees and roast for 1 more hour, adding more water to pan if evaporated. Raise oven temperature to 350 degrees and roast for 1 hour longer, for a total of 3 hours. Meat thermometer will register 145 degrees for medium rare, 160 for medium, or 170 for well-done.

Remove roast from oven and transfer remaining liquid from pan to a bowl. Raise oven temperature to 400 degrees and roast meat until nicely browned, about 15 minutes. Remove meat from oven and allow to rest for 10-15 minutes before slicing.

Strain the juices from the roasting pan, squeezing any liquid from onions and garlic. Skim any fat that rises to the top and add to a small saucepan or skillet with enough water to make 2 c. of liquid. Add flour and whisk vigorously until a thin paste is formed (add more flour if needed). Continue to cook sauce until thickened and add cream (if using). Serve sauce with lamb.

Per serving: 813 calories, 59 g fat, 25 g saturated fat, 201 mg sodium, 4 g carbohydrates, 60 g protein.

SERVING SUGGESTIONS:

Serve with roasted potatoes and rhubarb or blueberry jam.

TIP:

Lamb can also be roasted at 400 degrees for 2 hours to reduce cooking time.

IRELAND
IRISH STEW

1 / 1 / 1
COOK TIME: 2 HOURS, 5 MINUTES
ACTIVE PREP TIME: 10 MINUTES
MAKES 6 SERVINGS

THE BRONZE CAULDRON MADE ITS WAY TO IRELAND AROUND THE SEVENTH century, and it was not long afterwards that a simple stew of meat and root vegetables became the island's trademark recipe. In its earliest versions, the stew known as *ballymaloe* in Gaelic contained tough cuts of mutton or goat meat, which became tender with hours of slow-cooking, along with carrots, leeks, and turnips. When potatoes were introduced to Ireland from the New World, they quickly became the dominant ingredient, and a proper Irish stew cannot be made without them today. This recipe is considerably more complex than those enjoyed by the Hibernians of the Middle Ages.

3 lbs. boneless lamb, cut into pieces
¼ c. all-purpose flour
½ tsp. salt
½ tsp. ground black pepper
4 oz. bacon, chopped
3 small yellow onions, one chopped and two sliced
2 cloves garlic, minced
2 c. beef stock
1 tsp. sugar
3 lbs. red potatoes, peeled and quartered
2 large carrots, chopped
½ c. dark beer (such as stout)
1 Tbsp. fresh thyme
1 bay leaf
Chopped parsley, for serving

Season lamb with salt and pepper and place in a mixing bowl. Add flour and toss to coat evenly.

Cook bacon in a large Dutch oven over medium-high heat until crisp, about 5-7 minutes. Remove bacon from pot, reserving fat, and add lamb. Sauté lamb in bacon fat until brown on all sides, about 7-10 minutes. Remove lamb from pot.

Add chopped onion and garlic to pot and sauté until soft, about 5 minutes. Return meat and bacon to pot, along with beef stock and sugar. Reduce heat to low, cover, and simmer for 1-½ hours.

Add sliced onions, potatoes, carrots, beer, thyme, and bay leaf to pot. Continue to simmer for 20 minutes longer. Serve in bowls garnished with chopped parsley.

Per serving: 745 calories, 25 g fat, 9 g saturated fat, 1096 mg sodium, 48 g carbohydrates, 77 g protein.

SERVING SUGGESTION:

Serve with sourdough or Irish soda bread.

ITALY
RAGÙ ALLA BOLOGNESE

2 / 2 / 2
COOK TIME: 3 HOUS
ACTIVE PREP TIME: 10 MINUTES
MAKES 10-12 SERVINGS

ITALY IS ANOTHER COUNTRY WITH MANY REGIONAL CUISINES. WHILE IT IS difficult to choose one that represents the entire nation, pasta with meatballs and meaty Bolognese sauce certainly comes to mind. What may surprise many Americans is that traditional Italian Bolognese sauce contains no tomatoes—which is really not that surprising, considering that tomatoes were first brought to Italy from the New World long after Italians began eating pasta with sauce.

1 lb. pork spareribs, meat removed from bones and shredded
1 lb. Italian sausage, ground or chopped (with casings removed)
2 stalks celery, chopped
2 carrots, chopped

1 onion, chopped

4 oz. pancetta, finely chopped

3 Tbsp. butter

2 Tbsp. olive oil

4 cloves garlic, minced

2 bay leaves

1 Tbsp. fresh thyme

2 c. red wine

3 c. beef or chicken broth

½ c. whole milk

1 lb. fettuccine or pappardelle pasta, cooked

Combine celery, carrots, and onion in a blender or food processor. Pulse until vegetables are finely grated.

Heat butter in a skillet over medium heat. Add pancetta and cook for about 5 minutes. Add vegetables, reduce heat to low, and cook for 15-20 minutes.

While vegetables cook, heat olive oil in a Dutch oven or stockpot over medium-high heat. Add garlic and sauté 2-3 minutes or until fragrant. Add rib meat and sausage and cook until brown, about 15 minutes, breaking sausage into pieces. Add vegetable mixture to pot with meat, along with bay leaf and thyme. Add wine and continue to cook over medium-high heat, stirring constantly and scraping bottom of pan, until half of the wine has evaporated, about 15 minutes.

Add broth, cover, and simmer over low heat for 2 hours. Add milk and continue to cook until milk is warmed. Once ready, the sauce should be mostly dry and have very little liquid. Serve sauce over pasta.

Per serving: 916 calories, 65 g fat, 22 g saturated fat, 862 mg sodium, 31 g carbohydrates, 45 g protein.

VARIATION:

For a more traditional marinara-style sauce, add one 6-oz. can of tomato paste and one 28-oz. can of pureed tomatoes with broth, omit wine, and reduce broth by 1 cup.

KOSOVO BUREK

3 / 1 / 3
COOK TIME: 55 MINUTES
ACTIVE PREP TIME: 30 MINUTES
MAKES 6-8 SERVINGS

EVEN THOUGH IT IS STILL OCCUPIED BY ITS NEIGHBOR SERBIA, THE Republic of Kosovo declared its independence in 2008 and is largely recognized in the international community as an independent state. Kosovar cuisine incorporates many dishes from Serbia, Bosnia and Herzegovina, Albania, and other Balkan nations. One example is burek (also known as pite), a layered meat and phyllo pastry dish that can be assembled in a spiral shape, in stacked layers, or as rolled "cigars." This recipe uses the spiral shape.

1 lb. ground beef
12 large sheets phyllo pastry
¼ c. vegetable oil, plus more for sautéing and greasing pan
1 yellow onion, chopped
1 Tbsp. paprika
1 tsp. ground allspice
1 tsp. ground black pepper
2 eggs
¼ c. plain yogurt, divided
½ c. water

Heat vegetable oil in a heavy skillet over medium-high heat. Add onions and sauté until translucent, about 5 minutes. Add ground beef to pan along with paprika, allspice, and black pepper and cook until browned, about 10 minutes longer. Set aside to cool.

Preheat oven to 350 degrees. Grease a 10-inch round metal baking dish. Whisk together 1 egg, 2 Tbsp. yogurt, ¼ c. vegetable oil, and water. Unroll 2 sheets of phyllo pastry and brush with egg mixture to saturate. Spread ⅓ c. of ground beef mixture along near end of phyllo sheet. Roll phyllo sheet to form a log, and then roll from one end to form a spiral. Place phyllo and beef spiral in center of pan. Repeat with remaining phyllo sheets and ground beef mixture, wrapping each log around the center in pan to form a larger spiral until pan is filled.

Whisk together remaining egg and 2 Tbsp. yogurt and brush top of burek. Bake burek for 40 minutes or until top is golden brown. Allow to cool slightly, then cut into wedges to serve.

Per serving: 349 calories, 14 g fat, 4 g saturated fat, 301 mg sodium, 29 g carbohydrates, 25 g protein.

SERVING SUGGESTION:

Serve with plain yogurt on the side.

VARIATIONS:

For a spicier burek, replace allspice and black pepper with 2 tsp. red pepper flakes. Ground pork or lamb may be used in place of beef.

LATVIA
KARBONADE
WITH RASOLS

1 / 1 / 1
COOK TIME: 45 MINUTES
ACTIVE PREP TIME: 20 MINUTES
INACTIVE PREP TIME: 8 HOURS
MAKES 6 SERVINGS

THE FEUDAL SYSTEM ENDURED IN LATVIA FAR LONGER THAN IT DID ELSEWHERE in Europe–until the nineteenth century! Since most Latvian people were serfs, they ate food that was self-grown, high in calories, and rarely included spices, which were expensive and hard to find outside of major cities. Little has changed about Latvian food: heavy on local ingredients, pickling, fermenting, and fats, but light on spices and seasonings.

For karbonāde:
6 boneless pork chops
3 Tbsp. half and half
1 egg, beaten
½ c. all-purpose flour
1 c. bread crumbs
Salt and pepper, to taste
Oil, for frying
1 Tbsp. butter

Place pork chops between two pieces of plastic wrap and beat with a mallet or rolling pin until flattened and tenderized.

Combine egg and half and half. Season bread crumbs with salt and pepper. Dredge pork chops first in flour, then in egg mixture, and finally in breadcrumbs.

Heat oil in a heavy skillet over medium heat and add butter. Add pork chops and cook for 5 minutes on each side or until golden brown, with only a small amount of pink in the center.

Per serving: 386 calories, 20 g fat, 8 g saturated fat, 599 mg sodium, 22 g carbohydrates, 30 g protein.

For rasols:
2 lbs. potatoes, peeled and cubed
6 eggs
Water, for boiling
6 medium dill pickles, diced
1 apple, diced (optional)
¼ c. mayonnaise
2 Tbsp. sour cream
2 tsp. mustard
2 tsp. white vinegar
1 tsp. Worcestershire sauce
½ tsp. salt
¼ tsp. ground black pepper

Bring a pot of water to a boil and add potatoes. Reduce heat to medium and boil until potatoes are fully cooked, about 15-20 minutes. Drain and allow to cool.

Boil another pot of water and add eggs. Boil eggs until hard-cooked, about 12 minutes. Remove shells and cut eggs into cubes. Combine eggs, potatoes, pickles, and apple (if using) in a bowl.

Combine mayonnaise, sour cream, mustard, vinegar, Worcestershire sauce, salt, and pepper in a small bowl. Stir until smooth, adding more mayonnaise or sour cream if desired. Add to potato mixture and stir to coat. Cover with plastic wrap and refrigerate for 8 hours or overnight. Serve with karbonāde.

Per serving: 247 calories, 9 g fat, 3 g saturated fat, 1131 mg sodium, 34 g carbohydrates, 9 g protein.

VARIATION:

Pickled beets can be used in place of dill pickles in rasols.

TIP:

To make a sauce for the karbonāde, combine ½ c. mayonnaise with 4 finely minced anchovy filets and 1 clove garlic.

LIECHTENSTEIN KÄSKNÖPFLE

3 / 2 / 2
COOK TIME: 15 MINUTES
ACTIVE PREP TIME: 30 MINUTES
MAKES 4 SERVINGS

THERE ARE FEW FOODS MORE COMFORTING THAN MACARONI AND CHEESE, and this Liechtensteiner version is no exception. The unofficial dish of this tiny country sandwiched between Switzerland and Austria incorporates the cheese for which its neighbor to the west is known and its eastern neighbor's tiny spaetzle pasta. It may seem dauting at first to make your own spaetzle, but give it a try!

3 c. all-purpose flour

6 eggs, beaten

1 Tbsp. semolina

1 Tbsp. water, plus more for boiling

1 tsp. salt, plus more for boiling

8 oz. Gruyère cheese, grated

6 oz. Emmental cheese, grated

¼ c. plus 1 Tbsp. butter

2 small onions, sliced

Combine flour, eggs, semolina, 1 Tbsp. water, and salt and knead until a coarse dough is formed. Using a spaetzle press, potato press, or metal grater, press the dough through to form noodles.

Bring a large pot of salted water to a boil. Carefully add spaetzle and boil until pasta starts to float (this should take only a few minutes). Drain carefully.

While still hot, transfer one-third of the spaetzle to a large bowl and top with one-third of the cheeses. Do the same with the rest of the spaetzle and cheese, and allow cheese to melt.

Heat butter in a medium skillet over high heat. Cook onions until very brown and slightly crisp, about 7-8 minutes. Spread onions on top of käsknöpfle and serve.

Per serving: 844 calories, 36 g fat, 20 g saturated fat, 875 mg sodium, 83 g carbohydrates, 45 g protein.

VARIATIONS:

Other types of Swiss cheeses can be used in place of the Gruyère and Emmental, as can raclette, chevre, Cheddar, or blue cheese.

TIP:

If you don't want to make your own spaetzle, substitute 12 oz. of dried spaetzle for the first five ingredients and cook according to package directions.

LITHUANIA
CEPELINAI

Lithuania has a culinary tradition dating back over one thousand years, largely inspired by the country's nobility as well as its frigid climate and inaccessibility. Meat and game, especially pork, are mainstays, as are pickled and fermented foods. Since Lithuania has little arable land, many vegetables are foraged. Potatoes, sour cream, and bacon make these dumplings a classic Lithuanian dish whose name translates to "zeppelins" in reference to their shape.

6 lbs. Russet potatoes, peeled, divided
1 lb. ground pork
Water, for boiling
1 Tbsp. plus 1 tsp. salt, divided
2 large onions, finely chopped, divided
6 oz. thick-cut bacon, diced
Oil, for frying
1 c. sour cream
Salt and pepper, to taste

Cube 1 lb. of potatoes. Bring a pot of water to a boil and add cubed potatoes. Reduce heat to medium and boil until potatoes are tender, about 20-25 minutes. Drain and mash potatoes, and allow to cool.

Grate remaining potatoes using a box grater. Place grated potatoes in a cheesecloth and squeeze until all moisture is gone, reserving liquid. Potato liquid will separate into two layers: one clear liquid layer on top, and a layer of potato starch at the bottom of the bowl. Drain off top layer, reserving potato starch.

Combine grated potatoes, mashed potatoes, and potato starch. Add 2 tsp. salt and mix until a dough-like consistency is achieved. Divide potato mixture into 12 ball-shaped portions.

In a separate bowl, combine pork, half of one onion, and 2 tsp. salt. Mix thoroughly and divide into 12 ball-shaped portions.

Bring a stockpot of salted water to a boil. Flatten each potato ball slightly and place a meat ball on top. Fold edges of potato around meat ball until it is surrounded and seal.

Once water is boiling, reduce heat to medium and carefully lower dumplings into pot. Simmer for 20 minutes or until potato and meat are both cooked (you may need to cut one dumpling open to be certain).

Heat oil in a large skillet over medium heat. Sauté bacon and remaining onion for 5-10 minutes or until all fat has been cooked from bacon. Add sour cream and stir vigorously. Add water if necessary to achieve a sauce-like texture. Serve dumplings with gravy.

Per serving: 628 calories, 16 g fat, 8 g saturated fat, 419 mg sodium, 88 g carbohydrates, 34 g protein.

SERVING SUGGESTION:

Top with chopped dill, parsley, or green onions.

TIP:

To keep grated potatoes from browning while standing, sprinkle with citric acid.

LUXEMBOURG JUDD MAT GAARDEBOUNEN

3 / 3 / 2
COOK TIME: 2 HOURS, 15 MINUTES
ACTIVE PREP TIME: 25 MINUTES
INACTIVE PREP TIME: 8 HOURS
MAKES 6 SERVINGS

THE SMALLEST AND SOUTHERNMOST OF THE LOW COUNTRIES, LUXEMBOURG has a surprisingly large number of national dishes. One of the most well-known is

Judd mat Gaardebounen, which combines smoked pork with broad (fava) beans. This dish has its origins in the village of Gostingen (population 323), where broad beans are celebrated every summer at an annual Bean Feast.

2 lbs. smoked pork (neck meat)
Water, for boiling and soaking
4 carrots, sliced
2 stalks celery, sliced
1 onion, sliced
1 leek, white parts only, sliced
1 bay leaf
1 Tbsp. black peppercorns
1 tsp. whole cloves
6 oz. Moselle or Riesling wine
1 c. butter
1 c. all-purpose flour
2 lbs. fresh fava beans (not dried), peeled
½ c. fresh savory, finely chopped
Salt and pepper, to taste

Rinse pork with cold water for several minutes. Place pork in a deep dish, cover with cold water, and allow to soak for at least 8 hours, draining and replacing water once every 2 hours.

Place the pork in a Dutch oven and add enough cold water to cover. Bring to a boil, reduce heat to medium-low, and add carrots, celery, onion, leek, bay leaf, black peppercorns, cloves, and wine. Cover and simmer for 2 hours. Remove pork from pot and set aside, reserving 1 c. of the boiling water.

Bring a medium saucepan of water to a boil. Add fava beans and cook for about 2-3 minutes or just until soft. Drain beans and plunge into cold water to stop the cooking process.

Melt the butter in the saucepan used to cook beans over medium heat. Add flour and beat with a whisk until well blended. Add water as needed to bring the sauce to a thick but flowing consistency. Add fava beans and savory and stir until a chunky sauce is created (do not overcook beans to the point that they become mushy). Slice the meat and serve with sauce.

Per serving: 1107 calories, 41 g fat, 23 g saturated fat, 2055 mg sodium, 113 g carbohydrates, 70 g protein.

TIP:

If using dried fava beans (not recommended), soak 1 lb. beans in 3 qt. water overnight. Drain, rinse, and peel beans. Dried beans will need to be boiled for longer than fresh beans (up to 45 minutes).

MALTA
PASTIZZI

3 / 1 / 2
COOK TIME: 30 MINUTES
ACTIVE PREP TIME: 45 MINUTES
INACTIVE PREP TIME: 2 HOURS
MAKES 16 PASTIZZI

MALTA'S TINY SIZE, ITS CENTRAL LOCATION ALONG SEVERAL IMPORTANT trade routes, and the presence of the international Knights of St. John have led to Maltese cuisine being diverse, heavy with foreign influences, and reliant upon imports. Native cheeses and flaky, layered pastry both figure large in Malta's popular dishes. Pastizzi (singular: pastizz) are eaten both as a snack and as a meal in Malta, where they are sold at pastizzeria and from street vendors. Although the variations are endless, the most common fillings are cheese and peas. This recipe includes both.

For pastry:
2 c. all-purpose flour, plus more for flouring surface
1-½ c. water
Oil, for oiling surface
1 c. lard or vegetable shortening

Combine all ingredients and mix until a smooth dough is formed. Turn the mixture onto a floured surface and knead for about 15 minutes. Roll the dough into a log and cut into 8 portions. Cover portions with plastic wrap and allow to rest for 1 hour.

Take one of the 8 portions and stretch as thinly as possible into a long rectangular sheet of dough, using a rolling pin if necessary, onto an oiled surface. Spread 2 Tbsp. lard or shortening over the top of the sheet of dough. Starting at one end, roll the dough until you have a log. Stretch and roll out the second portion the same way. Place the dough log at the end of the rectangle and roll it up to form a thicker log. Do the same with the next 2 portions; then repeat the process using the remaining 4 portions.

Carefully and slowly cut each log into 8 portions using a serrated knife; the layers of the log should be preserved. Refrigerate the 16 portions for 1 hour.

For cheese filling:
2 c. ricotta cheese
½ c. grated Cheddar and Parmesan cheeses (any combination)
1 egg, beaten
2 Tbsp. fresh parsley

Combine cheeses, egg, and parsley and mix vigorously.

For pea filling:
One 15-oz. can English peas, drained
1 clove garlic, minced
1 small onion, finely diced
1 Tbsp. curry powder
Olive oil, for sautéing
¾ lb. corned beef (optional)

Heat oil in a skillet over medium-high heat. Sauté onion and garlic until onion is translucent, about 5 minutes. Add curry powder. If using corned beef, add to skillet and fry for 5 minutes longer.

Add peas to skillet and reduce temperature to medium-low. Using a potato masher or ladle, gently mash the peas. Stir until combined and heat until warmed.

Preheat oven to 425 degrees. Flatten each dough portion into a circle and place one generous spoonful of filling in the middle. Roll the sides upward to create an oval shape, then seal the dough around the filling. Squeeze the corners to make points. Place pastizzi on a lightly oiled baking sheet and bake for 20-25 minutes or until golden.

Per pastizz (cheese filling): 267 calories, 20 g fat, 10 g saturated fat, 162 mg sodium, 12 g carbohydrates, 8 g protein. Per pastizz (pea filling): 168 calories, 7 g fat, 2 g saturated fat, 401 mg sodium, 18 g carbohydrates, 9 g protein.

VARIATIONS:

Many variations on pastizzi fillings exist, including potatoes, eggplant, spinach, ground beef, pepperoni, and pesto or tomato sauce. Sweet pastizzi can be made using custard, pistachios or other nuts, and honey.

MOLDOVA TOCHITURA WITH MAMALIGA

1 / 1 / 2
COOK TIME: 50 MINUTES
ACTIVE PREP TIME: 10 MINUTES
MAKES 4 SERVINGS

A COUNTRY SANDWICHED BETWEEN ROMANIA AND THE UKRAINE, MOLDOVA pulls many of its national recipes from these two countries and others that surround it. Tochitură, a traditional Romanian stew, is served with tomato sauce, eggs, and sheep's cheese in Moldova. Mămăligă, Moldova's trademark dish, accompanies nearly every Moldovan meal.

For tochitură:
1 lb. pork (loin or shoulder), cut into small cubes
1 lb. smoked sausage, sliced
Oil, for frying
1 large onion, finely chopped

¼ c. water
½ tsp. salt
1 c. dry white wine
2 Tbsp. tomato paste
3 cloves garlic, minced
2 bay leaves
4 eggs
4 oz. mild feta cheese

For mămăligă:
2 c. water
1 Tbsp. plus 1-½ tsp. butter
½ tsp. salt
1 c. yellow cornmeal
Salt and pepper, to taste

Heat oil in a Dutch oven over medium-high heat. Add pork cubes and fry until lightly browned on all sides, about 5 minutes. Add onion, water, and salt to the pot. Cover, reduce heat to medium-low, and simmer for 20 minutes or until meat is tender. Add the sausage, wine, tomato paste, garlic, and bay leaves to pot. Stir, recover, and continue to simmer for 10 minutes longer.

Bring water, butter, and salt to a boil in a medium saucepan. While stirring, sprinkle cornmeal into boiling water a few spoonfuls at a time. Reduce heat to low and continue to stir until cornmeal thickens. Cover and simmer for 10 minutes, stirring occasionally.

Heat a little oil in a separate skillet over medium-high heat. Fry the eggs one at a time until desired doneness is reached (over-easy is traditional). Divide mămăligă between 4 plates and season with salt and pepper. Ladle hot stew on plate with mămăligă, cheese, and fried eggs.

Per serving: 1069 calories, 73 g fat, 33 g saturated fat, 2021 mg sodium, 32 g carbohydrates, 59 g protein.

VARIATION:

Use bacon in addition to or in place of sausage.

MONACO BARBAGIUANS

2 / 1 / 2
COOK TIME: 30 MINUTES
ACTIVE PREP TIME: 20 MINUTES
INACTIVE PREP TIME: 1 HOUR
MAKES ABOUT 40 BARBAGIUANS

STANDING ON LESS THAN ONE SQUARE MILE, MONACO IS ARGUABLY too small to have its own distinct cuisine. But the city-state definitely has a national dish: the savory cheese- and chard-filled pastries called barbagiuans (which in Monegasque means "Uncle Johns"). Barbagiuans are eaten year-round, but they are especially popular on November 19, when Monaco celebrates the Sovereign Prince's Day.

1 c. all-purpose flour
2 Tbsp. olive oil, plus more for frying
½ tsp. water
2 shallots, minced
1 medium onion, finely chopped
2 cloves garlic, minced
½ lb. Swiss chard (ribs removed), chopped
¼ c. grated Parmesan cheese
¼ c. ricotta cheese
Salt and pepper, to taste
1 Tbsp. fresh thyme

Place flour in a bowl and make a well in the center. Pour 2 Tbsp. olive oil and water in well and mix to combine. Knead until dough reaches a crumbly consistency. Cover in plastic wrap and refrigerate for at least 1 hour.

Heat olive oil in a skillet over medium heat. Sauté shallot, onion, and garlic until golden, about 3-4 minutes. Add chard and continue to cook until chard wilts. Remove from heat. Once cooled, stir in cheeses and season with salt and pepper.

Roll out the dough to a thin sheet with a rolling pin. Using a large round cookie cutter, cut circles from the dough and place a small spoonful of chard and cheese filling in the center of each circle. Fold the circles in half and wet to seal.

Pour olive oil to a depth of about ½-inch in a heavy skillet with high sides. Add thyme and heat oil to a high temperature. Reduce heat slightly and fry barbagiuans in batches until golden, about 4 minutes. Lift carefully from pan and allow to drain on paper towels before serving.

Per barbagiuan: 27 calories, 1 g fat, 0 g saturated fat, 27 mg sodium, 3 g carbohydrates, 1 g protein.

VARIATIONS:

Use spinach, mushrooms, butternut squash, or rice in place of chard.

MONTENEGRO JAPRACI

3 / 1 / 2
COOK TIME: 2 HOURS, 40 MINUTES
ACTIVE PREP TIME: 20 MINUTES
MAKES 6 SERVINGS

THE SMALL BALKAN NATION OF MONTENEGRO HAS A VARIETY OF NATIVE dishes that reflect its position as an Eastern European nation on the Adriatic coast. Japraci, one of many dishes in the region made from meat and rice rolled into leaves, is unique in that it uses raštan, a vegetable native to Montenegro, rather than the usual cabbage. Raštan is almost identical to collard greens, a dietary staple in parts of the United States.

2 lbs. collard greens (whole leaves only), cleaned and with stems removed
Water, for blanching and boiling
1 lb. veal shoulder or shank, cut into small pieces
1 medium onion, chopped
Oil, for frying
½ c. brown rice
2 Tbsp. fresh parsley
Salt and pepper, to taste

Clean collard greens thoroughly and remove stems. Bring a large pot of water to a boil. Place leaves in boiling water and cook for 2 minutes. Remove leaves from boiling water and immediately submerge in cold water to stop cooking process. Keep leaves in cold water until japraci are ready to assemble.

In a small saucepan, bring 1 c. water to a boil. Add rice, reduce heat to medium-low, cover, and simmer for 20-30 minutes or until fully cooked.

Heat oil in a large skillet over medium-high heat. Sauté onion until translucent, about 5 minutes. Add veal to pan and continue cooking until meat is browned, about 6-7 minutes. Add cooked rice and parsley and stir. Season with salt and pepper.

Take each collard green leaf and place a small amount of veal and rice filling at the widest end. Fold the edges over it and then roll in the other direction. Repeat with the remainder of leaves and filling. Use toothpicks or twine to hold rolls together if necessary.

Bring a large pot of water to a boil. Reduce heat to low and carefully lower each roll into the water. Cover and simmer over low heat for 2 hours.

Per serving: 277 calories, 12 g fat, 3 g saturated fat, 90 mg sodium, 22 g carbohydrates, 23 g protein.

SERVING SUGGESTION:

Serve with Greek yogurt and lemon slices.

VARIATIONS:

Use cabbage or kale leaves in place of collard greens.

THE NETHERLANDS HUTSPOT

1 / 1 / 2
COOK TIME: 30 MINUTES
ACTIVE PREP TIME: 15 MINUTES
MAKES 4 SERVINGS

IN 1573, AS THE EIGHTY YEARS' WAR RAGED BETWEEN THE LOW COUNTRIES and Spain, the Spanish general Francisco de Valdez attempted to capture the Dutch city of Leiden by placing it under siege. One year later, thousands of residents had starved to death, but the city was finally relieved as waters rose and Spanish forces retreated in fear. According to legend, the Leidenaars found several pots of potato and carrot stew that the Spanish had left behind when they fled, and a beloved Dutch comfort food was discovered. Today, hutspot is eaten in the Netherlands every October 3, the anniversary of the Siege of Leiden.

3 large Russet potatoes, peeled and coarsely chopped
4 large carrots, peeled and chopped
Water, for boiling
½ c. butter
4 shallots, peeled and sliced
8 thick slices bacon
1 c. whole milk
Salt and pepper, to taste

Place potatoes and carrots in a large saucepan and add enough water to cover by 1 inch. Bring to a boil, reduce heat to medium-high, and continue to boil until potatoes and carrots are tender, about 15 minutes. Drain and allow to cool slightly.

Melt ¼ c. butter in a skillet over medium heat. Add shallots and sauté until golden brown, about 5 minutes. Remove shallots from skillet, reserving any remaining butter.

Heat a separate skillet and add bacon. Fry bacon for about 10 minutes or until crispy and remove from pan, reserving bacon fat.

Place cooked potatoes and carrots in a large bowl. Use a hand mixer to whip the potatoes for about 3 minutes on medium setting. Add milk and remaining ¼ c. butter as well as butter from sautéing shallots and mix well.

Chop bacon into small pieces. Add half the bacon to the potato mixture and stir. Season with salt and pepper. To serve, divide mashed potato mixture between four bowls. Pour one spoonful of bacon fat over each portion and top with shallots and remaining bacon.

Per serving: 673 calories, 41 g fat, 21 g saturated fat, 1133 mg sodium, 56 g carbohydrates, 22 g protein.

VARIATIONS:

Hutspot can be prepared without bacon, or with cheese or sausage. A popular variation on hutspot, stamppot, uses kale, spinach, turnip greens, or other leafy vegetables instead of carrots.

NORTH MACEDONIA
TAVCE GRAVCE

2 / 2 / 2
COOK TIME: 3 HOURS, 10 MINUTES
ACTIVE PREP TIME: 10 MINUTES
INACTIVE PREP TIME: 8 HOURS
MAKES 4-6 SERVINGS

MACEDONIAN CUISINE FUSES INFLUENCES OF THE MEDITERRANEAN, Eastern Europe, and the Middle East. The name of North Macedonia's national dish, Tavče Gravče, means "beans in a frying pan." But these Balkan baked beans are traditionally baked in an earthenware pot. Its name probably reflects changes made in its preparation over time.

1 lb. dried cannellini (white kidney) beans
1-½ qt. water, plus more for soaking
2 Tbsp. butter
1 Tbsp. all-purpose flour
1 Tbsp. sweet paprika
2 large onions, chopped
1 c. cherry tomatoes, crushed
¼ c. sundried tomatoes, sliced
2 banana peppers, finely chopped
4 cloves garlic, crushed
1 Tbsp. dried mint
1 Tbsp. dried parsley
Salt and pepper, to taste
Chopped fresh parsley, for serving

Place beans in a bowl, cover with cold water, and soak for 8 hours or overnight. Drain and rinse beans.

Heat butter in a Dutch oven over medium heat. Add flour and paprika and cook, stirring vigorously, until flour is golden and mixture is smooth. Add beans, water, onions, tomatoes, peppers, garlic, mint, and parsley. Cook for at least 2 hours or until beans are tender and most of the liquid is evaporated.

Preheat oven to 350 degrees. Transfer bean mixture to a baking dish and season with salt and pepper. Bake uncovered for 1 hour. Garnish with parsley and serve.

Per serving: 294 calories, 5 g fat, 3 g saturated fat, 131 mg sodium, 69 g carbohydrates, 21 g protein.

VARIATION:

Add 1 lb. sliced, cooked sausage, ham, or bacon to beans before transferring to baking dish. Chorizo and kielbasa are good choices.

NORWAY
FÅRIKÅL

1 / 1 / 1
COOK TIME: 2 HOURS
ACTIVE PREP TIME: 10 MINUTES
MAKES 6 SERVINGS

FÅRIKÅL ("SHEEP IN CABBAGE") IS A SAVORY STEW OF LAMB, CABBAGE, AND peppercorns that has long been a mandatory element of Norway's frigid autumn months. It is also one of the few national dishes that was democratically chosen by its country's people. In 1972, a competition was held on the Norwegian Broadcasting Corporation (NRK)'s Nitimen cooking program in which fårikål emerged the winner. After Norway's food and agriculture minister sponsored a second competition in 2014, fårikål retained its title with 45 percent of the national vote.

4 lbs. lamb or mutton shanks, including bones
½ c. all-purpose flour
2 c. water

4 lbs. green cabbage, cut into wedges
2 Tbsp. black peppercorns
1 Tbsp. salt
Butter, for serving

Dredge meat in flour. Place water in a stockpot and add a layer of meat at the bottom. Cover it with a layer of cabbage, followed by a layer of peppercorns and salt. Repeat this process until all of the meat, cabbage, peppercorns, and salt have been added to the pot.

Bring pot to a boil. Cover, reduce heat to low, and cook about 2 hours or until meat is tender enough to fall from the bone. Divide between 6 bowls. Top each serving with a pat of butter and serve.

Per serving: 524 calories, 17 g fat, 6 g saturated fat, 1386 mg sodium, 27 g carbohydrates, 66 g protein.

SERVING SUGGESTION:
Serve with boiled potatoes (traditional), onions, celery, or carrots.

POLAND
PIEROGI

3 / 1 / 2
COOK TIME: 1 HOUR, 20 MINUTES
ACTIVE PREP TIME: 55 MINUTES
INACTIVE PREP TIME: 20 MINUTES
MAKES 8 SERVINGS

THE NAME PIEROGI COMES FROM A WORD MEANING "FEAST," AND THESE dumplings were originally eaten only on special occasions in Poland (they even have their own patron saint, St. Hyacinth). But today, they are eaten year-round and are a part of the regular Polish diet. According to some sources, pierogi (singular: pierog) were brought from China to Europe by Marco Polo; others say that the Mongols brought them to Eastern Europe from across Russia. Whatever the case, they are very versatile and can be filled with cheese, sauerkraut, potatoes, cabbage, mushrooms, ground beef, spinach, or lentils, among many other things. Dessert pierogi can even be made with fresh fruit and sugar.

1 lb. beef (chuck or brisket), cut into large pieces
2 Tbsp. salt, divided
Water, for boiling
3 carrots, chopped
1 leek, chopped
1 stalk celery, chopped
1 c. parsley, finely chopped, divided
2 medium onions, finely chopped, divided
Oil or butter, for sautéing
2 slices white bread
2 eggs, beaten
Salt and pepper, to taste
Pierogi dough (recipe below)

Bring a large stockpot of water to a boil. Add beef and 1 Tbsp. salt and reduce heat to medium. While beef simmers, add carrots, leek, celery, ½ c. parsley, and 1 onion. Reduce heat to low and simmer for 1 hour.

Heat oil or butter in a skillet over medium-high heat. Sauté remaining onion until very brown, about 7-8 minutes. Set aside.

When meat and vegetables are finished cooking, remove meat from broth and cut into smaller pieces. Take 1 c. of broth from pot and add to a small bowl with white bread. Once saturated, remove bread from broth and combine with meat and fried onion.

Process meat mixture in a meat grinder. (If you do not have a meat grinder, process in small batches in a food processor on a low setting.) Add eggs and remaining parsley to meat mixture and stir to combine. Season with salt and pepper to taste. If mixture is dry, add a small amount of broth.

Roll pierogi dough to a thickness of ⅛-inch on a floured surface. Use a large, round cookie cutter to cut circles from dough. Place a spoonful of meat filling on each circle, fold in half, and press edges to seal.

Bring another stockpot of water to a boil. Add remaining salt and reduce heat to medium-high. Carefully lower pierogi into water with a slotted spoon and boil until they float on the water's surface, then lift out and set aside.

Once all pierogi are cooked, heat oil or butter in a large skillet over medium-high heat. Add pierogi and fry until brown on both sides, about 2-3 minutes per side. Season with salt and pepper and serve.

For pierogi dough:
3 c. whole wheat flour
½ tsp. salt
¾ c. boiling water
¼ c. cold water
½ tsp. olive oil

Combine flour and salt and sift together in a large bowl. Add boiling water and stir with a fork until mixture is completely moistened and lumps are gone. Cover bowl with a cloth and allow to stand for 5 minutes.

Add cold water and stir to incorporate. Recover bowl and allow to stand for 15 minutes longer.

Add oil to dough and remove from bowl. Knead on a floured surface for at least 10 minutes or until dough is smooth, pliable, and slightly sticky.

Per serving: 360 calories, 9 g fat, 2 g saturated fat, 2129 mg sodium, 44 g carbohydrates, 25 g protein.

SERVING SUGGESTIONS:
Serve with fried onion cracklings and bacon (traditional) or with ketchup and mustard (nontraditional).

VARIATIONS:
For Ruskie (Ruthenian) pierogi: Fill with mashed potato, white curd cheese, and fried onion, and boil but do not fry. *For sauerkraut and mushroom pierogi:* Use 2 lbs. sauerkraut and 3 c. raw mushrooms for filling. *For berry pierogi:* Use strawberries, blueberries, and/or bilberries with a few Tbsp. of sugar, do not fry, and serve with whipped cream or vanilla ice cream.

PORTUGAL
COZIDO

1 / 1 / 1
COOK TIME: 3 HOURS, 40 MINUTES
ACTIVE PREP TIME: 15 MINUTES
MAKES 8 SERVINGS

Cozido is iberia's answer to the one-pot comfort stew, a staple

throughout Europe. The Portuguese version is distinguished by its use of various sausages and other cuts of pork (including some not in the regular American diet) along with beans, collard greens, and root vegetables.

2 lbs. pork shoulder, cut into pieces
1 lb. pork rib meat
½ lb. ham hock, cut into small pieces
1 lb. smoked sausage (preferably linguica), chopped
½ lb. bacon, chopped
3 bay leaves
4 qt. water
1 onion, quartered
4 carrots, peeled and sliced diagonally
2 turnips, quartered
2 leeks, chopped
1 large potato, peeled and cubed
2 tsp. salt
1 tsp. pepper
½ tsp. whole cloves
1 bunch collard greens, chopped

Heat oil in a large stock pot over medium-high heat. Add pork, sausage, and bacon and cook until brown, about 8-10 minutes. Add ham hock, bay leaves, and water and bring to a boil. Skim foam from surface, reduce heat to medium-low, and add onion.

Place lid over pot so that it is partially uncovered and simmer for 1-½ hours. Add

66 TASTING THE WORLD

carrots, turnips, leeks, potato, salt, and pepper and simmer for 1-½ hours longer. Add collard greens and simmer for another 30 minutes.

Per serving: 1248 calories, 82 g fat, 28 g saturated fat, 1947 mg sodium, 18 g carbohydrates, 102 g protein.

VARIATIONS:

For a vegetarian version (known in Portugal as cozido de grão), replace the meats with an equivalent amount of chickpeas. Or, use chicken in place of pork (Spanish cozido) or New World vegetables such as sweet potatoes and corn in place of turnips and leeks (Brazilian cozido).

ROMANIA
GHIVECI

1 / 1 / 1
COOK TIME: 45 MINUTES
ACTIVE PREP TIME: 10 MINUTES
MAKES 6 SERVINGS

ROMANIA IS PRIMARILY EASTERN ORTHODOX, AND DURING THE LENTEN season most refrain from eating meat. At this time, hearty vegetable stews such as ghiveci are often served as main courses. But ghiveci is most popular at the end of the summer months, when a bountiful harvest ensures that its ingredients are at their freshest and most robust.

2 large onions, chopped
4 large carrots, peeled and sliced diagonally
2 red bell peppers, seeded and chopped
2 green bell peppers, seeded and chopped
Olive oil, for sautéing
1 small cabbage, thinly sliced
3 large potatoes, peeled and chopped
3 cloves garlic, crushed
One 15-oz. can chopped tomatoes

2 c. water
1 tsp. dried thyme
½ tsp. paprika
Salt and pepper, to taste
One 12-oz. package frozen peas
2 Tbsp. fresh dill
2 Tbsp. fresh parsley
1 Tbsp. fresh lemon juice

Heat oil in a large Dutch oven over medium heat. Sauté onions, carrots, and bell peppers until onions and peppers are soft, about 5 minutes. Add cabbage, potatoes, and garlic and sauté for 3 minutes longer.

Add tomatoes (along with juice), water, thyme, and paprika. Season with salt and pepper and bring to a boil. Reduce heat to medium-low, cover, and simmer for about 30 minutes or until potatoes are tender.

Add peas, dill, parsley, and lemon juice. Recover and cook for 5 minutes longer and serve.

Per serving: 292 calories, 5 g fat, 1 g saturated fat, 150 mg sodium, 58 g carbohydrates, 8 g protein.

VARIATIONS:

When in season, eggplant, zucchini, green beans, and cauliflower may be used. If using tender vegetables, add them shortly before cooking is complete.

RUSSIA
BEEF STROGANOFF

2 / 1 / 2
COOK TIME: 20 MINUTES
ACTIVE PREP TIME: 10 MINUTES
MAKES 4 SERVINGS

THE CUISINE OF THE WORLD'S LARGEST COUNTRY IN AREA IS HIGHLY diverse, as can be expected. It pulls from the traditions of Eastern Europe, Central

Asia, and East Asia, all of which are its neighbors, as well as within its own borders. Interestingly, Russian cuisine is probably more divided by class than by region, with the traditional dishes of the aristocracy and peasantry forming two distinct culinary cultures. The most recognizable Russian dish outside of Russia, beef stroganoff falls neatly into the first category. Invented by a nineteenth-century French chef working in St. Petersburg and named for one of that city's oldest and wealthiest families, beef stroganoff combines a Russian standard—sliced beef cooked in sour cream—with Parisian cooking methods to perfectly embody pre-revolutionary Russia.

1 lb. beef sirloin or rump steak, cut into strips against the grain
1 large onion, thinly sliced
8 oz. baby portabella mushrooms, thinly sliced
Butter, for sautéing
¼ c. brandy
½ c. beef stock
1 tsp. mustard
1 bay leaf
Salt and pepper, to taste
1 c. full-fat sour cream
½ c. fresh parsley, chopped

Heat butter in a heavy skillet over medium-low heat. Sauté onions and mushrooms until brown, about 8 minutes. Remove onions and mushrooms from skillet. Add more butter and raise heat to high. Add steak and sear until brown on all sides, about 3-5 minutes. Reduce heat to medium-high.

Add brandy and cook until mostly evaporated, scraping bottom of pan constantly. Add beef stock, mustard, and bay leaf. Add onions and mushrooms back to pan and season with salt and pepper. Cook for 3 minutes longer. Remove from heat, stir in sour cream and parsley, and serve immediately.

Per serving: 436 calories, 23 g fat, 12 g saturated fat, 232 mg sodium, 8 g carbohydrates, 38 g protein.

SERVING SUGGESTIONS:

Serve with mashed potatoes or rice (traditional) or egg noodles (nontraditional).

SAN MARINO PIADINA

2 / 2 / 1
COOK TIME: 20 MINUTES
ACTIVE PREP TIME: 20 MINUTES
INACTIVE PREP TIME: 30 MINUTES
MAKES 6 SERVINGS

THE MICROSTATE OF SAN MARINO, ONE OF TWO LOCATED ENTIRELY within Italy's borders, shares a common culture with the northeastern Italian region that includes its culinary tradition. The piadina, a type of sandwich served on a thin flatbread, has been a part of this tradition since the early Renaissance. While this bread can be served with virtually any fillings, soft cheese and cured meats are the most Sammarinese.

4 c. all-purpose flour
2 tsp. baking powder
1 tsp. salt
¼ c. plus 1 Tbsp. lard
¾ c. whole milk
½ c. water
Oil, for frying
¾ lb. prosciutto, thinly sliced
¾ lb. stracchino or provolone cheese, sliced
3 c. baby arugula or spinach

Sift together flour, baking powder, and salt. Fold in lard until pea-sized lumps form, and then add water and milk. Knead on a floured surface for 10 minutes or until smooth and pliable. If dough becomes sticky, add more flour.

Place the dough in a bowl and cover with plastic wrap. Allow to sit at room temperature for 30 minutes to 1 hour. Divide dough into 6 portions. Use a rolling pin to flatten each into a circle to a thickness of ⅛ inch. Prick the surface of the dough with a fork to release air bubbles.

Heat a small amount of oil in a non-stick skillet until hot. Cook each dough circle for 1-2 minutes on each side until golden brown. Remove from pan. While flatbread is still hot, place one-sixth of prosciutto, cheese, and arugula or spinach on half of bread and fold over. Serve immediately.

Per serving: 724 calories, 33 g fat, 15 g saturated fat, 1585 mg sodium, 68 g carbohydrates, 36 g protein.

VARIATIONS:

Grilled steak or chicken, sausage, salami, shrimp, fresh mozzarella, feta, sundried tomatoes, mushrooms, eggplant, and sauces such as marinara or pesto can be used as fillings. For a nontraditional piadina, use peanut butter and jelly or sliced banana and hazelnut spread. Use olive oil in place of lard for a lighter, crisper piadina.

SCOTLAND
HOTCH POTCH

2 / 1 / 1
COOK TIME: 2 HOURS, 45 MINUTES
ACTIVE PREP TIME: 10 MINUTES
MAKES 6 SERVINGS

UNLIKE THE ENGLISH, THE SCOTTISH PEOPLE HAVE TRADITIONALLY BEEN nomadic to a degree, and their cuisine includes many dishes that can be carried for long periods without spoiling and prepared while traveling. Scotland's infamous national dish, haggis, includes at least one ingredient that cannot legally be purchased in the United States, sheep lungs. Hotch potch, known in the old Scots dialect as *hairst bree* (harvest broth), is a rich, comforting stew that is far more likely to appeal to an American palate.

2 lbs. lamb shanks, with bones
Oil, for frying
1-¾ qt. chicken stock, divided
1 bunch fresh parsley
4 sprigs fresh thyme
2 bay leaves
1-2 Tbsp. butter

8 green onions, sliced
3 carrots, peeled and finely chopped
6 oz. button mushrooms, quartered
1 lb. green peas, shelled, divided
1 small cabbage, shredded, divided
1 Tbsp. fresh mint, finely chopped
½ tsp. sugar
Salt and pepper, to taste

Heat oil in a Dutch oven over medium-high heat. Add lamb shanks and sear on all sides until brown, about 10 minutes. Remove from pan. Pour 1 c. of chicken stock in pot and cook until reduced by half, scraping all brown bits from the bottom of the pot.

Return lamb to pot along with remainder of chicken stock. Tie the parsley, thyme, and bay leaves together with a piece of twine, reserving a few parsley sprigs, and add to pot. Reduce heat to low, cover, and simmer for 1 hour, checking occasionally to skim any fat that rises to the top.

Heat butter in a skillet over medium-low heat. Sauté green onions until tender and translucent, about 3 minutes. Add carrots and mushrooms and continue to cook until carrots are soft, about 4-5 minutes.

Remove lamb shanks from pot. Slice meat from bones and cut into small pieces. Return to pot along with sautéed vegetables and ½ lb. of the green peas. Cover and simmer for 45 minutes longer. Add remainder of peas and cabbage to pot along with mint and sugar. Cover once again and simmer for 30 more minutes. Remove and discard bundle of herbs and season with salt and pepper. Garnish witrh remaining parsley to serve.

Per serving: 475 calories, 18 g fat, 6 g saturated fat, 526 mg sodium, 25 g carbohydrates, 53 g protein.

TIP:

Frozen peas may be used in this recipe, but they should be added at the very end and cooked only until thawed.

SERBIA CEVAPI

CEVAPI, OR MEAT AND ONION SAUSAGES, WERE BROUGHT TO SERBIA FROM the Ottoman Empire. They resemble the ground-beef kafta (p. 103) in many ways, and their name has the same origin as the Turkish word "kebab." In Serbia, ćevapi are a common street food and are very easy to prepare, as they do not have casings like most types of sausages.

1 lb. ground beef
1 lb. ground lamb
1 lb. ground pork
1 large onion, finely chopped
3 cloves garlic, finely chopped
3 Tbsp. sweet Hungarian paprika
1 Tbsp. ground black pepper
½ tsp. ground nutmeg
½ tsp. cayenne pepper (optional)
Olive oil, for coating

Combine beef, lamb, pork, onion, garlic, paprika, black pepper, nutmeg, and cayenne pepper (if using) in a large bowl. Cover and refrigerate for at least 4 hours or overnight.

Divide meat mixture into about 20-25 portions. Roll each portion between your hands into a 3- to 4-inch long, ¾-inch wide log. Refrigerate for 1 hour.

Prepare a charcoal grill, setting the rack about 6 inches above the heat. Lightly coat sausages with olive oil and cook over grill for 8 minutes, turning halfway through. Remove from grill and serve while hot.

Per serving: 373 calories, 14 g fat, 4 g saturated fat, 131 mg sodium, 5 g carbohydrates, 56 g protein.

SERVING SUGGESTIONS:

Serve with flatbread, sour cream, and roasted red bell pepper (traditional) or with French fries, chopped onions, and mustard (nontraditional).

TIP:

Sausages can be pan-fried for about 8 minutes instead of grilled.

SLOVAKIA
BRYNDZOVÉ HALUSKY

2 / 3 / 2
COOK TIME: 15 MINUTES
ACTIVE PREP TIME: 35 MINUTES
MAKES 4 SERVINGS

A NATIONAL DISH OF SLOVAKIA, BRYNDZOVÉ HALUSKY CAN BE COMPARED to a very sharp macaroni and cheese. It combines halušky, pasta made from potato dough, with a native cheese known as bryndza. Bryndza is made with sheep's milk, and it is very difficult to find a perfect substitute for its distinctive flavor and aroma. The Slovakian village of Turecká (population 147) hosts an annual festival and eating contest celebrating the dish.

2 lbs. potatoes, peeled and grated
1 egg, beaten
½ c. all-purpose flour
1 tsp. salt
Water, for boiling
4 oz. bacon (thick-cut or from a slab), diced
Oil, for frying
1 lb. bryndza (see Tips section for substitutes)
Chopped fresh parsley, for serving

Combine potatoes, egg, flour, and salt and knead until a dough is formed. Form potato mixture into spoon-sized dumplings.

Bring a large pot of water to a boil. Carefully lower dumplings to the water with a slotted spoon and boil until all dumplings are floating on the surface.

Heat oil in a small frying pan over medium-high heat. Add bacon and fry until brown and crisp, about 5 minutes. Remove bacon from pan and drain on paper towels.

Remove dumplings from water. When slightly cooled, stir bryndza into dumplings to combine. Serve topped with bacon and parsley.

Per serving: 539 calories, 22 g fat, 10 g saturated fat, 1407 mg sodium, 54 g carbohydrates, 30 g protein.

SERVING SUGGESTIONS:

Serve with fried onions or sauerkraut.

TIP:

If bryndza cannot be found, a substitute can be made by combining equal parts feta cheese and sour cream or fresh goat cheese and ricotta.

SLOVENIA
FIZOLOVA MINESTRA

1 / 1 / 1
COOK TIME: 15 MINUTES
ACTIVE PREP TIME: 35 MINUTES
INACTIVE PREP TIME: 8 HOURS
MAKES 6 SERVINGS

SOUPS ARE VERY POPULAR IN THIS BALKAN NATION, AND IT IS HARD TO believe that they are a relatively new addition to the country's culture. Among the most popular is one that originated in Italy, Slovenia's neighbor to the west, that is familiar to many Americans. Mineštra, as Slovenian minestrone is known, differs from the popular vegetable soup in that it includes meat and lacks a strong tomato base. But pasta, beans, and fresh vegetables are still key ingredients.

12 oz. dried beans (pinto, kidney, or a combination of the two)
Water, for soaking and boiling

1 qt. chicken broth
½ lb. pork ribs
1 ham bone
3 carrots, finely chopped
1 parsnip, finely chopped
1 stalk celery, finely chopped
1 ear sweet corn, removed from cob
1 bay leaf
8 oz. small pasta (such as shells)
½ tsp. salt
Olive oil, for sautéing
1 large onion, finely chopped
3 cloves garlic, minced
1 large tomato, peeled, seeded, and chopped
½ tsp. paprika
Salt and pepper, to taste
Chopped fresh parsley, for serving

Cover beans with cold water and allow to soak for 8 hours or overnight. Drain and rinse beans. Add beans to a stockpot along with broth, pork ribs, bone, carrots, parsnip, celery, corn, and bay leaf. Bring to a boil. Reduce heat to medium-low, cover, and simmer for 2 hours, stirring occasionally.

Shortly before cooking time ends, bring a smaller pot of water and salt to a boil. Add pasta and cook for 10 minutes. Drain pasta and add to stew. Remove ribs and bone from pot. Cut remaining meat from ribs and add back to pot.

Heat olive oil in a skillet over medium-high heat. Sauté onion and garlic until fragrant, about 3 minutes. Add tomato and paprika and sauté for 2 minutes longer. Add onion mixture to pot with other ingredients. Season with salt and pepper and garnish with chopped parsley before serving.

Per serving: 334 calories, 12 g fat, 3 g saturated fat, 447 mg sodium, 40 g carbohydrates, 20 g protein.

SERVING SUGGESTIONS:
Serve with polenta or with crusty white bread.

VARIATION:
Use smoked sausage, such as kielbasa, in place of rib meat.

SPAIN
PAELLA

3 / 2 / 2
COOK TIME: 1 HOUR, 40 MINUTES
ACTIVE PREP TIME: 15 MINUTES
INACTIVE PREP TIME: 20 MINUTES
MAKES 6-8 SERVINGS

RICE WAS BROUGHT TO SPAIN BY THE MOORS IN THE EIGHTH CENTURY.
Saffron, a spice produced from the stamens of the crocus flower and worth more than its weight in gold, was introduced shortly after. With those two pivotal ingredients, the evolution of Spain's national dish began and continues today. Paella's first incarnations included rabbit, snails, and three types of beans; shortly after, a non-halal version developed with pork and shellfish. Chicken, shrimp, and vegetables are included in most paella recipes found in Spain today.

1 lb. bone-in chicken thighs (skin-on)
1 lb. jumbo shrimp, unpeeled
1 lb. chorizo sausage, removed from casings and crumbled
2-½ c. paella rice
12 clams, mussels, or a combination
½ c. olive oil, plus more for sautéing
2 white onions, finely chopped
3 cloves garlic, crushed
4 red bell peppers, seeded and finely chopped
4 tomatoes, peeled, seeded, cored, and finely chopped
4 bay leaves

1 bunch fresh thyme
½ tsp. saffron threads
¼ c. hot water
1 Tbsp. smoked paprika
1-¾ qt. chicken broth
Chopped fresh parsley, to serve
Lemon wedges, to serve

Heat olive oil in a 16- to 18-inch paella pan over high heat. Add onions, garlic, bell peppers, tomatoes, bay leaves, and thyme and reduce heat to low. Cook over low heat for 1 hour or until mixture begins to darken and develop a paste-like consistency. Remove from pan and allow to cool.

Place saffron in hot water and allow to soak for at least 15 minutes. Water will become a deep yellow or orange-red color.

Add a little extra olive oil to paella pan (if needed). Brown chicken, shrimp, and sausage in pan for 5 minutes. Remove shrimp from pan and set aside. Return onion and tomato mixture to pan along with paprika, and cook for 5 minutes longer. Add rice to pan, a spoonful at a time, and stir to coat.

Slowly add broth and saffron mixture to pan, increase heat to high, and bring to a boil. Stir once and then cook for 15-20 minutes or until all liquid is absorbed. Halfway through cooking, add shrimp back to pan and stir.

Reduce heat to low and add shellfish hinge-side down, pushing them into the top of the rice slightly. Cook without stirring for 5-10 minutes longer or until shellfish have opened. A thin crust (called a socarrat) will form on the bottom of the pan. Remove paella from heat and allow to rest for 5 minutes. Garnish with parsley and serve with lemon wedges.

Per serving: 932 calories, 50 g fat, 13 g saturated fat, 1515 mg sodium, 33 g carbohydrates, 88 g protein.

VARIATIONS:

Paella can be made with only rice and meat, only rice and seafood, or only rice. Use an equal amount of firm, white-fleshed fish (such as monkfish) in place of chicken for a seafood version, or add vegetables such as olives, carrots, and peas.

SWEDEN
KÖTTBULLAR
AND GRAVY

2 / 2 / 2
COOK TIME: 55 MINUTES
ACTIVE PREP TIME: 20 MINUTES
INACTIVE PREP TIME: 30 MINUTES
MAKES 4 SERVINGS

AS WITH ANY NATIONAL DISH, THE SPECIFICS OF MAKING KÖTTBULLAR, OR Swedish meatballs, are hotly debated. One thing that is certain is that köttbullar was introduced to Sweden in the eighteenth century, after King Charles XII returned from a trip to Turkey with a recipe for a dish known to the Turks as *akçaabat kofta*. In a country where meat was often scarce, Swedes combined minced meat with stale bread soaked in cream to make their own version.

½ lb. ground beef
½ lb. ground pork
3 Tbsp. light cream or half-and-half
2 Tbsp. breadcrumbs
3 beef bouillon cubes, crushed
¼ tsp. ground allspice
1 egg, beaten
1 small yellow onion, finely grated
Butter, for sautéing
1-½ tsp. salt
1 tsp. ground black pepper
Chopped fresh parsley, for serving

Combine cream, breadcrumbs, bouillon, allspice, and egg and set aside. Heat butter in a heavy skillet over medium heat. Add onions and sauté until soft and translucent, about 3-4 minutes.

Add onions, meat, salt, and pepper to cream mixture and knead together just until blended. Chill in refrigerator for at least 30 minutes.

Use about 2 Tbsp. of meat mixture to form each meatball. Heat oil in a large skillet over medium-high heat and fry meatballs in batches for about 15 minutes per side, until golden brown and no longer pink in the center. Remove from pan and set aside while making the gravy.

Per serving: 288 calories, 13 g fat, 7 g saturated fat, 1175 mg sodium, 5 g carbohydrates, 35 g protein.

For the gravy:
1 c. heavy cream
1 Tbsp. cornstarch or arrowroot powder
1 c. beef stock
1-½ tsp. soy sauce
2 Tbsp. lingonberry jam

Whisk together cream and cornstarch. Add to the skillet used to fry köttbullar along with beef stock and soy sauce. Cook over medium-high heat, stirring constantly, for about 2 minutes. Stir in lingonberry jam. Garnish köttbullar with chopped parsley and serve with gravy.

Per serving: 144 calories, 11 g fat, 7 g saturated fat, 285 mg sodium, 10 g carbohydrates, 1 g protein.

SERVING SUGGESTIONS:

Serve with mashed potatoes (recommended), rice, or egg noodles and with additional lingonberry jam on the side.

SWITZERLAND
FONDUE

FRENCH, GERMAN, AND ITALIAN CULTURES HAVE ALL LEFT THEIR MARKS ON the people of Switzerland. But where cuisine is concerned, there are several foods that are distinctly Swiss, most famously cheese and chocolate. The earliest forms of Swiss fondue, first recorded in the early eighteenth century, incorporated eggs and wine as well as cheese. In the 1930s, the Swiss Cheese Union began vigorously promoting the version of fondue that became a national food of Switzerland. Served in a communal pot over an open flame and eaten with long forks, fondue has been popular in the United States as well as Switzerland since the mid-twentieth century.

1 large clove garlic, peeled and slightly crushed
1 lb. Emmentaler cheese, shredded
1 lb. Gruyère cheese, shredded
¼ c. cornstarch
2 c. Sauvignon Blanc or other dry white wine
2 Tbsp. lemon juice
2 Tbsp. cherry kirsch
1 tsp. dry mustard
¼ tsp. ground nutmeg

Combine cheeses and cornstarch in a large bowl, making sure that cheese is coated in cornstarch, and set aside.

Rub the inside of a fondue pot or other appropriate serving vessel (such as a large earthenware bowl) with garlic clove. Light heat source under pot. Add wine and lemon juice to pot and slowly bring to a simmer. Add cheeses slowly, one small handful at a time, and stir gently in a figure-eight motion until cheese is completely melted and smooth. Stir in kirsch, mustard, and nutmeg and serve.

Per serving: 733 calories, 47 g fat, 30 g saturated fat, 330 mg sodium, 15 g

carbohydrates, 46 g protein.

SERVING SUGGESTIONS:

Serve with cubes of chewy white bread. Other serving suggestions include fruits (such as apple slices), sausage, beef slices, and raw vegetables such as cherry tomatoes, carrots, and cauliflower.

VARIATION:

Substitute other cheeses such as fontina, gouda, cheddar, or Monterey Jack.

THE UKRAINE KRUCHENYKY WITH BORSCHT

2 / 3 / 2
COOK TIME: 1 HOUR, 20 MINUTES
ACTIVE PREP TIME: 20 MINUTES
MAKES 6 SERVINGS

SINCE TSARIST TIMES, THE UKRAINE HAS BEEN CALLED THE "BREADBASKET of Europe," owing to its rich dark soil. Locally-grown ingredients play a huge role in its cuisine. The beet soup known as borscht, a common dish throughout Eastern Europe and much of Asia, is known to have originated in the Ukraine.

For kruchenyky:
1-½ lb. lean pork loin, sliced into ⅓-inch cutlets and pounded
2 onions, sliced
1 lb. white button mushrooms, chopped
Olive oil, for frying and sautéing
1 c. crumbled bryndza (see Tips section for substitutes)
1-½ c. water
1 c. heavy cream
Salt and pepper, to taste

Heat olive oil in a heavy skillet over medium-high heat. Add onions and sauté until brown, about 5 minutes. Add mushrooms and continue to sauté until mushrooms are soft, about 10 minutes longer. Transfer sautéed onions and mushrooms to a bowl and add bryndza. Stir and season with salt and pepper.

Place about 2 large spoonfuls of mushroom mixture on the edge of each pork cutlet. Roll tightly and secure with toothpicks or twine. Repeat with remaining pork cutlets.

Heat about ½-inch of oil in a heavy skillet over medium heat. Sear pork rolls on all sides, starting with the seam side, in batches until golden brown.

Preheat oven to 375 degrees. Place pork rolls in a deep baking dish (stacking is okay) and pour water in the bottom of dish. Cover rolls with heavy cream and season with salt and pepper. Bake kruchenyky for 30 minutes. Serve immediately.

Per serving: 346 calories, 22 g fat, 11 g saturated fat, 87 mg sodium, 8 g carbohydrates, 30 g protein.

For borscht:
1-½ qt. beef bone broth or stock
1 lb. green cabbage, shredded
3 tomatoes, peeled, seeded, and chopped
1 large beet, peeled and finely chopped
1 medium onion, finely chopped
2 tsp. celery salt
½ tsp. ground black pepper
Juice of 1 lemon
1 Tbsp. sugar
Sour cream, for serving
Chopped fresh dill, for serving

Place broth or stock, cabbage, tomatoes, beet, onion, celery salt, and pepper in a large stockpot. Bring to a boil. Cover, reduce heat to medium-low, and simmer for 25 minutes, stirring frequently. Add lemon juice and sugar and simmer for 5 minutes longer. Garnish with dill and a dollop of sour cream and serve with kruchenyky.

Per serving: 58 calories, 1 g fat, 0 g saturated fat, 541 mg sodium, 13 g carbohydrates, 2 g protein.

SERVING SUGGESTION:

Serve with brown bread.

VARIATIONS:

Use pounded chicken cutlets in place of pork. Other vegetables may be used in filling, such as cabbage or carrots.

TIP:

If bryndza cannot be found, a substitute can be made by combining equal parts feta cheese and sour cream or fresh goat cheese and ricotta.

VATICAN CITY PASTA ALLA CARBONARA

2 / 2 / 2
COOK TIME: 20 MINUTES
ACTIVE PREP TIME: 15 MINUTES
MAKES 4 SERVINGS

THE MICRONATION OF VATICAN CITY, HOME OF THE ROMAN CATHOLIC CHURCH, is located entirely within the city of Rome. Italian food is geographically divided; in the northern part of the country, rich cream- and butter-based dishes are favored, while lighter tomato- and olive oil-based fare is more common in the southern region. Rome, located in the nation's center, can be seen as a middle ground of sorts, as the famous Roman dish pasta alla carbonara illustrates. Not as ancient as many other Italian dishes, carbonara made its way to urban Rome in the late 1940s.

1 lb. pancetta or cured bacon, coarsely chopped
Olive oil, for frying
1 lb. spaghetti or bucatini
Water, for boiling
3 eggs, beaten

¾ c. Pecorino Romano cheese, grated
Salt and freshly-ground pepper, to taste
Finely chopped fresh parsley, for serving

Boil a large pot of salted water. Cook pasta until *al dente*, about 9 minutes. Drain, reserving ½ c. of boiling water.

Meanwhile, heat olive oil in a heavy skillet over medium-high heat. Add pancetta or bacon and fry until crisp, about 5-10 minutes. Add pasta and reserved water to skillet and stir just until pasta and meat are well-mixed. Remove from heat.

In a small bowl, combine eggs and half of cheese. Season with salt and pepper and whisk together until thick and creamy. Pour egg mixture over pasta and stir quickly until pasta is coated.

Divide pasta between four bowls. Garnish with parsley and remaining cheese and serve.

Per serving: 1182 calories, 68 g fat, 25 g saturated fat, 3205 mg sodium, 66 g carbohydrates, 73 g protein.

VARIATION:
While not traditional, garlic is added to pasta alla carbonara outside of Italy.

WALES
CAWL CENNIN
WITH RAREBIT

LEEKS ARE ARGUABLY MORE IMPORTANT TO THE WELSH PEOPLE THAN THE potato is to the Irish; in fact, the leek is actually the national symbol of Wales! Cawl cennin, or "leek soup," celebrates one of the few vegetables that has traditionally grown well in the tiny British country. Meat has also been historically scarce in Wales, but dairy has not; another dish associated with Wales, the Welsh rarebit, was first recognized as a national dish in the fifteenth century.

For cawl:
½ lb. new potatoes, diced
½ lb. leeks (white parts only), diced
1 qt. chicken or vegetable broth
1 tsp. black pepper
½ tsp. salt
½ c. heavy cream
Chopped fresh parsley, for serving
Cracked black pepper, for serving

Bring broth to a boil in a stockpot. Add potatoes, leeks, pepper, and salt and reduce heat to low. Cover and simmer for 45 minutes or until potatoes and leeks are very tender.

Transfer soup to a blender or food processor and process until smooth. (Alternately, use an immersion blender to process.) Return to pot and stir. If needed, reheat soup but do not bring to a boil. Add cream and stir. Ladle soup into four bowls and garnish with parsley and cracked pepper.

Per serving: 165 calories, 7 g fat, 4 g saturated fat, 1075 mg sodium, 19 g carbohydrates, 7 g protein.

For rarebit:
4 thick slices rye bread, toasted
¼ c. butter
¼ c. all-purpose flour
1 c. dark beer (preferably 7 percent ABV or higher)
8 oz. sharp Cheddar cheese, grated
2 tsp. coarse mustard
2 Tbsp. Worcestershire sauce
2 tsp. ground black pepper

Melt butter in a heavy skillet over medium-high heat. Add flour, reduce heat to medium-low, and cook until a light roux is formed. Add beer to pan very slowly, constantly stirring, to make a sauce. Add cheese gradually, followed by mustard, Worcestershire sauce, and pepper. Continue to simmer until cheese is melted.

Move oven rack to 6 inches under broiler. Preheat broiler to High and place toast slices on a heavy baking sheet. Spoon cheese sauce over toast slices, keeping as much as possible from running onto the baking sheet. Broil toast until bubbly and brown on top. Serve with cawl.

Per serving: 412 calories, 31 g fat, 19 g saturated fat, 566 mg sodium, 14 g carbohydrates, 16 g protein.

THE MIDDLE EAST AND NORTH AFRICA

ALGERIA
CHAKHCHOUKHA

1 / 2 / 2
COOK TIME: 1 HOUR, 25 MINUTES
ACTIVE PREP TIME: 10 MINUTES
MAKES 8 SERVINGS

THE BERBERS, ALGERIA'S NATIVE PEOPLE, ARE A NOMADIC CULTURE. THIS is reflected in the fact that chakhchoukha, which the Berbers traditionally serve at special occasions, can easily be prepared using a single (rather large) pot. The dish's name is derived from the Chaouia word for "tearing into pieces," which suggests how it should be served—by laying small, torn pieces of *rougag* (a semolina-based flatbread) in the bottom of the bowl and pouring the rich stew on top, which the thin bread absorbs.

2 lbs. chicken, cut in medium-sized pieces
Olive oil, for frying
1 large onion, chopped
3 cloves garlic, minced
½ tsp. ground ginger
½ tsp. ground cardamom
½ tsp. ground mace
¼ tsp. ground allspice
¼ tsp. ground turmeric
1-½ qt. water or chicken broth, divided
4 carrots, sliced
2 small zucchini, sliced
1 potato, chopped
1 parsnip, sliced
1 large green chili, minced
One 15-oz. can chickpeas, drained and rinsed
One 15-oz. can diced tomatoes
Rougag or other flatbread (such as naan, lavash, pita, or chappati)
Salt and pepper, to taste

Heat olive oil in a large Dutch oven over medium-high heat. Add chicken, onion, garlic, ginger, cardamom, mace, allspice, and turmeric. Cook until chicken is no longer pink, about 7-10 minutes.

Add 4 c. of water or broth, carrots, zucchini, potato, parsnip, and chili to the pot. Reduce heat to low, cover, and simmer for 40 minutes.

Stir in chickpeas, tomatoes, and remaining water or broth. Cook for another 30 minutes, or until the chakhchoukha develops a thick "stew-like" consistency.

To serve, tear flatbread into pieces and divide between 8 bowls. Ladle chakhchoukha over bread pieces and serve.

Per serving: 329 calories, 5 g fat, 1 g saturated fat, 647 mg sodium, 30 g carbohydrates, 40 g protein.

SERVING SUGGESTION:

Serve with couscous (the national food of Algeria).

VARIATION:

For a vegan alternative, replace meat with additional potatoes or chickpeas and use vegetable broth in place of chicken broth.

BAHRAIN
MACHBOOS

2 / 2 / 2
COOK TIME: 55 MINUTES
ACTIVE PREP TIME: 10 MINUTES
MAKES 4 SERVINGS

ONE OF THE SMALLEST NATIONS ON EARTH, THE ISLAND OF BAHRAIN HAS little land for farming or grazing. While fresh local meats and vegetables may be in short supply, Bahrain's cooks take advantage of spices and crops such as dates, which are readily available. You'll need a fully stocked spice cabinet to make machboos, the country's national dish.

4 large, boneless chicken breasts

1-½ tsp. ground turmeric

1 tsp. ground cumin

2 Tbsp. baharat spice (see Tips section)

Olive oil, for sautéing and brushing

3 small onions, chopped

Juice and zest of two limes

2 tsp. ground cinnamon

3 tomatoes, quartered

2 cloves garlic

One 1-inch piece ginger root, peeled and julienned

½ c. fresh cilantro, chopped very fine

1 lb. basmati rice

1 qt. water

½ c. fresh lemon juice

3 Tbsp. butter

Combine turmeric, cumin, and baharat spice. Coat the chicken breasts with half of the spice mixture.

Heat olive oil in a large skillet or Dutch oven over medium-high heat. Sauté onions in olive oil until translucent, about 5 minutes. Add lime zest and juice.

Add chicken to the pan along with cinnamon and remaining spice mixture. Turn the chicken to make sure it is completely coated with oil and onions. Reduce heat to medium, cover, and cook for about 5 minutes.

Add tomatoes, garlic, and ginger. Continue to cook until chicken is cooked throughout, about 15-20 minutes. Add cilantro to pan in the last few minutes of cooking time.

Remove chicken from pan and add water and rice. Cook rice until all liquid is absorbed, about 15-20 minutes. Add lemon juice to the rice and dot with butter towards the end of cooking time.

As rice cooks, turn broiler to high. Place chicken on a baking sheet and brush with olive oil. Place chicken under broiler just until brown, about 2-5 minutes. Serve chicken on top of rice.

Per serving: 816 calories, 21 g fat, 8 g saturated fat, 170 mg sodium, 102 g carbohydrates, 51 g protein.

TIP:

If you cannot find pre-made baharat spice, you can make your own by combining 2 tsp. cardamom with 1 tsp. each of coriander, freshly ground black pepper, cloves, and paprika (to make 2 Tbsp.).

EGYPT
TA'AMEYA

2 / 2 / 2
COOK TIME: 20 MINUTES
ACTIVE PREP TIME: 15 MINUTES
INACTIVE PREP TIME: 8 HOURS, 10 MINUTES
MAKES 4-6 SERVINGS

IT IS BELIEVED BY MANY THAT FALAFEL ORIGINATED IN EGYPT IN THE

Middle Ages with Coptic Christians, who ate it as a meat substitute during Lent. Who invented it is a matter of dispute, but the deep-fried vegetarian street food that is now ubiquitous across the Middle East (and beyond) almost certainly has its roots in Egypt. While the more familiar Israeli variety is made from ground chickpeas, Egyptian falafel, known as ta'ameya, uses fava beans instead.

1 c. fava beans, dried and split
Cold water, for soaking
3 cloves garlic
1 small white onion
¼ c. fresh parsley, finely chopped
1 tsp. all-purpose flour
1 tsp. ground cumin
½ tsp. baking soda
¼ tsp. cayenne pepper (optional)
½ c. sesame seeds
Oil, for frying

Soak fava beans for 8 hours or overnight in cold water. Drain and pat dry. Place fava beans in a food processor with garlic, onion, parsley, flour, cumin, baking soda, and cayenne pepper (if using) and blend until slightly smooth.

Roll fava bean mixture into 1-inch balls. Roll each ball in sesame seeds until completely covered. Refrigerate for 10 minutes.

Heat 1 inch of oil in a heavy skillet over high heat until very hot. Reduce heat to medium and cook ta'ameya in batches for about 2-3 minutes per side. Drain on paper towels and serve warm with yogurt sauce.

Per serving: 391 calories, 30 g fat, 4 g saturated fat, 135 mg sodium, 24 g carbohydrates, 11 g protein.

For yogurt sauce:
1 c. plain yogurt
½ small cucumber, peeled
1 clove garlic
1 Tbsp. lemon juice

Place all ingredients in a food processor and blend until very smooth. Refrigerate until ready to serve.

Per serving: 41 calories, 1 g fat, 1 g saturated fat, 36 mg sodium, 5 g carbohydrates, 3 g protein.

SERVING SUGGESTIONS:
Serve with pita bread, tomatoes, and sautéed eggplant and garlic.

VARIATIONS:
Use cilantro in place of parsley, or substitute 2 Tbsp. of fresh mint for cucumber in yogurt sauce.

IRAN
CHELOW KABAB

3 / 1 / 3
COOK TIME: 50 MINUTES
ACTIVE PREP TIME: 15 MINUTES
INACTIVE PREP TIME: 8 HOURS
MAKES 6-8 SERVINGS

THE TERM "KABAB" IS USED TO APPLY TO A VARIETY OF MEAT DISHES IN THE Middle East, often grilled or cooked on a skewer. The Persian version is marinated in onions and garlic and served with chelow, rice that is fried and then steamed with butter. This preparation gives the rice a crispy golden crust, which is considered the best part of the dish (and is traditionally reserved for guests when served in Iran).

For kababs:
2 lbs. boneless lamb, cut into pieces and trimmed
2 large onions, coarsely chopped
4 cloves garlic
3 Tbsp. lemon juice
3 Tbsp. olive oil
2 Tbsp. ground coriander
2 tsp. ground cumin
Salt and pepper, to taste
Chopped fresh parsley, for serving

Place onions and garlic in a blender or food processor and puree until smooth. Add lemon juice, olive oil, coriander, and cumin. Season lamb with salt and pepper and add to onion mixture. Marinate in refrigerator for 8 hours or overnight.

Prepare a charcoal grill and thread meat onto metal or bamboo skewers (if using bamboo skewers, soak in water for 30 minutes first). Grill meat for about 15 minutes or until fully cooked. Slide meat off skewers and garnish with parsley.

Per serving: 316 calories, 16 g fat, 4 g saturated fat, 103 mg sodium, 5 g carbohydrates, 37 g protein.

For chelow:
1-¾ c. basmati or other long-grain white rice

1-½ qt.water
2 tsp. salt
3 Tbsp. butter, divided
1 Tbsp. olive oil
3 threads saffron

Rinse rice under cold water for at least 1 minute. Bring water and salt to a boil in a large pot. Add rice and continue to boil for about 5 minutes. Drain, reserving ¼ c. of cooking liquid, and rinse rice with warm water.

Heat cooking liquid, 2 Tbsp. butter, olive oil, and saffron in a heavy skillet over high heat. Add one-third of the rice to the skillet and spread in an equal layer on the bottom of the pan. Add the rest of the rice to the pan without stirring, and top with remaining butter. Cover with a large cloth and then with a lid, and cook over high heat for 3-4 minutes.

Once rice has begun to brown on the bottom, reduce heat to low. Continue cooking, covered with cloth and lid, for 20 minutes or until rice is fully cooked.

Remove from heat and uncover. Carefully invert rice onto a large platter, so that the crust on the bottom is facing upwards. Serve chelow with kababs.

Per serving: 82 calories, 7 g fat, 3 g saturated fat, 698 mg sodium, 5 g carbohydrates, 1 g protein.

VARIATION:

Traditionally, chelow is topped with a raw egg; a fried egg can be used.

IRAQ
SEMEÇ MASGÛF

1 / 2 / 2
COOK TIME: 40 MINUTES
ACTIVE PREP TIME: 10 MINUTES
INACTIVE PREP TIME: 30 MINUTES
MAKES 4 SERVINGS

THE MESOPOTAMIAN RIVER VALLEY, LOCATED BETWEEN IRAQ'S TIGRIS AND Euphrates Rivers, is famously called the "cradle of civilization." Carp from the Tigris

River are traditionally used in this Mesopotamian dish, which is enormously popular in Iraq and especially in Baghdad. Semeç masgûf is one of the few national dishes of the Middle East that uses fish as its main ingredient. While Iraqi street vendors usually roast this fish whole over an open flame in a metal basket, this recipe uses the oven instead.

2 lbs. carp or other freshwater white fish filets, butterflied
2 Tbsp. olive oil, plus more for sautéing
1 Tbsp. tamarind paste
1 tsp. ground black pepper
½ tsp. ground turmeric
Salt and pepper, to taste
2 onions, one finely chopped and one sliced
4 cloves garlic, minced
2 Roma tomatoes, peeled, seeded, and chopped
1 c. fresh parsley, finely chopped
1 c. water
One 6-oz. can tomato paste
¼ c. white vinegar
¼ c. lemon juice

Combine olive oil, tamarind paste, black pepper, and turmeric. Coat fish in mixture and season with salt and pepper. Marinate in the refrigerator for at least 30 minutes.

Heat olive oil in a large skillet over medium-high heat. Sauté chopped onion and garlic in olive oil until fragrant, about 3-4 minutes.

Add tomatoes, parsley, water, tomato paste, vinegar, and lemon juice to skillet. Simmer over medium-low heat for 5 minutes, stirring frequently.

Preheat oven to 425 degrees. Place fish on the rack of a roasting pan and spoon sauce on top. Top with sliced onions. Roast in oven for 25-30 minutes or until fully cooked.

Per serving: 579 calories, 24 g fat, 5 g saturated fat, 243 mg sodium, 34 g carbohydrates, 58 g protein.

Serve with white rice, spinach or parsley salad, and pomegranate seeds.

ISRAEL
ISRAELI SALAD
AND COUSCOUS

1 / 2 / 2
COOK TIME: 10 MINUTES
ACTIVE PREP TIME: 15 MINUTES
MAKES 6 SERVINGS

IN 1953, ONLY A FEW YEARS AFTER THE NATION OF ISRAEL BECAME independent, rice became scarce. Since rice was a staple food for many Jewish communities, a pasta substitute called ptitim was developed using wheat. Ptitim was first shaped in grains resembling rice, but over time it became available in other shapes as well. Today, ptitim is most recognizable in its pearl form, which people outside Israel commonly call "Israeli couscous."

2 c. Israeli couscous
3 c. water
1 pt. cherry tomatoes, halved
1 large seedless cucumber, finely chopped
1 yellow bell pepper, finely chopped
1 small purple onion, finely chopped
½ c. fresh parsley, finely chopped
¼ c. fresh mint, finely chopped
2 Tbsp. lemon juice
1 Tbsp. olive oil, plus more for sautéing
½ tsp. salt
¼ tsp. ground black pepper
3 oz. feta cheese, crumbled

Heat olive oil in a small pan over medium-high heat. Add couscous and sauté just until golden brown, about 2 minutes. Add water to pan and heat to a boil. Reduce heat to medium and simmer until couscous is cooked, about 8 minutes. Drain and rinse with cold water.

Combine tomatoes, cucumber, bell pepper, onion, parsley, and mint. In a separate bowl, combine lemon juice, olive oil, salt, and pepper. Add dressing to vegetables and toss to coat. Toss salad with couscous and feta cheese to combine.

Per serving: 309 calories, 6 g fat, 3 g saturated fat, 371 mg sodium, 53 g carbohydrates, 11 g protein.

VARIATIONS:

Add canned chickpeas (for extra protein), kalamata olives, or artichoke hearts.

KUWAIT
MUTABBAQ SAMAK

2 / 1 / 1
COOK TIME: 40 MINUTES
ACTIVE PREP TIME: 15 MINUTES
MAKES 4-6 SERVINGS

SITUATED AT THE FAR END OF THE PERSIAN GULF, THE TINY NATION OF Kuwait has a distinctive cuisine that combines Arab, Persian, Mediterranean, and Indian influences. This diffusion owes not only to its location, but also to its highly diverse international workforce. As a gulf nation, fish is more popular in Kuwait than it is in other parts of the Middle East. Mutabbaq samak, which features both fish and a spicy fish broth, is a classic Kuwaiti dish.

2 lbs. cod or haddock fillets
1 Tbsp. plus 1 tsp. curry powder, divided
1 tsp. ground cumin
Salt and pepper, to taste
Oil, for frying and sautéing
2 c. basmati rice

1 Tbsp. onion powder
2 tsp. ground turmeric, divided
1 tsp. black pepper
3 c. water
1 large onion, sliced
½ c. golden raisins
1 tsp. lime zest

Clean fish filets thoroughly and season with salt and pepper. Combine 1 Tbsp. curry and cumin and coat fish with curry mixture.

Heat about one-half inch of oil in a large frying pan over medium-high heat. Add fish filets and fry for 3-4 minutes on each side or until golden. Remove from pan and set on paper towels to drain excess oil.

Heat a small amount of oil in a large saucepan over high heat. Add rice, onion powder, 1-½ tsp. turmeric, and black pepper and stir. Cook for about 3 minutes or until rice is golden and spices are thoroughly blended. Add water and bring to a boil. Reduce heat to medium-low, cover, and simmer for 15 minutes or until rice is fully cooked.

In a skillet, heat a small amount of oil over medium-high heat. Add onion and sauté until translucent, about 5 minutes. Reduce heat to medium and add raisins, 1 tsp. curry powder, ½ tsp. turmeric, and lime zest and cook for 2-3 minutes or until raisins have begun to swell. Combine onion and raisins with rice and serve with fish.

Per serving: 550 calories, 5 g fat, 1 g saturated fat, 154 mg sodium, 75 g carbohydrates, 48 g protein.

SERVING SUGGESTIONS:
Serve with yogurt and flatbread.

VARIATION:
Other types of fish may be used in this recipe, such as salmon.

JORDAN MANSAF

Mansaf is not only Jordan's national dish, but also one that has historically played a great role in resolving conflicts. When Bedouin families or tribes have disagreements, the resolution process involves a meeting between the groups' leaders, at which a sheep is slaughtered and prepared to make mansaf. Once the conflict is resolved, both families or tribes gather and share the meal to celebrate the resolution. Jameed, yogurt made from fermented goat's milk, is used to make mansaf in Jordan. This recipe uses Greek yogurt in its place.

1 lb. lean lamb, cubed
Water, to cover
1 large onion, chopped
3 cloves garlic, chopped
¼ c. ghee or clarified butter
2 Tbsp. ground cumin
8 cardamom pods, crushed
1 tsp. whole cloves
One 2-inch cinnamon stick
2 bay leaves
2 c. plain Greek yogurt
1 Tbsp. cornstarch or arrowroot powder
½ c. fresh mint, chopped
2 tsp. sea salt

Place lamb in a dish and cover with enough water to cover. Cover with plastic wrap and refrigerate for about 6 hours. Remove from water and pat dry.

Heat ghee in a large Dutch oven over medium-high heat. Sauté onion and garlic for about 3 minutes. Move onion and garlic to one side of pot, add meat, and cook until slightly brown, about 5 minutes.

Add cumin, cardamom, cloves, cinnamon, and bay leaves to pot and stir to combine. Add enough water to cover all ingredients. Increase heat to high and bring to a boil. Continue to boil for 3 minutes, skimming off any fat that rises to the top. Reduce heat to low, cover, and simmer for 1 hour.

Strain the meat from the pot, reserving cooking liquid. Return meat to pot with ½ c. liquid. Pour rest of liquid into another pot and add yogurt. Simmer yogurt mixture over medium heat until a thick sauce forms.

Pour yogurt sauce over lamb and stir. Simmer over medium heat for 5 minutes. Add cornstarch or arrowroot powder and cook for an additional 5 minutes. Remove from heat and stir in mint and sea salt. Serve with rice.

Per serving: 354 calories, 19 g fat, 10 g saturated fat, 853 mg sodium, 10 g carbohydrates, 35 g protein.

For rice:
2 c. jasmine rice
3 c. water, plus 1 Tbsp. very hot water
5 threads saffron
2 Tbsp. ghee or clarified butter, plus extra for toasting, divided
1 tsp. sea salt
½ c. slivered almonds
½ c. pine nuts

Combine saffron threads with 1 Tbsp. hot water in a small bowl. In a medium pot, bring 3 c. water to a boil. Once boiling, add rice and saffron water. Reduce heat to low and add 1 Tbsp. ghee and salt. Cover and simmer for 20 minutes.

While rice is cooking, toast nuts. Heat a small amount of ghee in a small skillet over high heat and add almonds and pine nuts when hot. Toast over high heat just until brown. Fluff rice and top with toasted almonds and pine nuts.

Per serving: 447 calories, 19 g fat, 4 g saturated fat, 379 mg sodium, 61 g carbohydrates, 9 g protein.

SERVING SUGGESTIONS:
Serve with markook bread and dried Zante currants, if desired.

VARIATION:
Use beef in place of lamb.

LEBANON
KAFTA AND TABBOULEH

1 / 2 / 2
COOK TIME: 10 MINUTES
ACTIVE PREP TIME: 20 MINUTES
INACTIVE PREP TIME: 1 HOUR
MAKES 6 SERVINGS

IN THE UNITED STATES, LEBANESE IS PROBABLY THE MOST POPULAR OF all Middle Eastern cuisines. It is also one of the healthiest, relying on whole grains, fresh fruits and vegetables, lean meats, and meatless proteins such as chickpeas and nuts. Tabbouleh, a salad made from fresh parsley and bulgur wheat, is a perfect example.

For kafta:
2 lbs. lean ground beef or lamb
2 purple onions, finely chopped
1 c. fresh parsley, finely chopped
1 Tbsp. salt
½ tsp. ground allspice
½ tsp. ground black pepper

Combine meat, onions, parsley, salt, allspice, and pepper in a bowl and mix thoroughly. Divide the meat into 12 portions and roll each into a ball. Insert a skewer through each meatball and squeeze the meat around the skewer so that it is flat and log-shaped. (If using bamboo skewers, soak in water for 30 minutes first.)

Heat a gas grill to medium-high. Place skewers on grill and cook for about 4 minutes on each side.

Per serving: 300 calories, 10 g fat, 4 g saturated fat, 1270 mg sodium, 4 g carbohydrates, 47 g protein.

For tabbouleh:

⅓ c. wheat bulgur

1 c. hot water

4 c. fresh parsley, chopped

1 c. fresh mint, chopped

3 Roma tomatoes, seeded and chopped

1 small red onion, finely chopped

¼ c. lemon juice

¼ c. olive oil

Salt and pepper, to taste

Place wheat bulgur in boiling water and allow to soak for 1 hour or until water is completely absorbed.

Combine parsley, mint, tomato and onion. Add bulgur, followed by lemon juice, olive oil and salt and pepper, and mix thoroughly.

Per serving: 138 calories, 9 g fat, 1 g saturated fat, 34 mg sodium, 13 g carbohydrates, 3 g protein.

SERVING SUGGESTIONS:

Serve with hummus, pita bread, and fresh tomato and cucumber.

LIBYA
ASHARBAL LEEBIYA

1 / 1 / 2
COOK TIME: 30 MINUTES
ACTIVE PREP TIME: 10 MINUTES
MAKES 6-8 SERVINGS

THE CUISINE OF LIBYA IS HEAVY ON MEDITERRANEAN, ARABIC, AND AFRICAN influences. But its greatest influence comes from Italian cooking. This is no surprise, given that Italy was the first European country in the modern age to colonize Libya. Olive oil is a staple of Libyan cuisine, and it is difficult to find a Libyan meal that does not include large amounts of it. Many Libyan dishes such as asharbal Leebiya, or

"Libyan soup," also incorporate pasta.

1-½ lb. lean ground lamb
1-½ tsp. ground cinnamon
1 tsp. ground cumin
1 tsp. ground coriander
¼ tsp. red chili flakes
¼ tsp. ground allspice
1 large onion, chopped
3 cloves garlic, minced
Olive oil, for frying
2 tomatoes, peeled, seeded, and chopped
1 tsp. dried mint
1 tsp. paprika
½ c. tomato sauce
2 qt. beef broth
1 c. orzo or other small pasta
2 Tbsp. fresh parsley, finely chopped
2 Tbsp. lemon juice
Salt and pepper, to taste

Toast cinnamon, cumin, coriander, chili flakes, and allspice in a small, dry skillet over high heat for about 1 minute or until very fragrant. Remove from pan and set aside to cool.

Heat olive oil in a large Dutch oven over medium-high heat. Sauté onions and garlic for 5 minutes or until onion is soft. Add lamb and cook until browned, about 5 minutes longer, breaking up the meat.

Add spice mixture along with tomatoes, mint, and paprika and cook for about 5-6 minutes. Add tomato sauce and beef stock and bring to a boil. Add pasta, reduce heat to medium-low, and simmer until fully cooked, about 10 minutes.

Pour soup into bowls. Garnish with parsley, squeeze with lemon juice, and season with salt and pepper.

Per serving: 285 calories, 9 g fat, 2 g saturated fat, 1456 mg sodium, 24 g

carbohydrates, 27 g protein.

VARIATIONS:

Use chicken or beef in place of lamb, or potatoes in place of pasta. For a vegetarian version, replace meat with an equal amount of cooked lentils or chickpeas.

MOROCCO
TAJINE

2 / 2 / 2
COOK TIME: 1 HOUR, 25 MINUTES
ACTIVE PREP TIME: 10 MINUTES
INACTIVE PREP TIME: 1 HOUR
MAKES 4 SERVINGS

THE WORD "TAJINE" HAS TWO MEANINGS: A SLOW-COOKED, SAVORY STEW, AND the earthenware pot that is traditionally used to cook it. Probably one of the oldest recipes in this book, tajine was a favorite of the Bedouin nomads of northern Africa long before it was mentioned in the ninth-century Arabian classic *One Thousand and One Nights*. The distinctive pot known as a tajine consists of two parts: a flat, shallow circular base and a tall, cone-shaped lid. Many American retailers offer tajines, but this recipe can be prepared using any oven-safe lidded dish or pot.

4 chicken breasts or thighs, bone-in and skin on
1 Tbsp. olive oil, plus more for sautéing and frying
2 tsp. ground coriander
2 tsp. ground cumin
2 tsp. ground cinnamon
2 tsp. ground turmeric
2 tsp. salt
1 tsp. cayenne pepper (optional)
1-¼ qt. chicken stock
1 c. dried apricots, coarsely chopped
3 pods star anise
One 1-inch cinnamon stick

2 Tbsp. honey
1 large onion, chopped
6 cloves garlic, minced
1 c. canned chickpeas

Combine 1 Tbsp. olive oil, coriander, cumin, cinnamon, turmeric, salt, and cayenne pepper (if using) to form a paste. Rub chicken pieces with paste, including under the skin. Place chicken in a dish, cover with plastic wrap, and marinate for 1 hour.

In a medium saucepan, combine 2 c. chicken stock, apricots, star anise, cinnamon stick, and honey. Bring to a boil, reduce heat to medium-low, cover, and simmer for 10 minutes. Remove star anise and cinnamon stick.

Heat olive oil in a large skillet over medium heat. Fry chicken for about 4 minutes on each side or until brown. Place chicken in tajine or other lidded oven-safe pot and cover with apricot mixture.

Add more olive oil to the same skillet. Sauté onion, garlic, and chickpeas for about 5 minutes, scraping all brown bits from the bottom of the skillet. Add onion, garlic, and chickpeas to tajine along with remaining 3 c. of chicken stock.

Preheat oven to 350 degrees. Cover tajine with lid and transfer to oven. Bake for 1 hour. Check tajine after 30 minutes and add water or stock if dry.

Per serving: 582 calories, 18 g fat, 4 g saturated fat, 1181 mg sodium, 52 g carbohydrates, 56 g protein.

SERVING SUGGESTIONS:
Serve with couscous. Many contemporary Moroccans eat tajine with French fries.

VARIATIONS:
Lamb can be used in place of chicken. For a vegan version, replace meat with additional chickpeas or other legumes.

OMAN
LAMB AND DATE STEW

OMANI CUISINE IS A BIT DIFFERENT THAN MOST YOU WILL FIND IN THE Middle East. Indian, African, and even East Asian flavors are very prevalent, while Arabic staples like falafel and hummus are nowhere to be found. But like many other dishes found at this intercontinental crossroads, the foods of Oman are heavily spiced and feature halal meats such as lamb. Dates are also a staple here; before it became a major center for international trade, Oman was a culture of date farmers.

1-½ lb. lamb, cut into small pieces
2 tsp. crushed red pepper
1 tsp. ground turmeric
1 tsp. ground ginger
1 tsp. ground cinnamon
½ tsp. salt
Olive oil, for frying and sautéing
2 large red onions, chopped
3 cloves garlic, minced
3-½ c. beef broth
2 Tbsp. cold water
1 Tbsp. cornstarch
1 c. dates, pitted and chopped
¼ c. slivered almonds, toasted

Combine red pepper, turmeric, ginger, cinnamon, and salt. Rub spice mixture over the surface of the meat. Place meat in a dish, cover with plastic wrap, and marinate in refrigerator for at least 1 hour. Allow to return to room temperature before proceeding.

Heat oil in a Dutch oven over medium-high heat. Add meat and fry until brown on all sides, about 7-8 minutes. Add onions and garlic and sauté until onion is translucent, about 5 minutes.

Add broth to the pot and bring to a boil. Reduce heat to low, cover, and simmer for 2 hours or until meat is done. Uncover and skim any fat that has risen to the surface.

Add water to cornstarch and whisk with a fork until combined. Add to pot and stir. Add dates, cover, and simmer for 15 minutes. Garnish with almonds and serve.

Per serving: 339 calories, 13 g fat, 3 g saturated fat, 636 mg sodium, 31 g carbohydrates, 26 g protein.

SERVING SUGGESTION:

Serve with white rice.

PALESTINE MUSAKHAN

2 / 3 / 2
COOK TIME: 1 HOUR
ACTIVE PREP TIME: 20 MINUTES
INACTIVE PREP TIME: 3 HOURS
MAKES 4 SERVINGS

THE INGREDIENTS USED TO MAKE THIS NATIONAL DISH CELEBRATE THE bounty of the region of Palestine—sumac, pine nuts, and especially olive oil. The manner in which it is prepared takes advantage of the bright flavor of fresh olive oil, which is why it is served during the oil-pressing season every fall. To eat musakhan, use your fingers to tear a piece of flatbread and fold it around a bite of chicken and onion. Taboon bread, the traditional choice for musakhan, is named for the type of stone-lined oven that is used to bake it. In this recipe, a cast-iron skillet is used to bake the taboon, yielding similar results.

4 boneless chicken breasts, with skin (about 2 lbs.)
¾ c. extra-virgin olive oil, divided
¼ c. sumac, divided
1 Tbsp. ground cumin, divided

2 tsp. sea salt, divided
½ tsp. ground cinnamon
½ tsp. ground allspice
2 Tbsp. pine nuts
2 large yellow onions, sliced
1 Tbsp. fresh parsley, finely chopped
4 loaves taboon bread (recipe below)

Combine 2 Tbsp. olive oil, 2 tsp. sumac, 1 tsp. cumin, 1 tsp. sea salt, cinnamon, and allspice. Coat chicken breasts with spice mixture and refrigerate for at least 2 hours.

Preheat oven to 425 degrees. Set chicken on a rack above a roasting pan and roast for 30 minutes or until fully cooked.

While chicken is roasting, heat 2 Tbsp. olive oil in a skillet over medium-high heat. Add pine nuts and sauté until brown, about 3 minutes. Remove nuts from pan (reserving oil) and add 2 Tbsp. more olive oil along with onions and 1 tsp. salt. Sauté onions over medium-high heat until extremely soft, about 10 minutes, and add 2 Tbsp. sumac and 2 tsp. cumin.

To assemble musakhan, place taboon bread loaves under a broiler for about 3 minutes or until toasted. Place one loaf on each of four serving plates. Top with one chicken breast and one-quarter each of onion mixture and pine nuts. Sprinkle with parsley and remaining sumac and drizzle with remaining olive oil.

For taboon bread:
1-⅓ c. bread flour, plus more for flouring surface
1 tsp. salt
1 tsp. instant yeast
½ c. lukewarm water
2 tsp. olive oil

Sift together flour, salt, and yeast. Add water and olive oil and mix with your hands until a smooth dough is formed. Cover dough with plastic wrap and allow to stand for 1 hour or until doubled in size.

Preheat oven to 400 degrees and place a medium-sized cast-iron skillet in the oven to warm. Punch dough, knead slightly, and divide into four equal portions. Roll out each dough portion on a floured surface to form a circle about 6-8 inches in diameter. Place one dough circle in skillet and cook for 5-7 minutes. Remove from oven, set on wire rack to cool, and repeat with remaining dough.

Per serving: 773 calories, 52 g fat, 9 g saturated fat, 1645 mg sodium, 33 g carbohydrates, 46 g protein.

SERVING SUGGESTIONS:

Serve with plain yogurt and lemon slices.

VARIATIONS:

Musakhan can be made with a whole chicken, cut into parts, or with bone-in chicken legs and thigh quarters.

QATAR
THAREED

2 / 2 / 2
COOK TIME: 1 HOUR, 50 MINUTES
ACTIVE PREP TIME: 20 MINUTES
MAKES 8 SERVINGS

IN SPITE OF ITS LONG LIST OF INGREDIENTS, THAREED IS CONSIDERED TO be simpler than most Middle Eastern dishes because it is very light on the stomach. For this reason, it is often served during the month of Ramadan. Thareed is also mentioned in several of the hadiths attributed to the prophet Muhammad, who compared it to his favorite wife: "The superiority of Aisha to other women is like the superiority of thareed to other food" (*Sahih Al Bukhari* vol. 7, book 65, no. 329).

2 lbs. lamb stew meat, cut into pieces
1-½ qt. water
2 large onions, finely chopped
3 cloves garlic, minced
Oil, for sautéing

1 Tbsp. tomato paste
2 large potatoes, peeled and chopped
1 large carrot, peeled and chopped
4 tomatoes, seeded and chopped
Juice and zest of 2 limes
3 chicken bouillon cubes
2 Tbsp. baharat spice
1 tsp. ground cinnamon
1 tsp. ground turmeric
1 tsp. red curry powder
¼ tsp. cayenne powder
2 large zucchini or 1 large eggplant, chopped
Raqaq bread (recipe below)
½ c. chopped cilantro, for serving

Bring water to a boil in a stockpot. Add lamb, reduce heat to medium-low, and simmer uncovered for 1 hour, skimming fat as it rises to the top. Remove meat and set aside. Strain broth and reserve.

Heat oil in a Dutch oven over medium-high heat. Sauté onions for 5 minutes or until golden and translucent. Add garlic and sauté for 2-3 minutes longer.

Add tomato paste, potatoes, carrot, and tomatoes to pot and stir to combine. Add meat to pot along with lime juice and zest, bouillon cubes, and spices. Add enough broth to make the mixture soupy, and bring to to a boil. Reduce heat to medium and simmer for 20-30 minutes or until potatoes are tender. Add zucchini or eggplant and cook for 5-10 minutes longer.

To serve, place one piece of raqaq bread at the bottom of each of 8 shallow bowls. Ladle broth onto bread until saturated, then top with meat and vegetables. Garnish with cilantro and serve.

For raqaq bread:
2 c. all-purpose flour
2-¼ c. warm water
1 tsp. salt

Combine flour and salt in a mixing bowl and sift together. Add a few spoonfuls of water at a time, mixing constantly, until the mixture has the consistency of a thin batter.

Heat a non-stick skillet over medium heat. Scoop about ¼ c. of batter into the center of the pan and spread until it is very thin. Cook until the edges begin to peel away from the surface of the pan, and then turn and cook on the other side. Repeat with remaining batter.

Per serving: 454 calories, 11 g fat, 3 g saturated fat, 635 mg sodium, 49 g carbohydrates, 39 g protein.

TIP:

If you cannot find pre-made baharat spice, you can make your own by combining 2 tsp. cardamom with 1 tsp. each of coriander, freshly ground black pepper, cloves, and paprika (to make 2 Tbsp.).

SAUDI ARABIA LAMB KABSA

1 / 2 / 2
COOK TIME: 1 HOUR, 30 MINUTES
ACTIVE PREP TIME: 10 MINUTES
INACTIVE PREP TIME: 20 MINUTES
MAKES 6-8 SERVINGS

As WITH MOST ASPECTS OF SAUDI LIFE, THE ISLAMIC FAITH IS INTEGRAL to Saudi cuisine. This is reflected not only in its restrictions against pork and alcohol, but also its dedication to ancestral cooking practices stemming from the nation's nomadic past. Even those Saudis who live in urban centers cling to the same traditional dishes first eaten by goat and sheep herders. These include kabsa, a meat and rice combination that is regarded as Saudi Arabia's national dish.

2 lbs. boneless lamb, cut into large pieces
3 c. basmati rice
1-¼ qt. water, plus more for soaking
Oil, for sautéing

1 large onion, chopped

One 1-inch piece ginger, peeled and minced

4 cardamom pods, crushed

1 carrot, finely chopped

One 15-oz. can pureed tomatoes

2 Tbsp. tomato paste

1 Tbsp. ground coriander

1 tsp. paprika

1 tsp. ground cumin

1 tsp. ground black pepper

½ tsp. salt

Zest of 1 orange

Almonds, cashews, and/or raisins, for serving

Place rice in a bowl of water and allow to soak for 20-30 minutes. Drain and rinse. While rice is soaking, heat oil in a Dutch oven over medium-high heat. Sauté onion until translucent, about 5 minutes. Add lamb, carrot, cardamom, and ginger and sauté for 5 minutes longer or until lamb is browned, carrot is soft, and cardamom and ginger are fragrant.

Add water, tomatoes, tomato paste, coriander, paprika, cumin, black pepper, and salt. Cover and simmer over low heat for 1 to 1-½ hours or until meat is fully cooked and tender. Add rice and orange zest to pot and cook for 15-20 minutes longer or until rice is fully cooked. Garnish with nuts and raisins and serve.

Per serving: 581 calories, 12 g fat, 4 g saturated fat, 350 mg sodium, 71 g carbohydrates, 44 g protein.

SYRIA
KIBBEH
MABROUMEH

BAKED KIBBEH, ONE OF THE SIGNATURE DISHES OF THE LEVANT REGION, IS similar in many ways to other regional dishes (it's much like a non-vegetarian version of falafel). Dozens of versions exist in the Levant and throughout the Levantine diaspora of the United States and South America. This version is uniquely Syrian, having its origins in the nation's second-largest city, Aleppo.

1 lb. lean ground beef or lamb
1-½ c. fine bulgur wheat
2 red onions, finely chopped
2 tsp. salt
½ tsp. ground allspice
½ tsp. ground black pepper
¼ tsp. chili powder
Cold water, as needed
Olive oil, for sautéing
¼ tsp. ground cinnamon
¾ c. pistachio nuts, crushed
1 egg, beaten
¼ c. ghee or butter

Place bulgur wheat, 1 onion, 1 tsp. salt, ¼ tsp. allspice, ¼ tsp. black pepper, and chili powder in a blender or food processor and process until very fine.

Add half of meat to bulgur wheat mixture and knead until smooth. If mixture becomes dry, moisten with a small amount of cold water. Wrap dough in plastic wrap and refrigerate for 2 hours.

Heat olive oil in a skillet over medium-high heat. Add onions and sauté until softened, about 3-4 minutes. Add remaining meat, cinnamon, salt, black pepper, and allspice. Continue to cook until meat is thoroughly cooked and no longer pink, about 6-7 minutes. Remove meat mixture from pan. Combine with pistachio nuts and egg and mix well.

Preheat oven to 350 degrees. Remove bulgur wheat dough from refrigerator and divide into four portions. Flatten each portion slightly and place between two layers of plastic wrap. Use a rolling pin to roll to a thickness of about ¼ inch. Use a knife to cut each portion into a rectangular shape (about 6 inches by 12 inches).

Divide meat and pistachio mixture into four portions. Place each portion in the middle of one portion of dough and roll from the sides. Press the ends so that a solid, closed roll is created.

Coat each roll with ghee on all sides. Place rolls in an oven-proof dish and bake for 20 minutes or until golden. Remove from oven and allow to rest for 15 minutes before slicing and serving.

Per serving: 572 calories, 30 g fat, 12 g saturated fat, 1323 mg sodium, 35 g carbohydrates, 43 g protein.

SERVING SUGGESTIONS:

Serve with tabbouleh (p. 103), hummus or raita, and pomegranate seeds.

TUNISIA
LABLABI

1 / 1 / 2
COOK TIME: 1 HOUR, 15 MINUTES
ACTIVE PREP TIME: 15 MINUTES
INACTIVE PREP TIME: 8 HOURS
MAKES 6 SERVINGS

TUNISIAN CUISINE IS TYPICALLY MEDITERRANEAN, BASED ON HEALTHY regional ingredients and incorporating elements of the many cultures that have historically ruled the small North African country. But the native people's nomadic heritage lends itself to soups and stews, such as the thick and satisfying lablabi. Rich, spicy, and high in protein, Tunisians eat this stew throughout the day, sometimes even for breakfast.

1 lb. dried chickpeas
Water, for soaking and boiling
2 Tbsp. kosher salt
Olive oil for sautéing, plus more for serving
1 large onion, chopped
6 cloves garlic, minced
2 Tbsp. tomato paste
Juice of 1 lemon
¼ c. harissa, plus more for serving (see Tips section)
2 Tbsp. ground cumin
3 qt. chicken broth
½ lb. crusty white bread (preferably day-old), cut into pieces
6 eggs

Place chickpeas in a large bowl and add enough water to cover. Add salt to water and allow chickpeas to soak for 8 hours or overnight. Drain and rinse.

Heat olive oil in a Dutch oven over medium-high heat. Sauté onion until translucent, about 5 minutes. Add garlic and tomato paste and cook for another 2 minutes. Stir in lemon juice, harissa, and cumin.

Add chickpeas and broth and increase heat to high. Stir and bring to a boil. Reduce heat to medium-low and simmer uncovered for 1 hour or until chickpeas are tender.

Bring a large saucepan of water to a boil. Add eggs and cook over high heat for 5 minutes (soft-boiled). Remove eggs from pan and plunge into ice water to stop cooking. Peel eggs and set aside.

To serve, divide bread pieces between 6 bowls. Ladle soup over bread and top each serving with one egg (cut in half) and a spoonful each of olive oil and harissa.

Per serving: 604 calories, 19 g fat, 4 g saturated fat, 4568 mg sodium, 74 g carbohydrates, 36 g protein.

TIP:

To make your own harissa, soak 2 oz. of dried chilies in hot water overnight. Toast 1-½ tsp. cumin seeds, 1-½ tsp. coriander seeds, and 1 tsp. caraway seeds in a dry skillet. Place chilies and seeds in a food processor with 4 cloves garlic, 2 Tbsp. olive oil, 1-½ tsp. lemon juice, 1 tsp. salt, and ½ tsp. smoked paprika and pulse until smooth.

TURKEY SHISH KEBAB

1 / 2 / 2
COOK TIME: 12 MINUTES
ACTIVE PREP TIME: 20 MINUTES
INACTIVE PREP TIME: 4 HOURS, 30 MINUTES
MAKES 4 SERVINGS

WHILE SEVERAL DISHES IN THIS BOOK INCLUDE MEATS AND VEGETABLES skewered and baked or grilled over fire, the Turkish shish kebab is definitely the best known to most Americans. Its name comes from the Turkish word *şiş kebap*, meaning "skewered roasted meat." According to legend, the shish kebab originated in the fourteenth-century Ottoman Empire, when soldiers used their bayonets to grill meat over open flames. In Turkey, shish kebabs can include either meat or vegetables, but unlike in the United States, they are rarely cooked on the same skewer.

2 lbs. lamb loin, cut into 1-inch cubes
1 c. plain yogurt
Juice of 1 lemon
¼ c. olive oil, plus more for brushing
2 cloves garlic, minced
1 Tbsp. onion powder
1 Tbsp. sumac or za'atar seasoning
½ tsp. ground turmeric
½ tsp. ground coriander
½ tsp. ground cumin
½ tsp. red pepper flakes

2 onions, cut into eighths
2 green bell peppers, cut into large pieces
12 cherry tomatoes

Combine yogurt, lemon juice, olive oil, garlic, onion powder, sumac or za'atar seasoning, turmeric, coriander, cumin, and red pepper flakes. Place lamb cubes in a large bowl and cover with yogurt mixture. Marinate in refrigerator for at least 4 hours.

Preheat a charcoal or gas grill on high, placing the rack 4-5 inches above the flame. Thread lamb cubes and vegetable pieces on separate skewers (you will need at least six). If using bamboo skewers, soak in water for at least 30 minutes before threading. Brush vegetable skewers with olive oil. Grill skewers for 10-12 minutes or until vegetables are charred, turning frequently and brushing with olive oil when needed. Remove meat and vegetables from skewers and serve.

Per serving: 902 calories, 39 g fat, 11 g saturated fat, 325 mg sodium, 31 g carbohydrates, 103 g protein.

VARIATIONS:

Use beef, chicken, or swordfish in place of lamb.

TIP:

To prepare shish kebabs in the oven, place on a coated baking sheet and cook at 375 degrees for 30-40 minutes, turning every 10 minutes.

UNITED ARAB EMIRATES

MARAK LAHAM

WITH A FOREIGN-BORN POPULATION OF OVER 80 PERCENT, THE UNITED ARAB Emirates is the world's most cosmopolitan nation. Globalism is reflected in every aspect of the small Middle Eastern country's culture, including its cuisine. Indian, Chinese, and Southeast Asian foods are immensely popular, but traditional Emirati cuisine is fairly similar to that of other Middle Eastern countries. Marak laham, a hearty lamb stew, is a staple in many surrounding countries as well.

2 lbs. lamb stew meat, cut into 1-inch pieces
1 large purple onion, chopped
Oil, for sautéing
2 large tomatoes, seeded and chopped
One 1-inch piece ginger, peeled and grated
3 cloves garlic, minced
1-½ tsp. red curry powder
1 tsp. ground cumin
1 tsp. ground turmeric
½ tsp. ground cardamom
½ tsp. ground cinnamon
¼ tsp. red chili powder
1 bell pepper, chopped
½ c. fresh parsley, finely chopped
¼ c. tomato paste
1 dried black lime
2 green chilies, stemmed and cut in half

1-½ qt. chicken broth
2 large potatoes, peeled and coarsely chopped

Heat oil in a Dutch oven over medium-high heat. Add onion and sauté until translucent, about 5 minutes. Add lamb and continue to cook until brown on all sides, about 5 minutes longer.

Add tomatoes, ginger, garlic, curry powder, cumin, turmeric, cardamom, cinnamon, and chili powder. Mash tomatoes with the back of a spoon until a pulp-like consistency is reached. Add bell pepper and parsley, followed by tomato paste and broth, and then black lime and green chilies, stirring after each addition.

Reduce heat to low, cover, and simmer for 1-½ hours or until meat is tender. Add potatoes and simmer for another 30 minutes or until potatoes are fully cooked.

Per serving: 324 calories, 11 g fat, 3 g saturated fat, 152 mg sodium, 22 g carbohydrates, 35 g protein.

SERVING SUGGESTION:

Serve with rice or lavash bread.

VARIATIONS:

Use beef in place of lamb. Beef should be cooked longer to achieve desired tenderness. Other vegetables, such as zucchini and carrots, may be added with potatoes if desired.

YEMEN
SALTAH

3 / 2 / 3
COOK TIME: 50 MINUTES
ACTIVE PREP TIME: 30 MINUTES
MAKES 4 SERVINGS

THE COASTAL NATION OF YEMEN IS CULTURALLY DISTINCT FROM THE REST

of the Arab world in several ways, its cuisine being one of them. Saltah, its national dish, is highly unique in the way it is prepared: cooked in individual serving dishes over the stove until bubbling and then topped with hulba, a frothy and spicy blend of salsa and the Indian herb fenugreek.

1 large onion, chopped
12 cloves garlic, minced
Oil, for sautéing
2 tsp. salt
2 tsp. coriander powder
1 tsp. cumin seed
1 tsp. ground black pepper
6 tomatoes, seeded and chopped
½ lb. small okra pieces, sliced crosswise
4 potatoes, peeled and cut into large pieces
1-¼ qt. water or beef broth (plus more if needed)
Salt and pepper, to taste
½ c. hulba (recipe below)

Heat oil in a Dutch oven over medium-high heat. Add onion and garlic and sauté until browned, about 5-7 minutes. Add salt, coriander, cumin, and black pepper and continue to cook for 1 minute longer or until fragrant. Add tomatoes and cook until liquid has evaporated, about 5 minutes. Add okra, potatoes, and water or broth. Bring to a boil, reduce heat to medium-low, cover, and simmer for 25 minutes or until potatoes are fully cooked. Mash potatoes slightly so that all vegetables are bite-sized.

Divide stew between four oven-safe earthenware pots, adding water or broth if necessary. Heat each pot over medium-low heat until soup begins to bubble. When it reaches this stage, spoon one-fourth of the hulba over the surface of the soup. Repeat with each of the other pots and serve immediately.

For hulba:
3 Tbsp. ground fenugreek
Water, for soaking
1 small green bell pepper, chopped
1-2 small green chili peppers

1 clove garlic
1 Tbsp. lemon juice
½ tsp. ground coriander
½ tsp. salt
¼ tsp. ground cumin

Add fenugreek to a small amount of water in a small bowl. Allow to soak for 1 hour. Pour off water carefully, reserving fenugreek at bottom of bowl. Using a metal spoon, whip the fenugreek by hand until white and foamy, about 5-10 minutes.

Place bell pepper, chili peppers, garlic, lemon juice, coriander, salt, and cumin in a blender or food processor. Process until smooth. Add to fenugreek and stir.

Per serving: 302 calories, 5 g fat, 1 g saturated fat, 1491 mg sodium, 59 g carbohydrates, 10 g protein.

VARIATIONS:

Add other vegetables, such as squash and eggplant. A raw egg can be added to the stew immediately before the hulba.

AFRICA

ANGOLA
MUAMBA DE GALINHA

MUAMBA DE GALINHA, OR "CHICKEN WITH MOAMBE SAUCE," GETS ITS distinctive flavor and aroma from moambe, or palm fruit. This recipe uses palm soup base, an ingredient that can be found in some African grocery stores.

3 lbs. chicken, cut into pieces
Juice of 1 lemon
2-3 red chili peppers, seeded and chopped
3 cloves garlic, minced
Salt and pepper, to taste
¼ c. coconut oil
2 onions, chopped
2 bell peppers, seeded and chopped
One 15-oz. can crushed tomatoes
1 lb. squash (butternut or acorn) or pumpkin, chopped
½ lb. okra, sliced
One 12-oz. can palm soup base

Combine lemon juice, chili peppers, and garlic. Coat chicken with lemon juice mixture, and season with salt and pepper. Cover and marinate in refrigerator for at least one hour.

Heat coconut oil in a heavy skillet over medium-high heat. Add chicken to pan, reserving marinade, and fry until browned, about 5-10 minutes.

Remove chicken from oil. Add onions and bell peppers and sauté until onions are translucent, about 5 minutes. Add reserved marinade and tomatoes, reduce heat to low, and simmer for 5 minutes.

Return chicken to pan along with squash or pumpkin, okra, and palm soup base. Simmer uncovered over low heat for 25 minutes, stirring occasionally.

Per serving: 628 calories, 21 g fat, 13 g saturated fat, 208 mg sodium, 25 g carbohydrates, 87 g protein.

SERVING SUGGESTIONS:

Serve with white rice, polenta, or sweet potatoes.

VARIATION:

Use bacon grease or olive oil in place of coconut oil for a distinctly different flavor.

BENIN FRIED FISH WITH MOYO SAUCE

1 / 1 / 1
COOK TIME: 35 MINUTES
ACTIVE PREP TIME: 10 MINUTES
MAKES 4 SERVINGS

UNLIKE IN MANY OTHER WEST AFRICAN COUNTRIES, FRIED FOODS ARE popular in Benin, especially fish and chicken fried in peanut or palm oil. The Beninese eat fried fish and chicken with a variety of flavorful, tomato- or peanut-based sauces, such as the slightly spicy moyo sauce.

2 lbs. tilapia or other firm, white fish, filleted
½ c. coarsely-ground yellow cornmeal
Peanut oil, for frying
1 green bell pepper, seeded and finely chopped
2 small white onions, finely chopped
6 ripe tomatoes, peeled, seeded, and chopped
¼ c. chicken broth, or one chicken bouillon cube
1 Tbsp. lemon juice

Dredge fish fillets in cornmeal and shake off excess. Pour peanut oil in a heavy skillet to a depth of ¼-inch and heat over medium-high heat. Fry battered fish filets for 3-5 minutes on each side (depending on thickness) until fish flakes with a fork.

Heat additional peanut oil in a smaller skillet over medium-high heat. Sauté onions and bell pepper until onion is translucent and pepper is soft, about 5 minutes. Add tomatoes, chicken broth, and lemon juice. Reduce heat to low, cover, and simmer for 20 minutes or until sauce is smooth and thick.

Per serving: 419 calories, 17 g fat, 3 g saturated fat, 98 mg sodium, 25 g carbohydrates, 46 g protein.

SERVING SUGGESTIONS:

Serve with yams, rice, or couscous.

VARIATIONS:

This recipe can also be made with smoked or grilled fish, or with chicken. For a spicier moyo sauce, substitute bell pepper with 1-2 small, finely minced bird's-eye, habanero, or piri-piri chilies.

BOTSWANA SESWAA WITH MIELIEPAP

2 / 1 / 2
COOK TIME: 3 HOURS, 10 MINUTES
ACTIVE PREP TIME: 10 MINUTES
MAKES 6 SERVINGS

BOTSWANA BORDERS SOUTH AFRICA TO THE NORTH, AND THE PROMINENT Dutch and English influence on its cuisine mirrors its neighbor's. But Botswana's national dish, seswaa, is unique to that country. Made with beef, mutton, or goat meat, seswaa is simmered in a huge three-legged pot with a large amount of salt until tender. This recipe substitutes other seasonings for the excess salt.

For seswaa:
2 lbs. beef brisket or chuck, with bones

Vegetable oil, for frying
1 large onion, finely chopped
3 bay leaves
1 tsp. black peppercorns
Water, for boiling
Salt and pepper, to taste

Heat oil in a heavy skillet over medium-high heat. Fry meat until browned on all sides, about 10 minutes.

Place beef, onions, bay leaves, and peppercorns in a large stockpot and add enough water to cover. Bring to a boil, reduce heat to low, cover, and simmer for at least 3 hours or until meat is very tender.

Remove lid and continue to simmer until most of remaining liquid has evaporated. Remove bones. While still in pot, pound meat with a wooden spoon until shredded. If desired, brown shredded meat in oil.

Season with salt and pepper and serve with mieliepap.

Per serving: 312 calories, 12 g fat, 4 g saturated fat, 101 mg sodium, 3 g carbo-hydrates, 46 g protein.

For mieliepap:
2 c. white cornmeal
1-½ qt. water
Salt and pepper, to taste
Butter, to taste

Bring water to a boil in a large pot. Slowly add cornmeal to the water and boil for 3-4 minutes, stirring constantly until mixture becomes too thick to stir.

Reduce heat to low, cover, and simmer for 15-20 minutes. When done, the bottom of the mieliepap should be browned but not burned.

Per serving: 164 calories, 3 g fat, 1 g saturated fat, 28 mg sodium, 31 g carbohydrates, 3 g protein.

SERVING SUGGESTIONS:
Serve with cooked greens or root vegetables.

VARIATIONS:

For the seswaa, fatty cuts of lamb or goat meat can be used in place of beef. Grits or millet can be used in place of cornmeal.

BURKINA FASO
MAAN NEZIM NZEDO

1 / 1 / 1
COOK TIME: 40 MINUTES
ACTIVE PREP TIME: 5 MINUTES
MAKES 6-8 SERVINGS

ALTHOUGH BURKINA FASO IS LANDLOCKED, ITS POSITION IN THE BASIN OF the Niger River makes freshwater fishing an integral part of its economy. Burkinabè cuisine relies on West African staples such as peanuts, yams, and okra, which figure predominantly in this simple fish stew.

1-½ lb. perch, trout, or other freshwater fish filets, sliced into pieces
Vegetable oil, for frying
1 medium yellow onion, thinly sliced
One 15-oz. can tomato sauce
2 tsp. salt
½ tsp. cayenne pepper
1 lb. okra, sliced lengthwise
3 carrots, thinly sliced
1 small cabbage, shredded
1 c. brown rice, uncooked

Heat oil in a Dutch oven over medium-high heat. Add onion and cook until translucent, about 5 minutes. Add tomato sauce, salt, and cayenne pepper and bring to a boil. Add okra, carrots, and cabbage. Reduce heat to medium-low, cover, and simmer for 5 minutes.

While the vegetables are simmering, heat a small amount of oil in a frying pan over medium-high heat. Quickly cook fish pieces in oil until just slightly brown, about 2 minutes on each side.

Add fish to pot along with rice and stir. Simmer for an additional 25 minutes or until the rice is fully cooked and the fish flakes with a fork.

Per serving: 286 calories, 6 g fat, 1 g saturated fat, 885 mg sodium, 37 g carbohydrates, 21 g protein.

VARIATIONS:

Green beans may be substituted for some or all of the okra in this recipe. Fish stock may be used in place of vegetable oil.

BURUNDI PORK AND PEANUT STEW

2 / 1 / 2
COOK TIME: 1 HOUR, 40 MINUTES
ACTIVE PREP TIME: 10 MINUTES
MAKES 4 SERVINGS

BURUNDI IS SMALL AND AGRICULTURAL, WITH THE AVERAGE BURUNDIAN diet relying on vegetables rather than meat. The herding and breeding of animals is not common, so most meat dishes are made with bushmeat, which comes from non-domesticated animals that are hunted and is considered a great delicacy in many parts of sub-Saharan Africa. This pork and peanut stew would most likely be made from wild boar.

1 lb. pork shoulder with bone, cut into pieces
Salt and pepper, to taste
6 cloves garlic, minced
4 large carrots, cut into pieces
3 large tomatoes, seeded and chopped
2 medium yellow onions, chopped

1-2 chili peppers, seeded and minced

½ c. dry roasted peanuts, finely ground

One 1-inch piece fresh ginger, peeled and grated

2 Tbsp. oil or clarified butter

2 Tbsp. all-purpose flour

Place meat at the bottom of a large Dutch oven and season with salt and pepper. Add garlic, carrots, tomatoes, onions, peppers, peanuts, and ginger. Cover tightly and cook over low heat for 1 hour.

Remove meat and vegetables from pot, collecting juices separately. Heat oil or butter in pot over medium heat. Add flour and stir constantly until a light-brown roux is formed. Add juices from meat and vegetables to the pan slowly and stir to make a sauce. If necessary, add a small amount of water to the pan.

Add meat and vegetables back to the pan, and continue to cook over medium-low heat until all ingredients are fully cooked, about 30 minutes longer.

Per serving: 552 calories, 39 g fat, 10 g saturated fat, 138 mg sodium, 25 g carbohydrates, 27 g protein.

VARIATIONS:

Other types of meat can be used instead, such as lamb, goat, or any type of game, as well as other vegetables. For a spicier stew, add more chili peppers, or serve with hot sauce.

CAMEROON NDOLÉ

1 / 1 / 2
COOK TIME: 40 MINUTES
ACTIVE PREP TIME: 15 MINUTES
MAKES 4-6 SERVINGS

CAMEROON'S NAME COMES FROM THE PORTUGUESE WORD CAMARÕES, meaning "shrimp." Accordingly, shrimp is readily available in the coastal African country and is a staple of the local diet. A classic sub-Saharan dish that shows the cultural fusion of African, Portuguese, and French cuisine, ndolé takes its name from the bitter leaves that are traditionally used to make it. In this version, spinach is used as a substitute for the ndoleh leaves, which are difficult to find in the United States.

½ lb. stew beef, ground or finely chopped
½ lb. shrimp
1 c. peanuts, shelled
Water, for boiling
One 2-inch piece ginger, peeled and finely chopped
4 cloves garlic
1 c. vegetable broth
1 medium onion, sliced
1 lb. spinach, rinsed and coarsely chopped

Bring a small saucepan of water to a boil. Add peanuts and boil for about 10 minutes or until soft. Puree peanuts with ginger and garlic in food processor.

In a large saucepan, bring vegetable broth to a boil. Add beef and boil until cooked throughout. Add peanut paste, onion, and shrimp, in that order. Reduce heat to low and simmer gently for 20 minutes.

Add spinach to the stew and stir. Continue to cook just until spinach begins to wilt, about 2-3 minutes.

Per serving: 358 calories, 22 g fat, 5 g saturated fat, 364 mg sodium, 12 g carbohydrates, 32 g protein.

SERVING SUGGESTIONS:
Serve ndolé with brown rice and fried plantains.

VARIATIONS:
If desired, brown beef, shrimp, and onion before adding to stew (although in Cameroon, meats and vegetables are typically not browned). Crayfish tails may be used in place of shrimp.

CAPE VERDE CACHUPA

BEFORE BEING COLONIZED BY THE PORTUGUESE IN THE MID-FIFTEENTH century, Cape Verde was uninhabited. As both Europeans and enslaved Africans populated the archipelago's islands, native foods developed such as the stew cachupa, of which each island in Cape Verde has its own distinct version. Leftover cachupa is traditionally eaten with sausage and fried eggs for breakfast the next day.

2 c. hominy (corn groats), uncooked
½ c. dried black beans
½ c. dried lima beans
½ c. dried kidney beans
Salted water, for soaking
1-½ qt. chicken broth
6 cloves garlic, chopped, divided
1 onion, chopped, divided
2 bay leaves
2 Tbsp. olive oil
¼ lb. bacon, coarsely chopped
½ lb. smoked sausage (such as chorizo), coarsely sliced
2 tomatoes, seeded and chopped
1 small head cabbage, chopped
1 lb. winter squash, cut into cubes

   Soak hominy and beans for 8 hours (or overnight) in salted water. Place broth, 3 cloves garlic, half of the onion, bay leaves, and olive oil in a large pot. Drain hominy and beans, and add to pot. Bring to a boil, reduce heat to low, and add bacon. Cover and simmer for 2-½ hours, adding sausage to the pot after 1 hour. Check the pot frequently, adding additional water or broth as needed if liquid begins to reduce.

About 1 hour before cachupa is finished, sauté tomatoes and remaining onion and garlic cloves in a small frying pan. Add to pot after tomatoes have softened.

Thirty minutes before the cachupa is finished, add cabbage and winter squash. Remove cachupa from heat and allow to stand for 20 minutes before serving.

Per serving: 766 calories, 37 g fat, 11 g saturated fat, 1300 mg sodium, 74 g carbohydrates, 39 g protein.

SERVING SUGGESTIONS:

Garnish with chopped parsley and serve with Tabasco or piri-piri sauce if desired.

VARIATIONS:

Chicken, fresh tuna, or shrimp can be used in place of the sausage in this recipe. Meat can be omitted for a vegetarian version.

TIP:

To reduce cooking time, use one can each of canned and drained lima, black, and kidney beans and 3 c. of fresh or frozen white corn in place of hominy and beans.

CENTRAL AFRICAN REPUBLIC MBIKA WITH BEEF

2 / 3 / 3
COOK TIME: 45 MINUTES
ACTIVE PREP TIME: 20 MINUTES
MAKES 4 SERVINGS

IN THE CONGO RIVER REGION OF CENTRAL AFRICA, PLANTS FROM THE GOURD family are collectively called mbika. Pumpkins, melons, and squash are staples of central African cuisine, where cooks use not only their flesh but also their seeds, a valuable source of protein in a region where meat is not always plentiful.

2 lbs. stew beef, cut into small pieces

1 lb. raw, shelled pumpkin seeds
Oil, for frying
2-3 chili peppers, chopped
2 onions, chopped
1 bouillon cube, crushed
Water, as necessary
4 banana leaves

Spread pumpkin seeds on a baking sheet and bake until golden, about 5-7 minutes. Cool seeds completely, transfer to a food processor, and grind to a coarse flour.

Combine ground pumpkin seeds with bouillon in a small bowl. Add water and mix until a thick paste is formed.

Heat oil in a heavy skillet over medium-high heat. Fry meat, peppers, and onions until meat is brown, about 7 minutes. Add pumpkin seed paste to the pan and mix thoroughly.

Fold each banana leaf into a square shape, then fold in two to form a triangle. Spoon an equal amount of mbika and meat in the center of each banana leaf and fold to form a packet.

Preheat oven to 375 degrees. Bake banana leaf packets in the oven at 375 degrees (or on a hot outdoor grill) for 30 minutes or until completely warmed.

Per serving: 1083 calories, 76 g fat, 10 g saturated fat, 174 mg sodium, 20 g carbohydrates, 80 g protein.

VARIATIONS:

Other types of seeds, including sesame seeds and pepitas, can be used in lieu of the pumpkin seeds. Instead of beef, mbika can be made with smoked eel (traditional), chicken, or pork.

TIP:

Aluminum foil can be used instead of banana leaves to make packets.

CHAD
JARRET DE BOEUF

1 / 1 / 1
COOK TIME: 4 HOURS, 10 MINUTES
ACTIVE PREP TIME: 10 MINUTES
MAKES 4-6 SERVINGS

JARRET DE BOEUF, WHICH MEANS "BEEF SHIN," IS A TRADITIONAL FRENCH
method of preparing beef using shanks. The meat is simmered with vegetables in its
own broth, allowing the marrow to slowly flavor the meat. In this version from Chad,
a former French colony, the meat is prepared African-style (boiled without browning
first, and with no bones) and using local vegetables.

2 lbs. boneless beef shank or brisket, cut into medium-sized pieces
1 Tbsp. salt
Water, for boiling
½ tsp. cayenne pepper (or to taste)
½ tsp. ground black pepper
2 onions, chopped
2 cloves garlic, minced
2 carrots, chopped
1 eggplant, chopped
1 leek, chopped
1 sweet potato, peeled and chopped

Add salt to a large pot of water and bring to a boil. Add beef to the pot. Reduce
heat to low and simmer for 2 hours or until meat is completely cooked and tender.

Drain meat and return to pot. Cover with cold water and add cayenne pepper and
black pepper. Bring to a boil, reduce heat to low, and simmer for 1-½ hours longer.
Add onions, garlic, carrots, eggplant, leek, and sweet potato, along with more water
if needed. Simmer for 40 more minutes or until sweet potatoes are fully cooked.

*Per serving: 783 calories, 58 g fat, 22 g saturated fat, 1538 mg sodium, 20 g
carbohydrates, 45 g protein.*

SERVING SUGGESTIONS:

Serve with rice, millet, or polenta.

VARIATIONS:

Potatoes, celery, tomatoes, or other vegetables can also be used in this recipe.

COMOROS
POULET AU COCO

1 / 1 / 2
COOK TIME: 35 MINUTES
ACTIVE PREP TIME: 10 MINUTES
MAKES 4 SERVINGS

COMOROS IS A TINY ISLAND NATION OFF AFRICA'S EAST COAST, LYING HALFWAY between Madagascar and the coast of Mozambique. The former French colony served as a trading post between Europe and India in the nineteenth century. Coconuts and spices, prominent in this recipe, were traded from Comoros.

1 whole chicken, cut into parts (or 4 chicken breasts)
Peanut oil, for frying
6 cloves garlic, minced
1 onion, sliced
1 red bell pepper, seeded and sliced
1 Tbsp. curry powder
2 tsp. ground turmeric
One 15-oz. can coconut milk
1 bunch fresh parsley, finely chopped
4 c. cooked basmati rice, for serving

Heat peanut oil in a heavy skillet over medium-high heat. Brown chicken in oil until golden, about 5-7 minutes. Add garlic, onion, bell pepper, curry powder, and turmeric to the pan and fry for 5 minutes longer or until onion and bell pepper are soft.

Add coconut milk and parsley to the pan. Reduce heat to low, cover, and simmer for 20 minutes, stirring frequently and adding water if necessary. Serve chicken and sauce over rice.

Per serving: 704 calories, 46 g fat, 30 g saturated fat, 151 mg sodium, 29 g carbohydrates, 46 g protein.

SERVING SUGGESTIONS:

In Comoros, this dish is garnished with shredded coconut or chopped peanuts and served with sliced bananas as well as rice.

VARIATION:

For a distinctly different flavor, omit red bell pepper and add 1-2 chopped, seeded tomatoes (or 2 Tbsp. tomato paste) to the skillet with the onions and spices.

CONGO
COUPÉ-COUPÉ WITH
PILI-PILI SAUCE

2 / 2 / 2
COOK TIME: 3 HOURS
ACTIVE PREP TIME: 15 MINUTES
INACTIVE PREP TIME: 1 HOUR
MAKES 6-8 SERVINGS

COUPÉ-COUPÉ, WHOSE NAME MEANS "TO CUT" (IN REFERENCE TO THE STYLE in which it is served), is traditional Central African barbecue, marinated over low heat and served sandwich-style on baguette bread. Beef, chicken, goat, and even elephant are cooked this way to make this popular street food. The very hot and spicy pili-pili pepper is served with nearly everything in the Congo. It is similar in flavor to the Scotch bonnet pepper, which is easier to find in the United States.

For coupé-coupé:
3-4 lbs. beef brisket (shoulder, chuck, or flank)
1 beef bouillon cube

½ c. low-sodium soy sauce
Cayenne pepper, to taste
Baguette bread, for serving

Combine bouillon, soy sauce, and cayenne pepper. Pour marinade over meat and refrigerate for at least 1 hour. Reserve marinade.

Heat a charcoal grill or smoker. Cook marinated meat over low heat for at least 3 hours, brushing with reserved marinade every 20-30 minutes. Meat will be ready when a meat thermometer inserted in thickest portion reads 165 degrees. Slice meat diagonally and serve with pili-pili sauce on baguette bread.

Per serving: 738 calories, 15 g fat, 5 g saturated fat, 2052 mg sodium, 74 g carbohydrates, 75 g protein.

For pili-pili sauce:
10-15 red Scotch bonnet peppers
¼ c. extra-virgin olive oil
3 cloves garlic
Juice of 1 small lemon
¼ tsp. salt

Place all ingredients in a blender and process until smooth. If sauce is too thick, add a small amount of oil.

Per serving: 67 calories, 7 g fat, 1 g saturated fat, 82 mg sodium, 1 g carbohydrates, 0 g protein.

VARIATION:

Milder peppers such as red jalapenos can be used in place of the Scotch bonnet peppers if a less spicy sauce is desired.

TIP:

In Congo, Maggi® sauce is traditionally used to marinate meat cooked in this fashion. If available, it can be used in place of the soy sauce and bouillon.

DJIBOUTI SKOUDEHKARIS

COOK TIME: 1 HOUR, 10 MINUTES
ACTIVE PREP TIME: 10 MINUTES
MAKES 4 SERVINGS

THE TINY NATION OF DJIBOUTI REPRESENTS A CULTURAL CROSSROADS.

Situated in the Horn of Africa between Somalia and Ethiopia, a mere 18 miles separates it from Yemen. The influence of both African and Middle Eastern cuisines can be seen and tasted in Djibouti's national dish, skoudehkaris. The spices in this rice and lamb dish are reminiscent of biryani (p. 215), showing the South Asian influence that has endured in this part of the world as a remnant of the centuries-old spice trade.

1 lb. lamb (shank or shoulder), cubed
1 red onion, chopped
4 cloves garlic, minced
Oil, for sautéing
1 tsp. ground cloves
1 tsp. ground cardamom
½ tsp. ground cinnamon
½ tsp. ground cumin
¼ tsp. cayenne pepper
1 15-oz. can diced tomatoes
2 Tbsp. tomato paste
½ c. long-grain white rice
¼ c. fresh cilantro, chopped

Heat oil in a Dutch oven over medium-high heat. Add onions, garlic, cloves, cardamom, cumin, and cayenne pepper and sauté until onions are translucent and spices are fragrant, about 5 minutes. Add meat to the pot and cook until brown on all sides, about 5-6 minutes longer.

Preheat oven to 350 degrees. Add tomatoes and tomato paste to the pot. If the meat is not completely covered in liquid, add just enough water to cover. Cover pot and place in oven for 45 minutes or until meat is tender and fully cooked, adding more water if necessary.

Remove pot from oven and return to stovetop. Add rice to pot and stir. Cover and cook over medium-high heat until rice is fully cooked and all liquid is absorbed, about 15-20 minutes. Garnish with chopped cilantro and serve.

Per serving: 372 calories, 12 g fat, 4 g saturated fat, 104 mg sodium, 29 g carbohydrates, 35 g protein.

SERVING SUGGESTIONS:

Skoudehkaris can be served either as a stew or with Ethiopian injera bread (see recipe on p. 147).

VARIATIONS:

Beef, chicken, or shrimp may be used in place of lamb.

EQUATORIAL GUINEA JOLLOF RICE

1 / 1 / 1
COOK TIME: 1 HOUR, 15 MINUTES
ACTIVE PREP TIME: 10 MINUTES
MAKES 4 SERVINGS

EQUATORIAL GUINEA, A TINY COUNTRY IN WEST AFRICA, IS THE ONLY AFRICAN nation where Spanish is the official language. Its colonial heritage is reflected in this recipe for jollof rice, a popular dish throughout western Africa. Here it gets a Spanish treatment with the addition of saffron and smoked paprika–reminiscent of the dish upon which it was based, paella (p. 77).

1-½ lb. chicken, finely chopped
Oil, for frying
1 red bell pepper, chopped

1 yellow bell pepper, chopped
1 large onion, finely chopped
1 head garlic, peeled and cut in half
One 28-oz. can crushed tomatoes
1 Scotch bonnet pepper, seeds removed
3 Tbsp. tomato paste
1 cube chicken bouillon
2 c. water
1 Tbsp. ground turmeric
1 Tbsp. smoked paprika
¼ tsp. saffron strands, soaked in small amount of water
1-¾ c. basmati rice

Preheat oven to 425 degrees. Roast bell pepper, onion, and garlic in oven for 20 minutes or until onion and peppers are soft and blackened and garlic begins to liquefy. Set aside to cool.

Heat oil in a Dutch oven over medium-high heat. Add chicken and fry until brown, about 5 minutes. Remove from pot and set aside. Reduce heat to medium.

Place roasted vegetables in a blender or food processor and pulse until smooth. Transfer vegetable puree to pot and stir.

Place tomatoes and Scotch bonnet pepper in blender or processor and pulse until smooth. Transfer tomato mixture to pot, stir, and add chicken, water, turmeric, paprika, and saffron. Simmer uncovered for 20 minutes or until liquid is reduced by one-third. Add rice, reduce heat to low, cover, and simmer for 30 minutes or until rice is fully cooked and all liquid is absorbed. Fluff rice and serve.

Per serving: 416 calories, 8 g fat, 2 g saturated fat, 313 mg sodium, 47 g carbohydrates, 38 g protein.

VARIATION:

Omit chicken and bouillon for a vegan version.

ERITREA
ZIGINI

1 / 2 / 2
COOK TIME: 1 HOUR, 15 MINUTES
ACTIVE PREP TIME: 10 MINUTES
MAKES 6 SERVINGS

THE NATION OF ERITREA RECEIVED ITS INDEPENDENCE FROM ETHIOPIA ONLY
in 1993, and to many people the two countries' cuisines are very similar. The *tsebhi*,
or stew, served on injera (flat bread) forms the basis of both. But due to its coastal
location and its historical role in colonial commerce, Eritrea's dishes showcase the
impact of many lands. This heavily seasoned recipe reflects the influence of the spice
trade on this part of the world.

2 lbs. stew beef, cut into small pieces
1 Tbsp. paprika
1 tsp. ground ginger
1 tsp. ground fenugreek
1 tsp. ground black pepper
½ tsp. ground coriander seed
½ tsp. ground cardamom
½ tsp. salt
¼ tsp. ground allspice
2 onions, chopped
4 cloves garlic, minced
Oil, for sautéing
1 28-oz. can crushed tomatoes
2 cubes beef bouillon
1 Tbsp. tomato paste
½ c. red wine
¼ c. fresh cilantro, chopped (plus more for serving)

Combine paprika, ginger, fenugreek, black pepper, coriander seed, cardamom,
salt, and allspice in a small bowl. Set aside.

Heat oil in a Dutch oven over medium-high heat. Sauté onions until translucent, about 5 minutes. Add garlic to pot and sauté until fragrant, about 2 minutes longer.

Add beef to pot and cook until brown, about 5-10 minutes. Add spice mix, tomatoes, bouillon cubes, tomato paste, wine, and cilantro. Reduce heat to low, cover, and simmer for about 1 hour or until beef is tender. Garnish with cilantro and serve.

Per serving: 291 calories, 12 g fat, 1 g saturated fat, 671 mg sodium, 7 g carbohydrates, 35 g protein.

SERVING SUGGESTION:

Serve with Ethiopian injera bread (see recipe on p. 147).

VARIATION:

Use 2 lbs. chicken thighs instead of beef if desired.

TIP:

Two Tbsp. plus 2 tsp. of Berbere spice mix can be used in place of individual spices.

ESWATINI CHICKEN DUST

2 / 1 / 1
COOK TIME: 50 MINUTES
ACTIVE PREP TIME: 20 MINUTES
INACTIVE PREP TIME: 2 HOURS, 30 MINUTES
MAKES 4-6 SERVINGS

WITH THE POSSIBLE EXCEPTION OF THE UNITED STATES, THERE IS nowhere in the world where barbecue is more appreciated than in southern Africa. In countries such as Eswatini, the braai (from the Afrikaans word for "barbecue" or "grill") is a major social event. Braais are not unlike American potluck parties, where each guest brings a prepared side dish and the host takes charge of the meat on the grill. Chicken dust, a Swazi specialty, is one of many dishes cooked on the braai, often in the company of boerwors (sausage), kebabs, pork chops, steaks, and ribs.

1 whole chicken, spatchcocked and cut in half

2 Tbsp. smoked paprika

1 Tbsp. brown sugar

1 Tbsp. coarse sea salt

1 Tbsp. garlic powder

2 tsp. cayenne pepper

2 tsp. ground cumin

2 tsp. ground coriander

1-½ tsp. coarsely ground black pepper

1 tsp. dried thyme

¼ c. olive oil

Combine paprika, brown sugar, salt, garlic powder, cayenne pepper, cumin, coriander, black pepper, and thyme. Rub the paprika mixture over the entire surface of the chicken. Cover chicken with plastic wrap and marinate in refrigerator for 2 hours.

After removing chicken from refrigerator, allow to sit at room temperature for 15-20 minutes and then coat surface with olive oil.

Prepare a charcoal grill, with coals on one side of the grill, and use a brush to lightly oil the grates. Once grill is ready, place chicken on grill and cook for 25 minutes, then turn and cook for 25 minutes longer. Chicken is ready when a meat thermometer inserted in thigh registers 165 degrees.

Remove chicken from heat and allow to rest for 10 minutes. Cut into pieces and serve.

Per serving: 326 calories, 19 g fat, 4 g saturated fat, 1252 mg sodium, 5 g carbohydrates, 33 g protein.

SERVING SUGGESTIONS:

Serve with polenta and grilled vegetables, such as zucchini, butternut squash, or corn on the cob.

VARIATIONS:

Use leg quarters in place of a whole chicken; reduce cooking time accordingly. Increase cayenne pepper by 1-2 tsp. for spicier chicken.

ETHIOPIA
WAT WITH INJERA

3 / 2 / 3
COOK TIME: 1 HOUR
ACTIVE PREP TIME: 20 MINUTES
MAKES 8 SERVINGS

ETHIOPIAN CUISINE IS AMONG THE MOST UNIQUE AND DISTINCTIVE IN THE world. A typical Ethiopian meal will include several types of wat, or stew, including at least one meat variety with chicken, lamb, or beef such as this one. In addition, several varieties of bean, legume, or vegetable wat are served along with cooked and raw vegetables such as greens or tomatoes and ayib, a fresh Ethiopian cheese. Ethiopian dishes are never eaten using silverware. Instead, the food is served on a plate covered with a large, thin piece of spongy bread called injera. To eat the meal, one uses their hands to tear off pieces of injera, wrapping the contents in it.

For wat:

3 lbs. boneless chicken (breasts or thighs), cut into small pieces
½ lb. butter
2 onions, chopped
1 Tbsp. sugar
4 cloves garlic, minced
2 Tbsp. garam masala
1 Tbsp. ground red pepper
1 Tbsp. dried thyme
2 tsp. salt
2 tsp. ground fenugreek
1 tsp. ground cardamom
1 c. red wine
2 c. water
¼ c. plus 1 Tbsp. smoked paprika
3 Tbsp. tomato paste
Juice of 1 lime

Heat butter in a large Dutch oven over medium heat. Add onions and sugar and stir until onions are brown, about 7-10 minutes.

Add garlic, garam masala, red pepper, thyme, salt, fenugreek, and cardamom. Stir for about 2-3 minutes. Add wine and water to pot, followed by chicken, paprika, and tomato paste. Reduce heat to medium-low, cover, and simmer for 30-45 minutes or until chicken is tender.

Add lime juice to pot and mix thoroughly. To serve, unroll a piece of injera and spread over surface of plate. Ladle wat onto injera and serve immediately.

Per serving: 582 calories, 36 g fat, 18 g saturated fat, 906 mg sodium, 8 g carbohydrates, 51 g protein.

For injera:
3 c. all-purpose flour
1 c. buckwheat flour
2 Tbsp. baking soda
1 tsp. salt
1 qt. club soda
1 c. white vinegar
Oil, for frying

Blend flours, baking soda, and salt thoroughly. Whisk in club soda and vinegar until smooth.

Wipe a large skillet with oil and place over medium heat. Pour one ladle-sized scoop of batter onto pan and carefully swirl the pan until the batter forms a 9-inch circle. Cook for 1 minute on each side and remove from pan. Repeat until all batter has been cooked. After injera has cooled, roll up each piece and serve alongside wat.

Per serving: 242 calories, 3 g fat, 0 g saturated fat, 1239 mg sodium, 47 g carbohydrates, 7 g protein.

SERVING SUGGESTIONS:

Serve with collard greens, field peas, lentils, onions, tomato salad, hard-boiled eggs, lemon slices, and fresh cheese.

VARIATION:

Stew can be served with plain flatbread instead of injera.

GABON
POULET NYEMBWE

1 / 3 / 2
COOK TIME: 1 HOUR, 20 MINUTES
ACTIVE PREP TIME: 10 MINUTES
MAKES 6 SERVINGS

THE WORD NYEMBWE IS BANTU FOR "PALM OIL," AND THE SAUCE IN THIS recipe uses the palm nut as its main flavoring. Palm oil has a red sheen and a smoky flavor and is a staple in West African and sub-Saharan cooking. It is pressed from the flesh surrounding the fruit of the African palm tree, a task many African cooks still perform themselves. In the United States, palm nut sauce can be purchased in canned form in ethnic grocery stores.

2 lbs. boneless chicken (breasts or thighs)
Oil, for frying (preferably palm oil)
2 cloves garlic, minced
1 onion, chopped
2 Roma tomatoes, seeded and chopped
2 c. okra, cut into ½-inch pieces
1 chili pepper, sliced
1 c. chicken broth
One 16-oz. can palm nut sauce
Salt and pepper, to taste

Heat oil in a Dutch oven over medium-high heat. Add chicken and cook until brown, about 8-10 minutes. Set aside.

Add garlic and onion to pot and sauté until onion is translucent, about 5 minutes. Add tomatoes, okra, and chili pepper and cook 3-4 minutes longer. Add chicken broth to pot and simmer uncovered until broth is reduced by half. Add palm nut sauce and stir.

Add chicken to pot. Reduce heat to low, cover, and simmer for 1 hour, stirring occasionally. When chicken is fully cooked and tender, skim any oil that has risen to the top. Season with salt and pepper and serve.

Per serving: 634 calories, 44 g fat, 17 g saturated fat, 443 mg sodium, 11 g carbohydrates, 46 g protein.

SERVING SUGGESTIONS:
Serve with white rice, plantains, cooked greens, or mashed yams.

TIP:
Palm nut soup base can be used in place of palm nut sauce.

THE GAMBIA
CHUWE KONG

2 / 1 / 2
COOK TIME: 9 HOURS
ACTIVE PREP TIME: 10 MINUTES
INACTIVE PREP TIME: 8 HOURS
MAKES 4 SERVINGS

THE GAMBIA IS THE SMALLEST COUNTRY IN AFRICA'S MAINLAND AND IS almost completely surrounded by Senegal. The narrow country's borders run along the Gambia River, which accounts for nearly half of its geographic area. Fishing is a major industry in the Gambia, and fish and shellfish have a larger place in its cuisine than in those of other West African nations. Chuwe kong, or catfish stew, is one of many popular seafood dishes in the Gambia.

1-½ lb. catfish (about four 1-inch thick filets)
½ c. liquid smoke
3 onions, chopped
1 tomato, seeded and chopped
Oil, for sautéing
¼ c. tomato paste

1-¼ qt. water or chicken broth
3 cloves garlic, crushed
2 carrots, cut into 1-inch pieces
1 large sweet potato, peeled and chopped
½ head green cabbage, shredded
2 bay leaves
1 c. white rice
Salt and pepper, to taste

Rinse fish filets, pat dry, and place in a shallow dish. Season with salt and pepper and coat with liquid smoke. Cover with plastic wrap and allow to marinate in refrigerator for 8 hours or overnight.

Preheat oven to 150 degrees. Rinse marinade from filets and place on a rack in a roasting pan. Bake for 8 hours with oven door ajar, or until filets are opaque.

Heat oil in a Dutch oven over medium-high heat. Add onions and tomatoes and cook until soft, about 5-6 minutes. Add tomato paste and cook for 2 minutes longer. Add water or broth and garlic, carrots, sweet potato, cabbage, and bay leaves. Bring to a boil, reduce heat to medium-low, cover, and simmer for 30 minutes or until sweet potato is fully cooked.

Cut fish into small pieces and add to pot. Simmer for 15 minutes longer. Season with salt and pepper and serve.

Per serving: 634 calories, 21 g fat, 5 g saturated fat, 1336 mg sodium, 77 g carbohydrates, 34 g protein.

TIP:

To save time, fish may be smoked on a grill with charcoal or wood chips without marinating (omit liquid smoke).

GHANA
SHOKO

1 / 1 / 2
COOK TIME: 2 HOURS, 25 MINUTES
ACTIVE PREP TIME: 10 MINUTES
MAKES 4 SERVINGS

Most Ghanaian dishes are composed of a starch, such as rice or corn, and served with a filling, high-protein stew made with tomatoes and meat, fish, or beans. Shoko, traditionally made with goat meat, is a creative alternative to the common beef stew. The people of Ghana eat it with yellow rice or millet.

1 lb. beef stew meat, cubed
Oil, for frying
1 tsp. ground cardamom, divided
½ tsp. salt
½ tsp. ground black pepper
1 onion, chopped
3 cloves garlic, minced
1 tsp. brown sugar
1 15-oz. can diced tomatoes
1 c. beef stock
One 1-inch piece fresh ginger, peeled and grated
1 tsp. ground cumin
½ tsp. cayenne pepper
½ tsp. ground coriander
1-½ c. white rice
2-¼ c. water
½ tsp. ground turmeric
1 lb. fresh spinach, chopped and with stems removed

Heat oil in a Dutch oven over medium-high heat. Season beef with ½ tsp. cardamom, salt, and pepper. Fry beef in oil until brown on all sides, about 5-6 minutes. Remove beef from pot.

Add onions, garlic, and brown sugar to pot. Cook until onion is brown and caramelized, about 7-8 minutes. Add tomatoes and cook 5 minutes longer. Return beef to pot and add stock, ginger, cumin, cayenne pepper, and coriander. Reduce heat to low, cover, and simmer for 2 hours.

While stew is cooking, prepare rice. Add rice, water, and turmeric to a saucepan and bring to a boil. Reduce heat to medium-low, cover, and simmer until rice is tender and all liquid is absorbed, about 20 minutes. Add spinach to pot and cook until it wilts, about 5 minutes or less. Serve stew with rice.

Per serving: 482 calories, 12 g fat, 3 g saturated fat, 665 mg sodium, 50 g carbohydrates, 43 g protein.

SERVING SUGGESTIONS:

Serve with fried plantains and yams.

VARIATIONS:

Cayenne pepper can be omitted for a milder dish or substituted with 4 diced Serrano peppers or one Scotch Bonnet pepper.

GUINEA
POULET AU YASSA

2 / 1 / 2
COOK TIME: 45 MINUTES
ACTIVE PREP TIME: 10 MINUTES
INACTIVE PREP TIME: 8 HOURS
MAKES 6 SERVINGS

YASSA IS A DISH POPULAR THROUGHOUT WEST AFRICA THAT CAN BE MADE with any type of meat, but it is most commonly made with chicken or other fowl. The key to yassa is the marinade, which combines mustard, lemon juice, oil, and a large quantity of onions. Like so many West African dishes, yassa reflects the colonial influence on the region's cuisine: mustard and onions are both ingredients introduced to Africa by the Europeans.

6 large chicken cutlets (about 5 oz. each)

½ c. oil (preferably peanut oil), plus more for sautéing
4 onions, chopped
½ c. fresh lemon juice
½ c. apple cider vinegar
4 cloves garlic, minced
1 bay leaf
2 Tbsp. mustard powder
2 Tbsp. soy sauce
2 carrots, chopped (optional)
1 small cabbage, chopped (optional)
1 red chili pepper, sliced (optional)
Chopped parsley, for serving

Place chicken in a non-reactive dish. Combine oil, onions, lemon juice, vinegar, garlic, bay leaf, mustard powder, and soy sauce and pour over chicken. Cover with plastic wrap and marinate 8 hours or overnight. Reserve marinade.

Heat oil in a Dutch oven over medium-high heat. Add chicken and cook until brown on both sides but not fully cooked, about 5 minutes. Set chicken aside.

Remove onions from marinade, add to pot, and sauté until soft, about 5 minutes. Add remaining marinade with carrots, cabbage, and red chili pepper (if using) and bring to a boil. Continue to cook at medium-high heat, stirring frequently, until sauce has thickened, about 20 minutes.

Add chicken to pot. Reduce heat to medium-low, cover, and simmer until chicken is fully cooked, about 15 minutes. Garnish with chopped parsley and serve.

Per serving: 438 calories, 27 g fat, 5 g saturated fat, 425 mg sodium, 19 g carbohydrates, 31 g protein.

SERVING SUGGESTIONS:

Serve with with rice or couscous and sweet potatoes.

GUINEA BISSAU RED RED

1 / 1 / 1

COOK TIME: 1 HOUR, 15 MINUTES
ACTIVE PREP TIME: 10 MINUTES
INACTIVE PREP TIME: 1 HOUR
MAKES 6 MAIN-COURSE SERVINGS
OR 10 SIDE-DISH SERVINGS

THIS BLACK-EYED PEA AND OKRA STEW COMBINES TWO WEST AFRICAN staple foods. Originating along the African Gold Coast, this recipe came to the United States via the trade in enslaved people and became a staple of Southern as well as African cooking. Regardless of which side of the Atlantic Ocean it is enjoyed on, Red Red is great vegan comfort food.

1-½ c. dried black-eyed peas
Water, for boiling
1 onion, thinly sliced
Olive oil, for sautéing
One 1-inch piece fresh ginger, peeled and finely grated
1 clove garlic, minced
¼ tsp. cayenne pepper (or 1 minced habanero pepper)
One 28-oz. can crushed tomatoes
½ lb. small okras, cut into ½-inch pieces

Place black-eyed peas in a large pot and cover with water. Bring to a boil and continue to boil for 2-3 minutes. Remove from heat and allow to stand for 1 hour. Drain and rinse beans and return to pot.

Cover beans with cold water and bring to a boil. Reduce heat to low, cover, and simmer for 45 minutes or until beans are tender. Remove from heat and drain beans.

Heat oil in a Dutch oven over medium-high heat. Add onions and sauté until soft and transparent, about 5 minutes. Add ginger, garlic, and cayenne or habanero pepper and cook for 1 minute longer.

Add tomatoes, black-eyed peas, and okra to pot and bring to a boil. Reduce heat to medium-low, cover, and simmer until okra is cooked, about 20 minutes.

Per main-course serving: 183 calories, 3 g fat, 1 g saturated fat, 202 mg sodium,

39 g carbohydrates, 13 g protein.

SERVING SUGGESTION:

If serving as a main course, serve with white rice and fried plantains.

VARIATION:

Add 6 oz. of peeled crayfish tails.

IVORY COAST CALALOU

1 / 2 / 2
COOK TIME: 2 HOURS, 15 MINUTES
ACTIVE PREP TIME: 10 MINUTES
MAKES 6 SERVINGS

CALALOU IS COMMONLY SERVED IN THE CARIBBEAN, BUT IT HAS WEST African origins. One chief difference between African and American calalou is the greens, which in the African dish are not optional. Traditionally, West African calalou is made from amaranth, taro, or xanthosoma leaves. This version uses greens that are more readily available in the United States.

2 lbs. lean pork, cut into small pieces
1 onion, chopped
2 cloves garlic, minced
Oil, for frying
2 lbs. greens (spinach, swiss chard, or mustard, turnip, or collard greens, or a combination of these), stems removed
2 tomatoes, seeded and chopped
½ lb. okra, sliced
1-½ qt. water
1 c. dried shrimp (optional)
¼ tsp. cayenne pepper (optional)

Heat oil in a Dutch oven over medium-high heat. Sauté onions and garlic for

2-3 minutes. Add pork and continue to cook until pork is brown, about 10 minutes.

Add greens, tomatoes, okra, water, and shrimp and cayenne pepper (if using) to pot. Cover, reduce heat to low, and simmer for at least 2 hours, adding more water if necessary.

Per serving: 418 calories, 18 g fat, 6 g saturated fat, 163 mg sodium, 17 g carbohydrates, 47 g protein.

SERVING SUGGESTION:

Serve with white rice.

VARIATIONS:

Beef, chicken, or fish may be used in place of pork. Okra can be omitted if preferred.

KENYA
NYAMA CHOMA WITH UGALI AND KACHUMBARI

1 / 1 / 2
COOK TIME: 1 HOUR
ACTIVE PREP TIME: 10 MINUTES
INACTIVE PREP TIME: 2 HOURS
MAKES 4 SERVINGS

NYAMA CHOMA, WHOSE NAME IS SWAHILI FOR "ROAST MEAT," WAS FIRST prepared by hunters who cooked their game over open fires on expeditions. In Kenya, nyama choma is typically made from goat and involves nothing more than fresh meat, an open flame, and a little salt and pepper. You're likely to eat it with ugali, a cornmeal porridge, and kachumbari, a fresh tomato and onion salad.

For nyama choma:
2 lbs. beef short ribs
3 cloves garlic, minced
2 Tbsp. oil
1 Tbsp. ground turmeric

Salt and pepper, to taste

Season ribs with salt and pepper. Combine garlic, oil, and turmeric and rub onto the meat. Cover with plastic wrap and marinate in refrigerator for 2 hours.

Preheat oven to 350 degrees. Place ribs on rack of roasting pan and cook for 1 hour or until well done.

Per serving: 535 calories, 27 g fat, 9 g saturated fat, 137 mg sodium, 2 g carbohydrates, 66 g protein.

For kachumbari:
3 Roma tomatoes, seeded and diced
1 small purple onion, diced
2 stalks celery, diced
2 Tbsp. lime juice
2 Tbsp. fresh cilantro, finely chopped
¼ tsp. cayenne pepper
¼ tsp. black pepper

Combine tomatoes, onion, celery, lime juice, cilantro, cayenne pepper, and black pepper. Cover and allow to chill in refrigerator until ready to serve.

Per serving: 29 calories, 0 g fat, 0 g saturated fat, 13 mg sodium, 7 g carbohydrates, 1 g protein.

For ugali:
2 c. cornmeal, finely ground
1 qt. water
Butter (optional)

Bring water to a boil in a medium saucepan. Reduce heat to medium and slowly add cornmeal. Continue cooking for 3-4 minutes, stirring constantly to avoid lumps, until a thick consistency is reached. Add butter if desired. Serve roasted meat with ugali and salad on the side.

Per serving: 221 calories, 2 g fat, 0 g saturated fat, 21 mg sodium, 47 g carbohydrates, 5 g protein.

VARIATIONS:

Use one whole chicken, cut into parts, in place of ribs. Grill meat over an open flame instead of roasting in the oven.

LESOTHO
CAPE MALAY CHICKEN

2 / 2 / 2
COOK TIME: 40 MINUTES
ACTIVE PREP TIME: 10 MINUTES
MAKES 4 SERVINGS

THE TINY COUNTRY OF LESOTHO IS SURROUNDED BY SOUTH AFRICA, and while it may be small it is as culturally diverse as its larger neighbor. Curries are popular in Lesotho, showing the East Asian influence on Africa's southernmost palates. One example originated with the Cape Malays, an ethnic group descending from enslaved people who were brought to South Africa from Java by the Dutch East India Company in the seventeenth century.

4 chicken breasts, cut into large pieces
1 clove garlic, crushed
One ½-inch piece ginger, peeled and crushed
Oil, for sautéing and frying
1 small onion, finely chopped
One 15-oz. can chopped tomatoes
One 15-oz. can coconut milk
Lemon juice, to taste
Chopped cilantro, for serving

Heat oil in a medium saucepan over medium heat. Sauté onion, garlic, and ginger until onion is soft, about 3 minutes. Raise heat to high, add curry, and cook for 1 minute longer. Add tomatoes and coconut milk and stir. Reduce heat to medium-low and simmer, uncovered, until sauce is reduced by one-third, about 10 minutes, stirring frequently.

Heat a small amount of oil in a heavy skillet over medium-high heat. Add chicken pieces to pan and fry until golden brown, about 3-4 minutes each side. Add sauce to chicken, cover, and simmer over medium heat for 5 minutes or until chicken is fully cooked. Add a squeeze of lemon juice and stir.

Per serving: 611 calories, 46 g fat, 29 g saturated fat, 173 mg sodium, 9 g carbohydrates, 44 g protein.

For rice:
1 c. basmati rice
2 c. water
1-½ tsp. ground turmeric
1 small stick cinnamon
1 pod star anise

Add rice, water, turmeric, cinnamon, and star anise to a medium saucepan and bring to a boil. Reduce heat to medium low, cover, and simmer for 15 minutes or until rice is tender and all water has been absorbed.

Remove cinnamon stick and star anise from rice before serving. Garnish chicken with cilantro and serve with rice.

Per serving: 171 calories, 1 g fat, 0 g saturated fat, 6 mg sodium, 37 g carbohydrates, 3 g protein.

VARIATIONS:
Add vegetables such as potatoes, carrots, and peas to the chicken curry along with the sauce.

LIBERIA
PALAVA WITH SWEET POTATO PONE

2 / 3 / 2
COOK TIME: 1 HOUR, 25 MINUTES
ACTIVE PREP TIME: 15 MINUTES
MAKES 4 SERVINGS

FOUNDED IN 1822 AS A PLACE FOR FORMERLY ENSLAVED PEOPLE TO resettle, Liberia is the only country in Africa that has never been colonized. While Liberian cuisine may not reflect a European impact, it has been heavily influenced by the regional cuisine of the southern United States. Particularly, Liberia is the only country in West Africa where baking is a large part of the culinary tradition. The recipe for sweet potato pone included here is reminiscent of a dessert familiar to many Southerners in the United States, especially around Thanksgiving.

For palava:
1 lb. chicken, cut into small pieces
½ c. pumpkin seeds, ground
¼ c. water
2 Tbsp. red palm oil
1 medium onion, chopped
3 cloves garlic, crushed
One 1-inch piece fresh ginger, peeled and grated
5 Roma tomatoes, peeled, seeded, and chopped
1 Scotch bonnet pepper
1 lb. frozen spinach, chopped

Mix pumpkin seeds with water to form a paste. Set aside.

Heat 1 Tbsp. red palm oil in a Dutch oven over medium-high heat. Sauté onion, garlic, and ginger until onion is soft, about 4-5 minutes. Add chicken and cook for 2-3 more minutes or until brown on all sides. Add tomatoes and pepper to the pot. Continue to cook for about 6-7 minutes or until tomatoes have softened. Add pumpkin seed paste (do not stir). Reduce heat to medium-low, cover, and simmer for 20 minutes.

Uncover pot and stir thoroughly so that pumpkin seed paste is fully incorporated into the stew. Add spinach, recover, and cook for 10 minutes longer. Remove Scotch bonnet pepper and serve.

Per serving: 397 calories, 19 g fat, 6 g saturated fat, 175 mg sodium, 18 g carbohydrates, 42 g protein.

For pone:
2 lbs. sweet potatoes, peeled and cut into cubes
2 c. water, plus more for steaming
1 c. cane syrup
2 tsp. baking powder
2 tsp. ground ginger
1 tsp. ground nutmeg
1 tsp. vanilla extract
½ tsp. salt
¼ tsp. ground cloves
¼ tsp. ground cinnamon
Oil, for greasing baking dish

Place sweet potatoes in a steamer basket. Boil a pot of water, insert steamer basket, cover, and steam for about 7 minutes or until potatoes are soft. Set potatoes aside and allow to cool.

Preheat oven to 325 degrees. Place potatoes in a blender with water and pulse until smooth. (This may need to be done in batches.) Transfer potatoes to a large saucepan and add cane syrup, baking powder, ginger, nutmeg, vanilla, salt, cloves, and cinnamon. Cook over medium heat, stirring constantly, for about 10 minutes or until most of the mixture's moisture has evaporated.

Grease a 9- x 13-inch baking dish with oil and pour sweet potato mixture into dish. Bake for 25-30 minutes or until brown on top. Allow to cool before serving.

Per serving: 372 calories, 4 g fat, 1 g saturated fat, 321 mg sodium, 81 g carbohydrates, 4 g protein.

MADAGASCAR ROMAZAVA

An AFRICAN ISLAND LOCATED IN THE INDIAN OCEAN. MADAGASCAR IS home to the descendants of African, Indian, Southeast Asian, Chinese, and European settlers who arrived over the course of nearly four centuries. Rice is the cornerstone of the average Malagasy diet, usually heavily seasoned with ginger, vanilla, curry, garlic, or other native spices. But the country's cuisine also includes a number of special dishes, one of which is the meat and greens stew known as romazava. This dish was a favorite of the Malagasy royal family before the island was colonized by France in the late nineteenth century.

1 lb. beef stew meat, cut into cubes
1 lb. lean pork loin, cut into cubes
Peanut oil, for sautéing
2 c. beef stock
3 cloves garlic, crushed
One 1-inch piece ginger, peeled and crushed
1 Tbsp. all-purpose flour, sifted
2 tomatoes, finely chopped
2 Tbsp. tomato paste
3 Serrano chilies, sliced horizontally (optional)
1 lb. spinach, sliced and with stems removed
Salt and pepper, to taste

Heat peanut oil in a Dutch oven over medium-high heat. Cook beef and pork until brown, about 5-7 minutes. Add beef stock, garlic, ginger, flour, tomatoes, tomato paste, and peppers (if using) and stir until flour dissipates. Reduce heat to medium-low, cover, and simmer for 45 minutes.

Add the spinach to the pot. Cover and simmer for 10 minutes longer, or until spinach is completely wilted. Season with salt and pepper and serve.

Per serving: 356 calories, 15 g fat, 5 g saturated fat, 416 mg sodium, 7 g carbohydrates, 48 g protein.

SERVING SUGGESTIONS:

Serve with white rice and fresh sliced tomatoes.

VARIATIONS:

Use chicken in place of beef and/or pork, or use mustard greens in place of spinach.

MALAWI KANYENYA WITH NDIWO AND NSHIMA

1 / 1 / 2
COOK TIME: 25 MINUTES
ACTIVE PREP TIME: 15 MINUTES
INACTIVE PREP TIME: 20 MINUTES
MAKES 6 SERVINGS

LAKE MALAWI, WHICH FORMS MOST OF THE EASTERN BORDER OF THE SMALL nation of Malawi, is an abundant source of fish such as bream, salmon, and sardines. A typical Malawian meal will include fish, a fruit or vegetable relish, and the country's staple food, nshima.

For kanyenya:
Six 6-ounce pompano filets
1 c. all-purpose flour
1 c. water
2 cloves garlic, crushed
2 Tbsp. fresh lemon juice
1 tsp. salt
1 tsp. chili powder
Oil, for frying

Combine flour and water in a bowl, adding more water if necessary to form a thick paste. Add garlic, lemon juice, salt, and chili powder.

Dredge fish filets in flour mixture until well coated. Place battered filets in a shallow dish, cover with plastic wrap, and chill in refrigerator for 20 minutes.

Heat oil in a heavy skillet over high heat. Dredge filets once more in flour mixture and add to skillet. Fry for 5-8 minutes or until golden brown and crisp. Set fried filets on paper towels or a wire rack to cool.

Per serving: 306 calories, 16 g fat, 5 g saturated fat, 462 mg sodium, 17 g carbohydrates, 23 g protein.

For ndiwo:
1 small onion, chopped
2 cloves garlic, minced
Oil, for sautéing
2 Roma tomatoes, seeded and chopped
4 c. kale, finely chopped, with stems removed
¼ c. water

Heat oil in a medium skillet over medium-high heat. Sauté onion and garlic for 5 minutes or until onions are translucent. Add tomatoes, reduce heat to medium, and cook for 2 minutes longer. Add kale and water, cover, and simmer for 5 minutes or until kale is tender and has wilted.

Per serving: 56 calories, 2 g fat, 0 g saturated fat, 22 mg sodium, 8 g carbohydrates, 2 g protein.

For nshima:
2 c. white cornmeal
1-¼ qt. water
1 tsp. salt

Bring water to a boil in a medium saucepan. Add salt and reduce heat to medium. Add cornmeal to pan one spoonful at a time, stirring after each addition. Cook for about 3-4 minutes or until porridge is thick and all liquid is evaporated.

Per serving: 110 calories, 1 g fat, 0 g saturated fat, 592 mg sodium, 24 g

carbohydrates, 3 g protein.

VARIATION:

For extra texture and flavor, add 1 c. of roasted peanuts to ndiwo before serving.

MALI MAAFE WITH COUSCOUS

1 / 1 / 2
COOK TIME: 35 MINUTES
ACTIVE PREP TIME: 10 MINUTES
MAKES 4 SERVINGS

ONCE THE CENTER OF ONE OF THE WORLD'S MIGHTIEST EMPIRES, MALI IS much smaller than it once was. But its people take food very seriously; the average Malian spends half their income on food! Maafe is a very typical Malian dish, consisting of a grain or pulse (in this case, couscous) with a thick, protein-rich sauce. The Mandinka and Bambara people of Mali contributed maafe to the country's table. Its name literally means "peanut butter stew," and this recipe uses peanut butter as a chief ingredient.

1 lb. chicken (white or dark meat), cut into small pieces
Oil, for frying
1 medium onion, chopped
2 bay leaves
1 tsp. red chili flakes
2 cloves garlic, minced
1 jalapeno, minced
2 Tbsp. tomato paste
1 green bell pepper, coarsely chopped
¼ c. smooth peanut butter
4-½ c. water, divided

½ tsp. salt

1 c. wheat couscous

Heat oil in a Dutch oven over medium-high heat. Add chicken and fry until brown on all sides, or about 5 minutes (do not overcook). Remove chicken from pot. Add a little more oil to the pot and add onion, bay leaves, and chili flakes. Sauté over medium heat until onion is transparent, about 5 minutes. Add garlic and jalapeno and stir to combine. Add chicken back to pot with tomato paste and cook for 2 minutes longer.

Add 3 c. water and salt to pot. Stir, reduce heat to low, cover, and simmer for 20 minutes. Add peanut butter and bell pepper, cover again, and simmer for 5 minutes.

In a separate medium saucepan, prepare couscous. Bring remaining 1-½ c. water to a boil and remove from heat. Add couscous, cover, and allow to sit for 5-10 minutes or until all liquid has been absorbed. Fluff with a fork and serve with maafe.

Per serving: 436 calories, 8 g fat, 2 g saturated fat, 384 mg sodium, 50 g carbohydrates, 41 g protein.

VARIATIONS:

While it is traditional in Mali to pair maafe and couscous, rice or sweet potatoes may be used in the latter's place.

MAURITANIA CHUBBAGIN LÉLÉ ET RAABIE

2 / 2 / 2

COOK TIME: 40 MINUTES

ACTIVE PREP TIME: 15 MINUTES

MAKES 4 SERVINGS

SITUATED BETWEEN MOROCCO AND THE WEST AFRICAN COAST, MAURITANIA has a cuisine that reflects North and West African influences. Historically a caravan culture, the Mauritanians traditionally eat much of their food dried—the preferred manner of preservation for traveling long distances in the desert. But *chubbagin lélé et raabie*, a fish and vegetable stew, uses both fresh and dried ingredients.

1-½ lb. thick snapper or tilapia filets
2 cloves garlic, finely minced
3 Serrano chilies, finely minced
¼ c. fresh parsley, finely chopped
Oil, for frying
1 small onion, chopped
One 6-oz. can tomato paste
3 c. water
1 small eggplant, sliced
½ small cabbage, shredded
1 large sweet potato, chopped
½ c. dried fish (optional)
2 c. white rice

Combine garlic, chilies, and parsley in a small bowl. Rinse and pat dry fish filets. Using a filet knife, cut a slit in the center of each filet and stuff with garlic and chili mixture.

Heat a thin layer of oil in a Dutch oven over medium heat. Fry the fish filets for about 5 minutes per side. Remove from pot.

Add onion to pot and sauté until translucent, about 5 minutes. Add tomato paste, water, eggplant, cabbage, sweet potato, and dried fish (if using). Stir and add rice. Reduce heat to medium-low, cover, and simmer for 20 minutes or until rice is cooked and all liquid is absorbed (add more water if necessary).

Place fish filets on top of rice. Reduce heat to low, cover, and continue to simmer for 5 minutes. Serve rice and vegetables with fish.

Per serving: 644 calories, 8 g fat, 2 g saturated fat, 529 mg sodium, 104 g carbohydrates, 41 g protein.

VARIATIONS:
Use beef, lamb, seitan, or textured vegetable protein instead of fish.

MAURITIUS KITCHEREE

1 / 3 / 2
COOK TIME: 1 HOUR, 5 MINUTES
ACTIVE PREP TIME: 10 MINUTES
MAKES 4 SERVINGS

MAURITIUS, AN AFRICAN ISLAND IN THE INDIAN OCEAN, IS ONE OF THE most culturally diverse small nations in the world. While Christianity and Islam are well-represented, Mauritius stands as the only African nation where the majority of the population practices Hinduism. Ayurveda, the ancient Hindu system of natural and holistic medicine, is especially prevalent in Mauritius and places great emphasis on diet. Kitcheree, an Ayurvedic staple, is hailed as a cleansing, detoxifying, and nourishing food that promotes digestive health.

2 Tbsp. sesame oil
2 tsp. black mustard seed
2 tsp. cumin seed
1 tsp. fennel seed
1 tsp. fenugreek seed
2 bay leaves
2 tsp. ground turmeric
2 tsp. ground black pepper
1 tsp. ground coriander
2 c. yellow lentils
1 c. basmati rice
2 qt. water
3 cardamom pods
2 whole cloves
2 c. spinach, kale, or bok choy cabbage, chopped
1 c. carrots, chopped
Chopped fresh cilantro, for serving

Heat sesame oil in a large Dutch oven over medium-high heat. Add mustard, cumin, fennel, and fenugreek seeds and toast for 3-4 minutes. Add bay leaves, turmeric, black pepper, and coriander. Stir in lentils and rice and add water, cardamom, cloves, and vegetables. Bring to a boil, reduce heat to low, cover, and simmer for 1 hour or until a porridge-like consistency is achieved. Spoon into bowls, top with cilantro, and serve.

Per serving: 609 calories, 9 g fat, 1 g saturated fat, 43 mg sodium, 102 g carbohydrates, 30 g protein.

VARIATIONS:

Use quinoa, amaranth, millet, or grated cauliflower (one small head) in place of the rice. Broccoli, zucchini, asparagus, or sweet potatoes can be used. Add a small amount of cayenne pepper with the other powdered spices for extra heat.

MOZAMBIQUE PIRI-PIRI CHICKEN

2 / 3 / 2
COOK TIME: 40 MINUTES
ACTIVE PREP TIME: 20 MINUTES
INACTIVE PREP TIME: 4 HOURS
MAKES 4-6 SERVINGS

CHILIES ARE A MAJOR PART OF MANY SUB-SAHARAN AFRICAN DISHES, SO IT is surprising that they are not native to this part of the world. Portuguese explorers introduced chilies to Mozambique in the fifteenth century. The bird's-eye chili, a tiny red ball of fire, quickly became integral to Mozambican cuisine, where it is known by the Swahili word *piri-piri*. This recipe calls for five chilies, but feel free to use fewer (or more!) in accordance with your preference for heat.

One 4-lb. chicken, spatchcocked or cut into parts
5 bird's-eye chilies, stems removed and chopped (seeds intact)
11 cloves garlic, chopped, divided
1 small red bell pepper, chopped
¾ c. lemon juice, divided
½ c. white wine vinegar

1 Tbsp. brown sugar

1 Tbsp. tomato paste

2 tsp. dried oregano

2 tsp. dried thyme

2 tsp. salt

1 tsp. paprika

¾ c. peanut oil, divided

¼ c. fresh cilantro, chopped

One 2-inch piece ginger, peeled and chopped

1 shallot, chopped

1 tsp. kosher salt

1 tsp. ground black pepper

First, make piri-piri sauce. Place chilies, 8 cloves garlic, bell pepper, ½ c. lemon juice, vinegar, brown sugar, tomato paste, oregano, thyme, salt, and paprika in a food processor. Process until combined, and then gradually pour ½ c. peanut oil into food processor container until a smooth sauce is formed. Pour sauce into a jar and refrigerate immediately.

Place cilantro, ginger, shallot, and remaining 3 cloves garlic in food processor and process until combined. Add ½ c. of piri-piri sauce, remaining ¼ c. peanut oil and ¼ c. lemon juice, kosher salt, and pepper and process until blended.

Place chicken in a large plastic bag. Pour marinade over chicken and turn to coat, removing as much air as possible from bag before sealing. Marinate in refrigerator for at least 4 hours and preferably overnight.

Prepare a barbecue grill and place chicken on upper rack, skin side up. Set a pan below the rack to catch drips. Cook chicken over medium heat with grill lid closed, turning frequently, for 40 minutes or until a meat thermometer inserted in thickest part registers 165 degrees. Serve chicken with remaining piri-piri sauce.

Per serving: 548 calories, 41 g fat, 8 g saturated fat, 1507 mg sodium, 9 g carbohydrates, 34 g protein.

SERVING SUGGESTIONS:

Serve with French fries and a cucumber, tomato, and onion salad.

VARIATION:

Piri-piri sauce can also be used on barbecued pork or beef ribs.

TIP:

As far as heat is concerned, 1-3 chilies will produce a low heat; 4-6 a medium heat; and 7-10 a very high heat.

NAMIBIA
WORS WITH CHAKALAKA

1 / 2 / 1
COOK TIME: 30 MINUTES
ACTIVE PREP TIME: 10 MINUTES
MAKES 4-6 SERVINGS

IN NAMIBIA, FORMERLY GERMAN SOUTH WEST AFRICA, THE GERMAN AND Dutch colonial influence is evident in the prevalence of sausage. *Boerewors*, a word meaning "farmer's sausage," is a cultural staple in southern Africa. This pork and beef sausage includes a large proportion of fat and spices, especially coriander, and is formed into a large spiral. Boerewors is cooked over the grill (braaied) in its spiral form without cutting into smaller pieces and served with a spicy relish called chakalaka.

2 lbs. beef and pork sausage, uncooked and in casings
3 Tbsp. butter
1 large onion, chopped
Olive oil, for sautéing
2 cloves garlic, minced
One 1-inch piece ginger, peeled and minced
1 tsp. salt
1 tsp. ground coriander
1 tsp. ground black pepper
½ tsp. paprika
¼ tsp. ground cumin

¼ tsp. ground cloves
¼ tsp. ground nutmeg
¼ tsp. ground allspice
¼ tsp. cayenne pepper (optional)
2 large tomatoes, seeded and diced
Zest of 1 lemon

Heat butter in a large skillet over medium-high heat. Add sausage and cook for about 20 minutes, turning frequently, until golden brown.

In another skillet, heat olive oil over medium-high heat. Sauté onion for 6-8 minutes or until soft, translucent, and very fragrant. Add garlic and ginger and cook for 1-2 minutes longer.

Add salt, coriander, black pepper, paprika, cumin, cloves, nutmeg, allspice, and cayenne pepper (if using), followed by tomatoes and lemon zest. Stir until all ingredients are combined and tomato is warm. Serve chakalaka with sausage.

Per serving: 731 calories, 62 g fat, 21 g saturated fat, 1879 mg sodium, 7 g carbohydrates, 37 g protein.

SERVING SUGGESTIONS:

Serve with polenta or bread.

VARIATION:

Sausage can be cooked on a grill instead of pan-fried.

NIGER
FOY CIREY RICE

1 / 1 / 2
COOK TIME: 45 MINUTES
ACTIVE PREP TIME: 10 MINUTES
MAKES 4 SERVINGS

A LARGELY RURAL COUNTRY WITH FEW URBAN AREAS, NIGER'S AGRICULTURE suffers from frequent drought. Its staple foods include millet, sorghum, beans, and peanuts; while rice is grown plentifully along the Niger River, it is regarded as a status food only eaten on special occasions such as Muslim holy days. On such occasions, rice is usually served with thick, flavorful sauces, such as the Foy Cirey ("red sauce") whose recipe is included here.

2 large onions, chopped
3 cloves garlic, minced
Oil, for sautéing
¼ c. tomato paste
4 tomatoes, peeled, seeded, and chopped
2 green bell peppers, chopped
1 Scotch bonnet pepper, minced
½ c. chicken or vegetable stock
Salt and pepper, to taste
Green onions, sliced diagonally, for serving
6 c. cooked rice (recipe below)

Heat oil in a large saucepan over medium-high heat. Sauté onions and garlic for about 3-4 minutes. Add tomato paste, reduce heat to medium-low, and continue to cook for 5-6 minutes longer.

Add tomatoes, bell peppers, Scotch bonnet pepper, and stock to saucepan. Cover and simmer for 15-20 minutes or until vegetables are tender. Season with salt and pepper.

For rice:
2 c. long-grain white rice
1 c. coconut milk
1 c. chicken broth
½ c. tomato sauce

Add coconut milk, broth, and tomato sauce to a large saucepan and bring to a boil. Add rice, stir well, and reduce heat to medium. Cover and simmer for 15 minutes or until rice is fully cooked (add more liquid if necessary). Serve sauce over rice, garnished with green onions.

Per serving: 469 calories, 14 g fat, 9 g saturated fat, 57 mg sodium, 66 g carbohydrates, 21 g protein.

VARIATIONS:

Serve sauce over chicken instead of rice. Couscous can be used in place of rice.

NIGERIA
AYAMASE

3 / 3 / 3
COOK TIME: 2 HOURS, 10 MINUTES
ACTIVE PREP TIME: 15 MINUTES
MAKES 4 SERVINGS

FOOD IS CELEBRATED IN AFRICA'S MOST POPULOUS AND ECONOMICALLY dominant country, Nigeria. Soups and stews are the cornerstone of its cuisine, and palm oil its most prevalent flavor. Ayamase, an extremely time- and labor-intensive dish, showcases the Yoruba commitment to richness and spice. Fermented locust beans are difficult to find in the United States (they are most often carried at African food stores), but ayamase cannot be made without them.

1 lb. stew beef, cut into small pieces
1-½ c. palm oil
Water, for boiling
1 large red onion, chopped
½ c. fermented locust beans
6 green bell peppers, seeded and coarsely chopped
1 red bell pepper, seeded and coarsely chopped
3 Scotch bonnet peppers, seeded
1 c. beef stock
1 Tbsp. ground turmeric
1 Tbsp. ground crayfish (optional)

Heat palm oil in a stainless steel pot (this is important), covered, over medium heat for 12 minutes. Remove from heat and set aside. Do not remove lid until oil is completely cooled.

Bring a large saucepan of water to a boil. Add beef and boil for 30 minutes or until beef is fully cooked.

Place bell peppers and Scotch bonnet peppers in a blender and process until smooth (add a minimal amount of water if necessary). Transfer pepper puree to a saucepan and cook over medium heat until as much liquid as possible has evaporated. This may take up to 1 hour.

Heat palm oil over medium heat (do not allow oil to smoke). Add onions and sauté until translucent, about 5 minutes. Add locust beans and sauté for about 5 minutes longer or until the oil begins to bubble. Add beef and peppers and fry for 5 more minutes. Add stock, turmeric, and crayfish (if using) and stir; cover, reduce heat to low, and simmer for 10 minutes. Stew should be extremely thick before serving. If there is still too much moisture present, continue to simmer uncovered until it has evaporated.

Per serving: 739 calories, 62 g fat, 27 g saturated fat, 205 mg sodium, 21 g carbohydrates, 29 g protein.

SERVING SUGGESTIONS:
Serve with rice and hard-boiled eggs (customary in the Yoruba culture).

RWANDA
RWANDAN BEEF STEW

1 / 2 / 2
COOK TIME: 1 HOUR, 20 MINUTES
ACTIVE PREP TIME: 10 MINUTES
MAKES 8 SERVINGS

RWANDAN FOOD HINGES ON LOCALLY-SOURCED INGREDIENTS, SUCH AS plantains, cassava, beans, and sweet potatoes. Unlike many other African cuisines, it is very mild and neither hot nor spicy. In Rwanda, where meat is scarce, a meat-based dish such as this rich stew would most likely be served on a special occasion.

2 lbs. stewing beef, cut into pieces
1 onion, chopped
Peanut oil, for sautéing
1 qt. beef broth or water
3 green plantains, peeled and cut into chunks
One 15-oz. can chopped tomatoes
1 green bell pepper, seeded and chopped
¼ c. fresh lemon juice
1 tsp. salt
¼ tsp. dried sage
¼ tsp. dried thyme
¼ tsp. ground black pepper

Heat peanut oil in a Dutch oven over medium-high heat. Sauté beef and onion until beef is brown on all sides, about 7-8 minutes.

Add broth or water, plantains, tomatoes, bell pepper, lemon juice, salt, and spices. Cover and cook over low heat for 1-½ hours, stirring occasionally and adding more liquid if necessary.

Per serving: 286 calories, 10 g fat, 3 g saturated fat, 949 mg sodium, 9 g carbohydrates, 39 g protein.

VARIATIONS:

Use potatoes or sweet potatoes in place of plantains.

SÃO TOMÉ AND PRINCIPE CHICKEN WITH COFFEE SAUCE

2 / 1 / 2
COOK TIME: 30 MINUTES
ACTIVE PREP TIME: 10 MINUTES
INACTIVE PREP TIME: 1 HOUR
MAKES 4 SERVINGS

SÃO TOMÉ AND PRINCIPE, TWO SMALL ISLANDS IN THE GULF OF GUINEA, are sometimes called the "islands of cocoa and coffee." Coffee was first cultivated by Portuguese colonizers in the late fifteenth century, and many entrepreneurs still own coffee fields on the islands today. It is used as a main ingredient in many dishes, including as a sauce for chicken, beef, and desserts.

4 boneless, skinless chicken breasts
1 Tbsp. soy sauce
1 Tbsp. hoisin sauce
Salt and pepper, to taste
Olive oil, for frying
2 cloves garlic, minced
¼ c. strong brewed coffee
¼ c. white wine
1 Tbsp. tomato paste
2 tsp. brown sugar
1-½ tsp. apple cider vinegar
½ tsp. Worcestershire sauce

Place chicken breasts in a shallow dish and cover with soy sauce and hoisin sauce. Season with salt and pepper, cover with plastic wrap, and allow to marinate in the refrigerator for at least 1 hour.

Heat olive oil in a large skillet over medium heat. Cook chicken breasts until fully cooked, about 8-10 minutes on each side. Remove from pan and set aside.

Add garlic and sauté until fragrant, about 2 minutes. Reduce heat to medium-low and add coffee, wine, tomato paste, brown sugar, vinegar, and Worcestershire sauce. Simmer for about 3 minutes or until liquid is reduced by half. Add chicken to the pan, allowing sauce to caramelize and coat the chicken. Serve immediately.

Per serving: 332 calories, 14 g fat, 3 g saturated fat, 423 mg sodium, 5 g carbohydrates, 41 g protein.

SERVING SUGGESTIONS:

Serve with rice or boiled potatoes.

VARIATION:

Add ¼ c. heavy cream for a creamier sauce.

SENEGAL
THIEBOUDIENNE

2 / 2 / 2
COOK TIME: 1 HOUR, 20 MINUTES
ACTIVE PREP TIME: 25 MINUTES
INACTIVE PREP TIME: 30 MINUTES
MAKES 4 SERVINGS

THIEBOUDIENNE, ONE OF SENEGAL'S NATIONAL DISHES, HAS A FRENCH-sounding name that is phonetically similar to the dish's Wolof name, *ceebu jën* (rice and fish). In many ways, thieboudienne is much like another popular African dish, jollof rice (see p. 142), except that it uses fish instead of chicken. Those familiar with Creole cuisine may notice a striking similarity between thieboudienne and many dishes native to Louisiana.

4 red snapper or tilapia filets
2 c. jasmine rice
1-¾ qt. water, plus more for soaking
1 bunch parsley
6 cloves garlic, finely minced
2 shrimp or fish bouillon cubes
2 Scotch bonnet peppers, finely minced

2 tsp. ground black pepper
1 tsp. salt
1 onion, sliced
One 6-oz. can tomato paste
4 carrots, peeled and chopped
1 eggplant, chopped
1 sweet potato, peeled and chopped
Oil, for frying
Lime wedges, for serving

Soak the rice in water for 30 minutes. Drain and rinse rice. Crumble the rice with your fingers until it is mostly broken into smaller pieces. Set aside.

Preheat oven to 375 degrees. Place parsley, 3 cloves garlic, 1 bouillon cube, 1 Scotch bonnet pepper, 1 tsp. black pepper, and salt in a food processor and process until a paste is formed. Create a slit in the side of each fish filet and stuff with parsley mixture. Bake fish filets for 25-30 minutes or until fish flakes with a fork.

Heat oil in a Dutch oven over medium-high heat. Sauté onion until translucent, about 5 minutes. Add tomato paste and remaining garlic and Scotch bonnet pepper to pot and sauté for 2 minutes longer.

Heat more oil in a separate skillet over medium-high heat. Sauté carrots, eggplant, and sweet potato until brown but not completely cooked, about 5 minutes. Add sautéed vegetables to pot along with remaining bouillon cube, black pepper, and water. Reduce heat to medium-low, cover, and simmer until vegetables are almost fully cooked, about 20 minutes.

Add broken jasmine rice to pot. Make sure that the water remaining in pot covers the rice; add more if it does not. Simmer for another 15-20 minutes or until rice is tender and all liquid is absorbed. Serve fish and rice with lime wedges.

Per serving: 756 calories, 11 g fat, 2 g saturated fat, 818 mg sodium, 105 g carbohydrates, 59 g protein.

VARIATIONS:

Vegetables such as cabbage, potatoes, and okra may also be used.

TIP:

If using tender vegetables, add them to the pot later in the cooking process.

SEYCHELLES SEYCHELLOIS FISH CURRY

2 / 1 / 2
COOK TIME: 35 MINUTES
ACTIVE PREP TIME: 10 MINUTES
MAKES 4 SERVINGS

THE SMALLEST COUNTRY IN AFRICA BY POPULATION, SEYCHELLES IS A widely-spaced archipelago of 115 islands, two-thirds of which are uninhabited. Since its largest island is nearly one thousand miles from the African mainland, the people of Seychelles rely on local ingredients such as fish and coconut as dietary staples. Seychellois cuisine is heavy on spices such as curry for a similar reason: electricity did not make it to most of Seychelles until well into the twentieth century, so other means of food preservation were used.

1 lb. red snapper or grouper filets, cut into large pieces
1 medium onion, chopped
2 Tbsp. curry powder
1 tsp. ground cinnamon
Oil, for sautéing
1 medium tomato, peeled, seeded, and chopped
1 small eggplant, chopped
4 cloves garlic, minced
1 Tbsp. ground turmeric
½ c. chicken or fish broth
1 c. full-fat coconut milk
Lime wedges, for serving

Chopped fresh parsley, for serving

Heat olive oil in a large, heavy skillet over medium-high heat. Sauté onion, curry powder, and cinnamon for 3-4 minutes or until onion begins to soften. Add tomato, eggplant, garlic, and turmeric and cook for 2 minutes longer.

Add broth to skillet. Continue to cook until about half of the broth is evaporated, about 2-3 minutes, scraping the bottom of the pan. Add coconut milk, reduce heat to medium, and simmer for 2 minutes or until curry and coconut milk are well combined.

Add the fish to the sauce. Cover and simmer for about 6-10 minutes or until fish is cooked throughout, turning halfway through.

Per serving: 407 calories, 21 g fat, 14 g saturated fat, 92 mg sodium, 18 g carbohydrates, 39 g protein.

For creole rice:
1-½ c. basmati rice
3 c. water or broth
3 Tbsp. minced onion
1 clove garlic, minced
1-½ tsp. curry powder
½ tsp. ground ginger
1 dash cloves
1 red chili, diced (optional)
Oil, for sautéing
1 Tbsp. ground turmeric
¼ tsp. ground cinnamon
Salt and pepper, to taste

Bring rice and water or broth to a boil in a medium saucepan. Reduce heat to low, cover, and simmer for 15 minutes or until rice is tender and liquid is absorbed.

Heat oil in a small skillet over medium-high heat. Sauté onion, garlic, curry, ginger, cloves, and chili (if using) until fragrant, about 2-3 minutes. Reduce heat and add turmeric and cinnamon. Combine onion mixture with rice and stir. Season with salt and pepper.

Serve creole rice with curry and garnish with lime wedges and parsley.

Per serving: 212 calories, 4 g fat, 1 g saturated fat, 9 mg sodium, 40 g carbohydrates, 4 g protein.

VARIATIONS:

For a chicken curry, use a combination of breasts and thighs, cut into pieces and browned before simmering in sauce. Chicken will need to cook for longer than fish. Use vegetable broth and potatoes or sweet potatoes, peeled and cut into large chunks, in place of fish for a vegan version.

SIERRA LEONE FRIED STEW

1 / 2 / 2
COOK TIME: 45 MINUTES
ACTIVE PREP TIME: 10 MINUTES
MAKES 4 SERVINGS

As IN MANY WEST AFRICAN NATIONS, SIERRA LEONEAN CUISINE REVOLVES around stew. Most stews are made with chicken or fish and served over rice or other starches, such as cassava or fufu. Sierra Leone's people love spicy foods served with local ingredients, such as fresh vegetables and palm oil. Make sure you have plenty of oil on hand to make this Sierra Leonean staple—it's not just for frying, but adds a strong flavor as well.

2 lbs. chicken breasts, cut into pieces
Palm oil, for frying
1 large onion, finely chopped
1 green bell pepper, finely chopped
3 small eggplants, finely chopped
1 carrot, grated
2 cloves garlic, minced
1 dried red chili, ground (optional)
1-½ tsp. smoked paprika

1 tsp. dried thyme
One 15-oz. can tomato puree
1 c. chicken or vegetable broth
1 tsp. salt
1 bay leaf
Chopped parsley, for serving

Heat palm oil in a Dutch oven over medium-high heat. Add chicken and sauté, scraping the brown bits from the bottom of the pot, for about 5 minutes.

Add onion, bell pepper, eggplants, carrot, garlic, chili (if using), paprika, and thyme and continue to cook until all ingredients are crisp, about 7 minutes longer. Add tomato puree, broth, salt, and bay leaf to pot. Cover, reduce heat to medium-low, and simmer for 20-30 minutes. Garnish with parsley and serve.

Per serving: 730 calories, 23 g fat, 7 g saturated fat, 878 mg sodium, 51 g carbohydrates, 84 g protein.

SERVING SUGGESTION:

Serve with rice.

VARIATIONS:

Use fish filets instead of chicken. Any vegetables can be used in or omitted from fried stew (except for onions and bell peppers, which are mandatory).

SOMALIA
CHICKEN SUQAAR

2 / 3 / 3
COOK TIME: 25 MINUTES
ACTIVE PREP TIME: 15 MINUTES
MAKES 4-6 SERVINGS

FORMING MOST OF THE GEOGRAPHIC AREA KNOWN AS THE HORN OF AFRICA, Somalia's location on the Arabian Sea and Indian Ocean made it a major center for the spice trade in ancient times and later a key player in cross-continental commerce.

The Somali dish suqaar incorporates a spice mix called xawaash, which combines many of the spices that passed through Somalia's ports in the Middle Ages.

1-½ lb. boneless chicken thighs, cut into strips
Oil, for sautéing
1 onion, sliced
1 potato, peeled and sliced thinly
1 carrot, peeled and sliced thinly
1 tsp. xawaash (see Tips section)
1 tsp. paprika
1 tsp. salt
¼ tsp. ground turmeric
¼ c. water
1 orange or yellow bell pepper, sliced
Salt and pepper, to taste
Hot sauce, for serving (optional; recipe below)

Heat oil in a heavy skillet over medium-high heat. Add onion, potato, and carrot and sauté for 8 minutes or until potatoes are softened. Remove vegetables from pan.

Add chicken to pan and season with xawaash, paprika, salt, and turmeric. Saute chicken for 3-4 minutes or until brown. Add cooked vegetables back to pan along with water. Reduce heat to medium-low, cover, and simmer for 5 minutes longer. Add bell pepper to pan and continue to simmer until chicken is completely cooked, about 3-5 minutes longer. Season with salt and pepper and serve with hot sauce, if desired.

Per serving: 211 calories, 11 g fat, 3 g saturated fat, 537 mg sodium, 14 g carbohydrates, 17 g protein.

For hot sauce:
2 green chili peppers, coarsely chopped (about ½ c.)
1 Scotch bonnet chili, coarsely chopped
1 clove garlic
½ small onion, chopped
½ tsp. salt

Juice of 1 lemon

2 Tbsp. white vinegar

½ bunch fresh cilantro, chopped

Place all ingredient in a blender in the order that they are listed. Blend until smooth. Serve with suqaar.

Per serving: 6 calories, 0 g fat, 0 g saturated fat, 234 mg sodium, 2 g carbohydrates, 0 g protein.

SERVING SUGGESTIONS:

Serve with injera bread (traditional, see p. 147 for recipe) or basmati rice (more common today). Serving suqaar with spaghetti noodles, a nod to Somalia's colonial Italian history, is not unheard of.

TIP:

To make your own xawaash, you will need 2 Tbsp. cumin seeds, 2 Tbsp. coriander seeds, 1-½ tsp. black peppercorns, 1-½ tsp. ground turmeric, 1 tsp. cinnamon, 6 cardamom pods, and 3 whole cloves. Toast all ingredients except turmeric in a dry skillet over medium heat for 4-5 minutes. Once cooled, grind toasted spices and mix with turmeric. Makes about ¼ c. of xawaash.

SOUTH AFRICA BOBOTIE

2 / 2 / 2

COOK TIME: 1 HOUR, 15 MINUTES

ACTIVE PREP TIME: 15 MINUTES

MAKES 6 SERVINGS

SOUTH AFRICA, A NATION WITH ELEVEN OFFICIAL LANGUAGES, PROBABLY fits the term "melting pot" better than any other country in the world. Generally speaking, South African cuisine can be divided into two categories: indigenous and non-indigenous. The latter combines influences from literally every corner of the world: England, France, the Netherlands, India, and Southeast Asia, to name a few.

Of the non-indigenous dishes enjoyed in South Africa, bobotie is possibly the only one that is not eaten in any other country (which, in a sense, makes it "indigenous" as well).

2 lbs. ground lamb
2 slices fresh white bread
1 c. whole milk
Olive oil, for sautéing
1 onion, finely chopped
1 carrot, finely chopped
2 cloves garlic, crushed
One 2-inch piece ginger, peeled and grated
2 Tbsp. curry paste
½ c. golden raisins
2 Tbsp. slivered almonds, toasted
2 Tbsp. mango or peach chutney
Salt and pepper, to taste
1 c. beef or lamb stock
Juice of 1 lemon
2 bay leaves
2 eggs
½ tsp. ground turmeric

Preheat oven to 350 degrees. Tear bread slices into pieces. Place bread in milk and allow to soak.

Heat olive oil in a heavy skillet over medium-high heat. Sauté onion and carrot for 4-5 minutes. Add garlic and ginger and continue to cook until fragrant, about 2 minutes longer. Add lamb to pan and cook for 5-6 minutes or until completely browned. Add curry paste, raisins, almonds, and chutney and season with salt and pepper. Stir to combine and cook for 2 minutes longer.

Squeeze milk from soaked bread pieces (reserving milk) and add bread to meat mixture along with stock, lemon juice, and bay leaves. Cover and simmer for 10 minutes.

Pour meat mixture into a 9 x 13-inch oven-proof dish, cover with foil, and bake for 25 minutes.

Beat eggs and combine with reserved milk and turmeric. Pour egg mixture over meat mixture and return to oven. Cook for 20-25 minutes longer, uncovered, until eggs are set and topping is golden brown.

Per serving: 454 calories, 20 g fat, 6 g saturated fat, 312 mg sodium, 19 g carbohydrates, 48 g protein.

VARIATION:

Use lean beef instead of lamb.

SUDAN
DAMA DE POTAATAS

2 / 1 / 1
COOK TIME: 40 MINUTES
ACTIVE PREP TIME: 15 MINUTES
MAKES 6 SERVINGS

A LARGE COUNTRY WITH A DESERT CLIMATE AND A NOMADIC CULTURE, Sudan borders Egypt and Ethiopia and is separated from the Arabian Peninsula by the Red Sea. Accordingly, stews form the backbone of its cuisine. Dama de Potaatas, or potato stew, is made with beef as well as potatoes and is not unlike many Western beef stews. However, you'll find that it takes not nearly as long to prepare.

1 lb. beef stew meat or sirloin, cut into small pieces

6-8 onions, chopped

Oil, for sautéing

2-½ qt. water, divided

6 tomatoes, chopped

4 medium potatoes, cubed

1 green bell pepper, chopped

2 tsp. salt

1 tsp. cardamom

1 tsp. cinnamon
½ c. tomato paste
5 cloves garlic, crushed

Heat oil in a large Dutch oven over medium heat. Add onions and sauté until golden, about 5 minutes. Add 1-½ qt. water and simmer until water is mostly evaporated, about 10 minutes.

Place onion mixture in a blender and pulse until blended. Return to pot and add tomatoes.

In a separate pan, heat more oil and sauté potatoes over medium-high heat until brown, about 5 minutes. Remove potatoes and add meat. Brown meat until seared on all sides, about 5 minutes.

Add meat to pot along with bell pepper, salt, cardamom, and cinnamon. Sauté until ingredients are coated with spices, then add tomato paste and remaining water and stir. Add potatoes and garlic, cover, and simmer for 10 minutes or until potatoes are fully cooked.

Per serving: 355 calories, 8 g fat, 2 g saturated fat, 866 mg sodium, 45 g carbohydrates, 29 g protein.

SERVING SUGGESTIONS:

Serve with flatbread or rice.

VARIATIONS:

Use lamb or mutton in place of beef, or add other vegetables such as carrots.

TANZANIA MSHIKAKI WITH MANDAZI

Tanzania is geographically large compared to other African nations, and its land area comprises both inland Africa and the coast of the Indian Ocean. As such, its food is diverse and varies depending on region. Mshikaki, a popular street food made from skewered meat, combines Arab and Indian spices like cumin, cardamom, turmeric and coriander with the traditional Swahili method of charring meat. Tanzanians eat mandazi, a lightly-sweetened fried dough, with mshikaki as well as virtually every other type of food.

For the mshikaki:
2 lbs. beef sirloin, cut into 1-inch pieces
¼ c. tamarind paste
6 cloves garlic, peeled and minced
One 1-inch piece fresh ginger, peeled and grated
2 Tbsp. oil, plus more for grilling
1 Tbsp. ground cumin
1 Tbsp. ground black pepper
1 tsp. ground turmeric
1 tsp. chili powder (optional)
½ tsp. ground cardamom
½ tsp. ground coriander
¼ tsp. salt

Combine tamarind paste, garlic, ginger, oil, cumin, black pepper, turmeric, chili powder (if using), cardamom, coriander, and salt. Add more oil if necessary to make a thick paste. Rub paste into surface of meat. Place meat in a shallow dish, cover with plastic wrap, and marinate in refrigerator for 6 hours.

Soak 12 bamboo skewers in water for at least 30 minutes. (Skip this step if using metal skewers.) Thread meat onto skewers.

Prepare a charcoal grill and use a brush to lightly oil the grates. Once grill is ready, place skewers on grill and cook for 10-15 minutes or until completely cooked and slightly charred, turning halfway through cooking.

Per serving: 416 calories, 17 g fat, 5 g saturated fat, 246 mg sodium, 7 g carbohydrates, 56 g protein.

For the mandazi:
2 c. all-purpose flour
¼ c. sugar
2 Tbsp. coconut flakes
2-½ tsp. baking powder
½ tsp. salt
½ tsp. ground cardamom
½ tsp. ground cinnamon
1 egg, beaten
½ c. evaporated milk
3 Tbsp. butter, at room temperature
Oil, for frying

Combine flour, sugar, coconut flakes, baking powder, salt, cardamom, and cinnamon in a large bowl. In a separate bowl, whisk together egg, milk, and butter. Slowly add egg mixture to flour mixture, stirring until dough is smooth but not sticky.

On a floured surface, roll dough to a 1-inch thickness and cut into about 12-15 triangle-shaped pieces.

In a heavy skillet or Dutch oven, pour oil to a depth of 2 inches and bring to a temperature of 350 degrees over medium heat. Carefully fry dough triangles in batches for 3-5 minutes each or until golden brown. Drain mandazi on paper towels and serve warm with mshikaki.

Per serving: 530 calories, 33 g fat, 9 g saturated fat, 324 mg sodium, 52 g carbohydrates, 8 g protein.

SERVING SUGGESTIONS:

In Tanzania, mshikaki is sometimes eaten with French fries and fried eggs instead of mandazi.

VARIATIONS:

Ground beef can be used in place of sirloin. Form meat into meatballs before placing on skewer, combining with egg or breadcrumbs if necessary. If desired, vegetables such as bell peppers and onions may be grilled on skewers along with meat.

TIP:

A mixture of two parts soy sauce to one part lemon juice or rice vinegar may be used in place of tamarind paste.

TOGO
KOKLO MEME

1 / 2 / 2
COOK TIME: 45 MINUTES
ACTIVE PREP TIME: 15 MINUTES
INACTIVE PREP TIME: 4 HOURS
MAKES 4 SERVINGS

TOGOLESE CUISINE COMBINES AFRICAN STAPLE FOODS SUCH AS MAIZE AND yams with the cooking styles of the French and Germans, their former colonizers. A traditional dish such as koklo meme, or chicken with chili sauce, is likely to be served with a French baguette and German beer in addition to standard West African side dishes like fufu and millet. The Togolese are known for their love of chilies, and this recipe fits the bill.

1-½ lb. bone-in chicken legs and thighs
1 small onion, coarsely chopped
One 3-inch piece fresh ginger, peeled and grated
5 cloves garlic
1 Scotch bonnet pepper
2 Tbsp. red palm oil

2 Tbsp. lemon juice
1 tsp. salt

Place onion, ginger, garlic, pepper, palm oil, lemon juice, and salt in a blender. Puree until smooth. Marinate chicken in onion mixture for at least 4 hours or overnight.

Preheat broiler to high, and place oven rack a few inches below heat. Set chicken pieces on a metal rack in a roasting pan, reserving remaining marinade. Broil chicken for 5-7 minutes, then turn and broil other side for 3-5 minutes. Chicken should be completely seared and slightly blackened on both sides. Turn off broiler and reposition oven rack to center of oven.

Preheat oven to 350 degrees. Brush chicken with half of reserved marinade and bake for 15 minutes. Turn chicken, brush with remaining marinade, and cook for 15-20 minutes longer or until chicken is fully cooked.

Per serving: 372 calories, 16 g fat, 7 g saturated fat, 694 mg sodium, 3 g carbohydrates, 51 g protein.

SERVING SUGGESTIONS:

Serve with cornmeal or polenta, beans, fresh tomatoes and onions, and French bread.

UGANDA MATOKE WITH PEANUT SAUCE

2 / 2 / 2
COOK TIME: 45 MINUTES
ACTIVE PREP TIME: 10 MINUTES
MAKES 4-6 SERVINGS

MATOKE, ALSO KNOWN AS THE EAST AFRICAN HIGHLAND BANANA, ARE a starchy type of banana that is a staple food throughout the Lake Victoria region. Cooked and eaten while still unripe, matoke are prepared many ways. But this recipe, which uses a thick peanut sauce, is unique to Uganda. Since matoke are difficult to find in the United States, plantains or very green bananas can be used in their place.

For matoke:
4 matoke, plantains, or green bananas, peeled and cut into 1-inch pieces
1 tsp. cumin seed
½ tsp. mustard seed
Oil, for sautéing
2 onions, finely chopped
2 c. beef stock or water
1 carrot, peeled and finely grated

Sauté the cumin and mustard seeds in a dry skillet over medium-high heat for about 1 minute or until fragrant. Add a small amount of oil to the pan. Once the oil is hot, add onions and continue to cook until translucent, about 3-4 minutes. Add carrot and cook until soft, about 2-3 minutes longer.

Add matoke, plantain, or green banana pieces and beef stock or water to skillet and reduce heat to medium-low. Simmer uncovered for 20 minutes or until matoke is tender. Transfer matoke to a medium bowl. Using a potato masher, mash matoke until smooth.

For peanut sauce:
1-½ c. peanuts, roasted
Olive oil, for sautéing
2 cloves garlic, finely minced
1 small onion, finely chopped
2 tomatoes, peeled, seeded, and chopped

Place peanuts in a blender or food processor. Process until ground to a fine powder. Set aside.

Heat a small amount of olive oil in a saucepan over medium heat. Sauté garlic until fragrant, about 1-2 minutes. Add peanut powder and stir until a paste is formed.

Heat more oil in a separate skillet over medium-high heat. Sauté onion until brown, about 5 minutes. Add tomatoes and cook until soft, about 3 minutes longer. Add tomatoes and onions to saucepan with peanut mixture and stir. Reduce heat to low, cover, and simmer 10 minutes, stirring frequently.

Divide matoke between 4 plates. Ladle peanut sauce over matoke and serve.

Per serving: 350 calories, 21 g fat, 3 g saturated fat, 334 mg sodium, 36 g carbohydrates, 11 g protein.

VARIATION:

Add 1-4 chopped red chilies or a dash of red chili flakes with the carrot if more heat is desired.

ZAMBIA
IFISASHI WITH NSHIMA

2 / 2 / 2
COOK TIME: 35 MINUTES
ACTIVE PREP TIME: 15 MINUTES
MAKES 4 SERVINGS

THE STAPLE FOOD OF ZAMBIA IS NSHIMA, A PORRIDGE MADE FROM CORNMEAL

and eaten throughout southern Africa. Nshima is most often eaten by itself, but is sometimes accompanied by "relishes" such as ifisashi, a blend of spinach, other vegetables, and peanuts. Zambians eat ifisashi with their hands, using a bit of nshima as a "utensil."

For ifisashi:
2 lbs. spinach, rinsed and chopped
1-½ c. raw peanuts
½ c. water, plus more for steaming
1 white onion, sliced
2 tomatoes, sliced
Salt and pepper, to taste

Place 1 c. of peanuts in a blender and pulse until ground to a fine powder. Add water, a little at a time, until a paste is formed.

Layer onions, tomatoes, and spinach in a Dutch oven. Add a small amount of water for steaming. Cover and cook over low heat for 20 minutes or until spinach is wilted.

Spread peanut paste over the top of spinach mixture. Cover and continue to cook for 10 minutes. Remove lid and stir.

Per serving: 281 calories, 19 g fat, 3 g saturated fat, 191 mg sodium, 19 g carbohydrates, 17 g protein.

For nshima:
2 c. white cornmeal
1-¼ qt. water
1 tsp. salt

Bring water to a boil in a medium saucepan. Add salt and reduce heat to medium. Add cornmeal to pan one spoonful at a time, stirring after each addition. Cook for about 3-4 minutes or until porridge is thick and all liquid is evaporated.

Sprinkle remaining peanuts on top of ifisashi. Serve with nshima.

Per serving: 110 calories, 1 g fat, 0 g saturated fat, 592 mg sodium, 24 g carbohydrates, 3 g protein.

VARIATIONS:

Use turnip or mustard greens, collards, or kale in place of spinach (adjust cooking time as needed for hardier greens). Add sweet potato, cabbage, pumpkin, or other vegetables along with onions and tomatoes. Ifisashi can be served with rice or polenta instead of nshima.

ZIMBABWE
SADZA NEHUKU

LIKE MANY OTHER SOUTHERN AFRICAN COUNTRIES, ZIMBABWE HAS A stiff, cornmeal-based porridge, sadza, as its national dish. Sadza can be rolled into balls and dipped in soups and stews. Sadza neHuku, or sadza with chicken, pairs the national dish with a creamy, heavily seasoned stew of chicken in tomato sauce, another of Zimbabwe's culinary specialties.

1-½ lb. chicken (with or without skin), cut into medium-sized pieces
2 c. water, divided
1 tsp. salt
Oil, for frying
1 clove garlic, sliced
One ½-inch piece ginger, peeled and minced
1 small onion, chopped
1 tomato, chopped
½ small green bell pepper, chopped
¼ c. crème fraîche

Place chicken in a medium-sized saucepan with 1 c. of water and salt. Bring to a boil, reduce heat to medium-low, cover with lid ajar, and simmer for 10-15 minutes.

Heat oil in a heavy skillet over medium-high heat. Remove chicken from pot, reserving any remaining liquid, and fry chicken pieces for 5-10 minutes or until browned on all sides. Add garlic, ginger, and onion and continue to cook until onion is soft, about 2-3 minutes. Add tomato and bell pepper and cook for 2-3 minutes longer.

Add remaining 1 c. water, reserved liquid, and crème fraîche. Reduce heat to medium-low, cover, and simmer for 5 minutes longer.

Per serving: 222 calories, 8 g fat, 3 g saturated fat, 468 mg sodium, 3 g

carbohydrates, 34 g protein.

For sadza:
3 c. coarse white cornmeal, plus more if needed
1 qt. water, divided

Combine cornmeal with 1 c. water in a Dutch oven and stir until a paste-like consistency is reached. Boil remaining 3 c. water in a separate pot.

Place pot with cornmeal over high heat and gradually add boiling water to pot, stirring constantly. Once mixture has reached a boil, reduce heat to low, cover, and simmer for 15 minutes.

Remove lid and check sadza. If any moisture remains, add more cornmeal until all moisture has been absorbed. Recover and continue to simmer over low heat for 5 minutes longer. Serve with chicken in shallow bowls.

Per serving: 74 calories, 1 g fat, 0 g saturated fat, 7 mg sodium, 16 g carbohydrates, 2 g protein.

SERVING SUGGESTION:
Serve with cooked spinach or other greens.

CENTRAL ASIA

AFGHANISTAN
KABULI PULAO

AFGHANISTAN IS A DIVERSE NATION, LYING AT THE CROSSROADS OF IRAN, Russia, and India. Nowhere is this more clearly reflected than in the nation's cuisine. But Afghani cuisine is unique in its own right, imbued with elaborate flavors, aromas, and textures. Afghanistan's national dish, kabuli pulao, is a sensory delight.

2-½ lbs. lamb, cut into large pieces
Oil, for sautéing
1 large onion, chopped
1-½ tsp. ground cumin
1 tsp. garam masala
1 tsp. salt
½ tsp. ground turmeric
1 c. beef broth
2-½ c. basmati rice
1 tsp. brown sugar
2 carrots, julienned
1 c. golden raisins
½ c. almonds, blanched
½ c. pistachios, blanched
2 c. water

Heat oil in a large skillet over medium-high heat. Sauté onion until brown, about 5 minutes. Add meat pieces to the fried onion and cook until lightly browned on both sides, about 5 minutes longer. Add cumin, garam masala, salt, and turmeric to the meat and fry until the oil separates and rises to the top, about 2-3 minutes. Add water and bring to a boil. Reduce heat to low, cover, and simmer 1 hour or until meat is tender (do not overcook).

Meanwhile, heat more oil in a separate skillet over medium-high heat. Fry the carrots until soft, about 2 minutes. Add brown sugar and sauté for 1 minute longer. Remove from pan and set aside.

Add raisins to pan and sauté until they begin to swell, about 2-3 minutes. Remove from pan and set aside.

Sauté almonds and pistachios until brown, about 2 minutes. Remove from pan and set aside.

When meat has finished cooking, remove it from the pan, set aside, and skim any excess fat and oil from the surface. Add rice and stock to the pan, raise heat to high, and bring liquid to a boil. Reduce heat to low, cover, and simmer until rice is fully cooked, about 15-20 minutes.

Preheat oven to 300 degrees. Place meat in an oven-safe serving plate. Layer with rice, carrots, raisins, and nuts, and bake for 5 minutes.

Per serving: 924 calories, 28 g fat, 7 g saturated fat, 852 mg sodium, 92 g carbohydrates, 75 g protein.

SERVING SUGGESTIONS:

Serve with naan or lavash bread.

VARIATIONS:

Use beef or chicken in place of lamb. Adjust cooking time accordingly to avoid overcooking. For a vegan alternative, omit meat and use vegetable broth.

ARMENIA
HARISSA

1 / 3 / 2
COOK TIME: 2 HOURS
ACTIVE PREP TIME: 15 MINUTES
INACTIVE PREP TIME: 8 HOURS
MAKES 6 SERVINGS

ARMENIA HAS A RICH CULINARY TRADITION THAT IS NEARLY AS OLD AS agriculture itself; the small nation is not far from the Fertile Crescent, where cattle breeding and the cultivation of grains began. Armenian cuisine is characterized by complicated cooking methods, complex spices, and the near absence of cooking fats. The rather simple harissa is an exception to the first two rules. Commonly served on Easter Day, this wheat porridge has been prepared in Armenia for thousands of years.

1-½ lb. chicken, cut into large pieces
2 c. chicken broth
1 qt. water, plus more for soaking
2 c. whole wheat kernels (wheatberries)
2 Tbsp. paprika
2 Tbsp. ground cumin
Salt and pepper, to taste
Butter, to taste

Soak wheat kernels in water for 8 hours or overnight. Rinse and drain after soaking.

Combine chicken, broth, water, and wheat kernels in a large pot and bring to a boil. Reduce heat to low, cover, and simmer for 2 hours, stirring frequently.

Shred chicken with two forks. Add cumin and paprika, and season with salt and pepper. Stir vigorously until harissa has a smooth consistency. Serve topped with a pat of butter.

Per serving: 282 calories, 10 g fat, 4 g saturated fat, 357 mg sodium, 13 g carbohydrates, 37 g protein.

SERVING SUGGESTIONS:

Serve with lavash bread and Armenian salad (tomatoes, cucumber, bell pepper, and onion).

VARIATIONS:

Bulgur wheat or barley can be used in place of wheat kernels if necessary. Lamb or mutton may be used instead of chicken.

TIP:

If using unsoaked wheat kernels, add 2 hours to cooking time.

AZERBAIJAN PLOV

1 / 2 / 2
COOK TIME: 1 HOUR, 30 MINUTES
ACTIVE PREP TIME: 10 MINUTES
INACTIVE PREP TIME: 40 MINUTES
MAKES 4 SERVINGS

AZERBAIJAN'S CUISINE IS AMONG THE MOST DISTINCTIVE IN WESTERN Asia. It includes several familiar dishes, such as kebabs and plov (pilaf). While these are common to the region, Azeri versions include unique ingredients such as aromatic herbs, fresh greens, and spices such as saffron. Azeri plov is distinguished by the fact that the rice and other ingredients are cooked separately and combined before serving.

2 lbs. lamb, deboned and cut into pieces
1-¼ c. long-grain basmati rice
Salted water, for soaking
Olive oil, for frying
3 cloves garlic, minced
2 small onions, chopped
2 carrots, chopped
¾ c. dried apricots, dates, or a combination
½ c. chestnuts
1-½ tsp. ground cumin
3-½ c. water, divided
½ tsp. ground saffron
1 c. beef stock

Soak rice in salted water for 30 minutes. Meanwhile, heat olive oil in a heavy skillet over medium-high heat. Fry lamb in olive oil until browned, about 5-7 minutes. Add garlic, onions, and carrots and cook until golden, about 6 minutes. Stir in apricots, chestnuts, cumin, and 3 c. of water; reduce heat to low, cover, and simmer for 1 hour.

Drain rice and stir in saffron. Transfer to a saucepan, add remaining water and stock, and bring to a boil. Reduce heat to medium-low, cover, and simmer until rice is tender, about 10 minutes. Remove from heat and let stand 10 minutes longer. Serve rice topped with lamb mixture.

Per serving: 717 calories, 21 g fat, 7 g saturated fat, 377 mg sodium, 59 g carbohydrates, 70 g protein.

VARIATIONS:

Chicken or beef can be substituted for lamb. For a vegan version, omit meat and use vegetable stock. Macadamia nuts or hazelnuts can be used in place of chestnuts.

BANGLADESH
REZALA

2 / 2 / 2
COOK TIME: 30 MINUTES
ACTIVE PREP TIME: 10 MINUTES
INACTIVE PREP TIME: 1 HOUR
MAKES 4 SERVINGS

REZALA IS ONE OF MANY DISHES REFLECTING THE ISLAMIC MUGHAL influence on Bangladesh and eastern India, which dates to the sixteenth century. Fragrant, full of flavor, and not overly spicy, rezala is usually reserved for special occasions. While usually made with mutton, beef rezala is especially popular in Bangladesh during the Muslim holiday of Eid-al-Adha, during which cattle are sacrificed to commemorate the prophet Ibrahim's willingness to follow God's orders to sacrifice his own son.

2 lbs. beef stew meat, cut into small pieces
¼ c. plain yogurt
One 1-inch piece fresh ginger, peeled and grated
4 cloves garlic, minced
1 tsp. ground coriander
1 tsp. chili powder
¼ c. cashews, coarsely ground
Oil, for sautéing
1 large onion, finely chopped

1 stick cinnamon, broken
6 green cardamom pods
4 whole cloves
2 bay leaves
8 green or red chilies, seeded
2 Tbsp. fresh lime juice
2 Tbsp. kewra water (optional)
1 tsp. sugar
2 Tbsp. ghee or butter
½ c. water (more if needed)

Combine the yogurt, ginger, garlic, coriander, chili powder, and cashews. Coat the beef with yogurt mixture and marinate in refrigerator for at least 1 hour.

Heat oil in a heavy skillet over medium-high heat. Sauté the onion, cinnamon, cardamom, cloves, and bay leaves until onion is soft and spices are fragrant, about 3-4 minutes.

Add the marinated beef to the pan and cook for about 2 minutes longer. Reduce heat to medium-low, cover, and simmer for 10 minutes. Add water to pan if meat becomes dry. Add the chilies, lime juice, kewra water (if using), and sugar to the pan and simmer until sauce thickens, about 3-4 minutes. Add ghee or butter and water and simmer for another 10 minutes. Remove from heat and serve.

Per serving: 593 calories, 28 g fat, 11 g saturated fat, 171 mg sodium, 10 g carbohydrates, 72 g protein.

SERVING SUGGESTIONS:

Serve with basmati rice or with naan or roti bread.

VARIATIONS:

Chicken or lamb may be used in place of beef. Paneer (fresh curd cheese) can be used in place of meat for a vegetarian version.

GEORGIA KHACHAPURI

3 / 1 / 2
COOK TIME: 25 MINUTES
ACTIVE PREP TIME: 25 MINUTES
INACTIVE PREP TIME: 1 HOUR, 30 MINUTES
MAKES 4 SERVINGS

THE NATIONAL DISH OF GEORGIA, KHACHAPURI, HAS OFTEN BEEN COMPARED to pizza; it is essentially a soft, chewy dough filled with cheese. And like pizza, the variations on this dish are endless. Georgians traditionally use two cheeses to make khachapuri: the fresh, mild imeruli cheese and the aged, tangy sulguni cheese. Since these cheeses are difficult to find in the United States, this recipe substitutes mozzarella and feta. Khachapuri makes an excellent appetizer, breakfast, or snack.

3-½ c. all-purpose flour

1 Tbsp. sugar

1 tsp. yeast

1 tsp. salt

1 c. water

½ c. whole milk

1 Tbsp. olive oil, plus more for coating bowl

3 c. mozzarella cheese, shredded

1-½ c. feta cheese, crumbled

¼ c. fresh tarragon, finely chopped

¼ c. fresh dill, finely chopped

5 eggs

Sift together flour, sugar, yeast, and salt and add to the bowl of a stand mixer with a paddle attachment. Heat water and milk to 115 degrees (use a kitchen thermometer to measure temperature) and add to flour mixture. Mix on medium speed until dough is smooth and pliable, and then add oil to dough and mix for 1 minute longer.

Coat a deep, nonreactive bowl with oil. Place dough inside bowl and cover with plastic wrap. Allow dough to rest for 1 hour or until it doubles in size. Remove wrap and punch dough, recover with wrap, and allow to sit for 30 minutes longer.

Preheat oven to 450 degrees. Combine mozzarella and feta cheeses, tarragon, and dill. Divide dough into 4 portions and roll each into a 9-inch circle. Roll edges upward to create a wall around the sides of the dough and pinch edges to form an oval with pointed ends. Place the 4 dough circles on a baking sheet lined with parchment paper or nonstick foil.

Divide cheese mixture between dough circles, filling each with an even layer of cheese. Crack 1 egg, mix with a little water, and use to brush rolled-up edges. Bake for 15 minutes or until cheese melts and crust begins to brown.

With the back of a spoon, create a small well in the center of each cheese-filled dough circle. Crack 1 egg and drop into each well. Return to oven and cook for about 6 minutes longer, or until egg is set and partially cooked (it will continue to cook upon standing).

To serve, mix together cheese and egg. Tear pieces of crust from edges and dip in cheese and egg filling.

Per serving: 706 calories, 28 g fat, 12 g saturated fat, 1247 mg sodium, 83 g carbohydrates, 31 g protein.

VARIATIONS:

Any cheese can be used to make khachapuri. Toppings such as sausage, chicken, bacon, or mushrooms may be added.

INDIA
LAMB VINDALOO

2 / 2 / 2
COOK TIME: 1 HOUR
ACTIVE PREP TIME: 20 MINUTES
INACTIVE PREP TIME: 8 HOURS
MAKES 4 SERVINGS

IT IS DIFFICULT TO CHOOSE A SINGLE DISH TO REPRESENT 1.3 BILLION people, 8,000 years of history, over 500 languages, and at least 40 distinct cuisines. To say that Indian cuisine has been influenced by the country's history is an extreme understatement; it is more accurate to say that Indian cuisine has had a great impact on the history of the world, as its characteristic spices were the driving force behind the age of exploration. To represent India in this cookbook, I have chosen a personal favorite, a specialty of the small southwestern coastal province of Goa. Like most Indian dishes, vindaloo includes a wide variety of spices, but it's definitely not a dish for those who can't handle more than a little heat.

2 lbs. boneless lamb, cut into medium-sized pieces
6 dry red chilies
10 whole cloves
1-½ tsp. mustard seeds, divided
1 tsp. poppy seeds
1 tsp. cumin seeds
½ tsp. whole black peppercorns
One 2-inch piece fresh ginger, peeled and chopped
15 cloves garlic, peeled
3 fresh green chilies, chopped
½ c. white wine vinegar
1 Tbsp. tamarind paste
2 tsp. sea salt
¼ c. vegetable oil
4 large onions, sliced
1 cinnamon stick
2 tsp. red chili powder
1 tsp. ground turmeric
2 tsp. dark brown sugar
2 c. hot water

Heat a small skillet over medium heat. Add red chilies, cloves, 1 tsp. mustard seeds, poppy seeds, cumin seeds, and peppercorns and toast for 2 minutes or until very fragrant. Remove from heat and allow to cool completely, then grind to a fine powder using a spice grinder or a mortar and pestle. Set aside.

Place fresh ginger, garlic, green chilies, white wine vinegar, tamarind paste, and sea salt in a blender and puree until smooth. Set aside.

Coat lamb pieces with dry spice mixture on all sides. Place in a shallow bowl and cover with wet spice mixture. Cover with plastic wrap and refrigerate for at least 8 hours.

Heat vegetable oil in a large heavy skillet or Dutch oven over medium-high heat. Add cinnamon stick and remaining ½ tsp. mustard seeds and cook for about 1 minute. Add onions and sauté until deep brown, about 5-7 minutes. Add red chili powder and turmeric to pan and cook one minute longer.

Add lamb pieces to pan and raise heat to high. Sauté lamb in hot oil for 10 minutes, then reduce heat to low. Cover and simmer for 20 minutes longer, stirring frequently. Sprinkle with brown sugar and simmer for 5 minutes longer. Slowly add hot water to the pan and simmer just until lamb is fully cooked and a meat thermometer inserted in center of thickest portion registers 150 degrees.

Per serving: 652 calories, 31 g fat, 9 g saturated fat, 1137 mg sodium, 23 g carbohydrates, 67 g protein.

SERVING SUGGESTION:

Serve with basmati rice (traditional) or boiled potatoes (nontraditional).

VARIATIONS:

Vindaloo can also be made with chicken, goat, or pork. It is interesting to note that while pork is eschewed by Muslims and most Hindus, it is popular in Goa, where a significant percentage of the population is Roman Catholic.

KASHMIR ROGAN JOSH

2 / 2 / 2
COOK TIME: 1 HOUR, 25 MINUTES
ACTIVE PREP TIME: 10 MINUTES
INACTIVE PREP TIME: 8 HOURS
MAKES 4 SERVINGS

KASHMIR, LOCATED IN THE NORTHERNMOST PART OF INDIA, LIES IN THE Himalayans between Pakistan and China, two countries that have disputed the region since the mid-twentieth century. While the Buddhist, Hindu, and Sikh regions are all well-represented, four centuries of Muslim control left a great impression on Kashmir's culture and especially its cuisine. The name of Rogan Josh, a dish of Mughal origins, means "red meat" in Urdu. Traditionally, its characteristic red color comes from Kashmiri chilies; paprika, which has a similar flavor and aroma, is used in their place in this recipe.

2 lbs. boneless lamb, cut into cubes
¾ c. plain yogurt
¼ c. ghee or oil
One 2-inch cinnamon stick
1 Tbsp. whole cardamom pods
1-½ tsp. whole cloves
1 tsp. black peppercorns
2 bay leaves
2 onions, chopped
2 Tbsp. garlic paste
2 Tbsp. ginger paste
1 Tbsp. paprika
2 tsp. ground coriander
2 tsp. garam masala
1 tsp cumin
¼ tsp. turmeric
¼ tsp. cayenne pepper
2 c. beef stock
1 c. water
Chopped cilantro, for serving

Place lamb in a large bowl and coat with ½ c. yogurt. Cover with plastic wrap and marinate in refrigerator for 8 hours or overnight.

Heat ghee or oil in a large Dutch oven over medium-high heat. Add cinnamon stick, cardamom, cloves, peppercorns, and bay leaves and fry until spices begin to darken, about 3-4 minutes. Add onions and fry until brown and translucent, about 5 minutes. Add garlic and ginger pastes and cook for another 1 minute, stirring constantly. Finally, add paprika, coriander, garam masala, cumin, turmeric, and cayenne pepper. Continue to cook until spices are very fragrant, about 2-3 minutes.

Add lamb and yogurt mixture to pot and fry until lamb is brown on both sides, about 10 minutes. Add beef stock and water and stir. Reduce heat to low, cover, and simmer for at least 1 hour or until lamb is cooked and sauce is thick. Stir remaining ¼ c. yogurt into sauce and garnish with chopped cilantro to serve.

Per serving: 628 calories, 31 g fat, 15 g saturated fat, 607 mg sodium, 15 g carbohydrates, 70 g protein.

SERVING SUGGESTION:

Serve with white basmati rice, cucumber and tomato salad, and extra yogurt.

VARIATIONS:

Lamb can be replaced with beef (brisket is preferred) or goat meat. For a vegetarian version, substitute meat with an equal amount of tempeh or cooked lentils.

KAZAKHSTAN
BASTURMA

2 / 2 / 3
ACTIVE PREP TIME: 20 MINUTES
INACTIVE PREP TIME: 7 DAYS
MAKES 4 SERVINGS

KAZAKHSTAN IS VERY LARGE IN SIZE AND JUST AS SPARSE IN POPULATION.
Many of its people are nomadic, like their Mongol ancestors, grazing their horses and sheep on the vast desert steppe. Horses have been bred in Kazakhstan for centuries for meat and milk, and today horsemeat is still a staple of many Kazakh diets. Horse sausage, fermented mare's milk, and kuyrdak, in which horse organ meats are stir-fried with onions and peppers, are all enjoyed in Kazakhstan. But basturma, cured and eaten by herders on the move, is made from mutton instead.

2 lbs. mutton or lamb, trimmed of fat
1 c. plus 1 tsp. kosher salt, divided
4 cloves garlic, minced

3 Tbsp. ground fenugreek
1 Tbsp. sweet paprika
1 tsp. cayenne pepper
1 tsp. ground black pepper
½ tsp. ground cumin
½ c. water

Use a knife to cut holes in meat. Place in a deep baking dish and pack with 1 c. kosher salt, making sure to coat the meat entirely. Cover with plastic wrap and refrigerate for 2 days. Check meat regularly to make sure salt has not been absorbed by the meat; if so, add more salt so that there is always a thick coating.

Remove meat from refrigerator and rinse thoroughly, being careful to remove all salt. Wrap meat in several layers of paper towels and place between two large cutting boards. Place weight on top cutting board and allow to sit in a cool, dry place for 1 day.

Using a metal hook or a piece of twine laced through the end of the meat, hang the meat in a well-lit area where it will not be disturbed for 2 more days.

Combine 1 tsp. kosher salt, garlic, fenugreek, paprika, cayenne pepper, black pepper, cumin, and water in a food processor and grind to form a paste. Spread the paste on the surface of the meat. Hang to dry for 2 days longer. Slice meat against the grain and serve.

Per serving: 507 calories, 23 g fat, 8 g saturated fat, 762 mg sodium, 8 g carbohydrates, 67 g protein.

SERVING SUGGESTION:

Serve with cucumbers and tomatoes.

VARIATION:

Beef, such as sirloin or top round, can be used in place of mutton.

KYRGYZSTAN
BESH BARMAK

3 / 1 / 2
COOK TIME: 2 HOURS, 30 MINUTES
ACTIVE PREP TIME: 20 MINUTES
INACTIVE PREP TIME: 30 MINUTES
MAKES 4 SERVINGS

BESH BARMAK, SOMETIMES CALLED "CENTRAL ASIAN LASAGNA," IS A PASTA
dish eaten by the nomadic people of the Steppe region. Its name means "five fingers"
and is a reference to the traditional way of eating it–with the hands. Kyrgyz nomads
and herders share a ritual of serving besh barmak to guests, in which the best cuts
of meat are given to the oldest and highest-ranking at the table. When celebrating
special occasions, the head of the lamb used to prepare the dish is served to the
guest of honor.

2-½ lbs. lamb, with bones
1 large onion, sliced into rings
1 c. water, plus more for boiling
3 c. all-purpose flour
2 eggs, beaten
½ tsp. salt
Chopped fresh parsley, for serving

Place meat and half of the onion in a large stockpot with enough water to cover.
Bring to a boil, reduce heat to low, and simmer for at least 2 hours, skimming fat
from surface when necessary.

As the lamb cooks, prepare the dough for the noodles. Combine flour, water,
eggs, and salt and knead until a pliable dough is formed. Place dough in a covered
bowl and allow to sit for 30 minutes.

On a flour-dusted surface, divide dough into smaller portions and roll each
portion into a thin layer. Cut each layer into 4-inch squares.

Remove meat and onions from pot and set aside. Boil remaining half of onion
for about 2 minutes or until slightly softened, then remove and set aside.

Bring stock to a boil. Cook noodles in batches for 7-8 minutes each. As the noodles are cooking, remove meat from bone and cut into small pieces.

When noodles are finished cooking, divide them between 4 plates, covering each plate with noodles. Place meat on top of noodles, and onions on top of meat. Garnish with parsley and serve.

Per serving: 704 calories, 16 g fat, 5 g saturated fat, 456 mg sodium, 75 g carbohydrates, 61 g protein.

SERVING SUGGESTION:

To serve this meal in the traditional manner, strain the cooking liquid through a fine sieve and divide between 4 bowls. Serve broth alongside meat and noodles.

MALDIVES KULHIMAS

1 / 2 / 2
COOK TIME: 25 MINUTES
ACTIVE PREP TIME: 10 MINUTES
MAKES 4 SERVINGS

A DISPARATE CHAIN OF OVER ONE THOUSAND ISLANDS IN THE INDIAN OCEAN, the Maldives drift over 300 miles from India, their closest mainland neighbor. Accordingly, the island nation's cuisine centers around locally-available food and especially three native staples: tuna, coconuts, and starches (including rice, sweet potatoes, and cassava). Tuna is not a common accompaniment to curry and chili for most Americans, but to the Maldivians it is ubiquitous.

1 lb. fresh tuna, cut into small pieces
1 medium onion, sliced
Juice and zest of 1 lime
1 Scotch bonnet chili, seeded and diced
One ½-inch piece ginger, peeled and cubed
3 cardamom pods, crushed
2 Tbsp. red curry powder
½ c. grated coconut

Oil, for frying
¾ c. full-fat coconut cream
2 bay leaves
Chopped cilantro, for serving

Place onion, lime juice and zest, Scotch bonnet chili, ginger, cardamom, curry powder, grated coconut, and half the coconut cream in a blender or food processor and pulse until smooth. Add a little water or lime juice if necessary to achieve a saucy texture.

Heat oil in a large skillet over medium heat. Add tuna and fry until golden, about 3 minutes per side. Add onion sauce and remaining coconut cream and stir. Reduce heat to low, cover, and simmer for 20 minutes or until tuna is fully cooked. Garnish with cilantro and serve.

Per serving: 391 calories, 27 g fat, 15 g saturated fat, 67 mg sodium, 7 g carbohydrates, 32 g protein.

SERVING SUGGESTIONS:

Serve with rice or sweet potatoes.

VARIATION:

Two Tbsp. of chili powder may be substituted for Scotch bonnet chili.

PAKISTAN BIRYANI

3 / 2 / 2
COOK TIME: 1 HOUR, 10 MINUTES
ACTIVE PREP TIME: 20 MINUTES
MAKES 4 SERVINGS

BIRYANI, THE NATIONAL DISH OF PAKISTAN, IS DIFFERENT FROM MANY OTHER dishes from the region in that its components are cooked separately. It is served as two layers of rice with a layer of meat in the center. This dish is popular not only in Pakistan but also throughout Central Asia and the Islamic diaspora, originating in the kitchens of the Mughal Empire in the sixteenth century. Pakistani biryani is distinguished by its myriad of spices and its use of chicken.

1 lb. chicken breasts
1 c. basmati rice
2-½ c. water, plus more for boiling and soaking
2 bay leaves
One 4-inch cinnamon stick
5 whole cloves
5 cardamom pods
1-½ tsp. salt
2 large onions, finely chopped
Oil, for sautéing
1 tsp. black peppercorns
2 large tomatoes, peeled, seeded, and chopped
1 tsp. ginger paste
1 tsp. garlic paste
1 tsp. chili powder
1 tsp. ground cumin
1 tsp. ground coriander
1 tsp. garam masala
½ tsp. ground turmeric
2 c. plain yogurt
5 plums, chopped
3 Tbsp. whole milk
5 saffron threads
3 jalapeno chilies, chopped
½ c. fresh cilantro, chopped
½ c. fresh mint, chopped
2 Tbsp. lemon juice

Place chicken breasts in a large saucepan and add enough water to cover. Bring to a boil, reduce heat to low, cover, and simmer until chicken is fully cooked, about 15 minutes. Remove from heat and allow to cool completely, then shred chicken with two forks.

Place rice, water, 1 bay leaf, ¼ of cinnamon stick, 2 cloves, 2 cardamom pods, and ½ tsp. salt in a medium saucepan and bring to a boil. Cover, reduce heat to medium, and simmer for 20 minutes or until rice is cooked. Set aside.

Heat oil in a large skillet over high heat. Add onion, peppercorns, and remaining cardamom, cloves, cinnamon stick, and bay leaf and reduce heat to medium. Sauté until onion is translucent, about 5 minutes. Add tomatoes, ginger and garlic pastes, chili powder, cumin, coriander, garam masala, and turmeric and sauté for 5 minutes longer.

Add shredded chicken, yogurt, and remaining 1 tsp. of salt. Cook over medium heat until sauce has thickened, about 5-10 minutes. Meanwhile, place plums in a small amount of water to soak and add saffron threads to milk.

Spread half of the rice on the bottom of a large Dutch oven. Ladle the chicken and yogurt mixture over the rice. Top first with plums (drained), followed by jalapeno chilies, cilantro, mint, and lemon juice, in that order. Add remaining rice on top and sprinkle with saffron-milk mixture.

Cover pan with aluminum foil and then cover with lid. Cook over low heat for 15-20 minutes. Invert biryani onto large platter and serve.

Per serving: 608 calories, 15 g fat, 4 g saturated fat, 797 mg sodium, 69 g carbo-hydrates, 47 g protein.

SERVING SUGGESTIONS:

Serve with chopped cilantro, boiled eggs, raisins, nuts, and tomatoes.

VARIATIONS:

Use lamb, beef, shrimp, or lentils in place of chicken.

SRI LANKA SHRIMP CURRY

1 / 2 / 2
COOK TIME: 25 MINUTES
ACTIVE PREP TIME: 10 MINUTES
MAKES 4 SERVINGS

SRI LANKAN FOOD IS OFTEN COMPARED TO THAT OF ITS NEIGHBOR TO THE north, India. While the two cuisines have many ingredients and basic dishes in common, Sri Lankan fare is distinguished by its use of extremes–very spicy, very sweet, and very sour (and often all three at once). This seafood dish incorporates what could be called the Holy Trinity of Sri Lankan cooking: tamarind, coconut milk, and curry.

1-½ lb. large shrimp, peeled and deveined
1 large onion, chopped
3 cloves garlic, crushed
Oil, for sautéing
1 Tbsp. red curry powder
1 tsp. ground turmeric
½ tsp. salt
One 2-inch cinnamon stick, broken in half
One 1-inch piece ginger, peeled and minced
One 15-oz. can coconut milk
One 15-oz. can crushed tomatoes
½ c. shredded coconut
2 Tbsp. tamarind paste
1 Tbsp. brown sugar
Juice of 1 lemon
2 red chilies, finely chopped (optional)
¼ c. roasted cashews, for serving

Heat oil in a large, heavy skillet over medium-high heat. Add onion and cook for 5-6 minutes or until brown and translucent. Add garlic, curry powder, turmeric, salt, cinnamon stick, and ginger and cook for 2 minutes longer, stirring constantly.

Add coconut milk, tomatoes, coconut, tamarind paste, brown sugar, lemon juice, and red chilies (if using) and stir. Reduce heat to medium-low and cook for 8-10 minutes or until liquid is reduced by one-third.

Add shrimp to pan and continue to cook until shrimp are opaque, about 5-6 minutes. Garnish with cashews and serve.

Per serving: 496 calories, 28 g fat, 19 g saturated fat, 377 mg sodium, 25 g carbohydrates, 37 g protein.

SERVING SUGGESTION:

Serve with rice.

VARIATIONS:

Use boneless chicken thighs (2 lbs.) in place of shrimp. If using chicken, cover pan after adding and cook for 30 minutes or until done. Use potatoes, carrots, and other vegetables in place of meat for a vegetarian version. Adjust cooking time and cook until vegetables are tender.

TAJIKISTAN
QURUTOB

3 / 1 / 3
COOK TIME: 3 HOURS, 15 MINUTES
ACTIVE PREP TIME: 35 MINUTES
INACTIVE PREP TIME: 1 HOUR, 30 MINUTES
MAKES 8 SERVINGS

TUCKED BETWEEN AFGHANISTAN, UZBEKISTAN, KYRGYZSTAN, AND CHINA, THE tiny republic of Tajikistan has a cuisine that reflects those of its neighbors. Qurutob is one of the few dishes that are distinctly Tajik. It can be made with meat, as it is here, or without it; mandatory ingredients include fried onions, qurut (a soft, salty yogurt cheese) and fatir (a dense, buttery flatbread). Like other nomadic peoples, Tajiks typically eat dishes such as qurutob with their hands, using torn pieces of fatir as utensils.

For qurutob:
1 lb. lamb (shoulder meat or shank, with bone)
2 c. plain yogurt
½ tsp. salt
1 tsp. ground cumin
1 tsp. ground coriander
1 tsp. paprika
½ c. olive oil, divided
One 15-oz. can crushed tomatoes, drained
1 large onion, sliced
¼ c. water
Chopped parsley, for garnish
Chopped basil, for garnish
Fatir (recipe below)

Preheat oven to 300 degrees. Pour yogurt into a 9 x 9-inch glass baking dish. Bake yogurt in oven for 1-½ hours or until most of the liquid has evaporated. After yogurt has finished cooking, transfer to a colander lined with cheesecloth to drain off any excess whey. Combine strained yogurt with salt, return to baking dish, and cook for 30 minutes longer.

Combine cumin, coriander, and paprika and coat surface of lamb with spices. Heat ¼ c. olive oil in an oven-safe pot or Dutch oven over high heat. Add lamb and sear for about 3 minutes on each side until browned. Add tomatoes, place pot in oven (it can cook alongside the yogurt), and bake for 2-½ hours.

Remove pot from oven, transfer lamb and tomatoes to a separate dish (reserving juices), and return to stovetop. Add remaining ¼ c. olive oil and heat over medium-high heat. Add onions and sauté for 5 minutes or until translucent and wilted. Crumble baked yogurt over onions and add water and juices from lamb and tomatoes. Once the sauce begins to thicken and become slightly lumpy, return lamb and tomatoes to pot and stir to combine.

For fatir:
1 c. all-purpose flour, plus more for flouring surface

1 tsp. salt
½ c. water
1 egg
½ c. butter, at room temperature, plus more for greasing baking sheet
1 tsp. sesame seeds (optional)

Sift together flour and salt and add to the bowl of a stand mixer with a paddle attachment. Slowly add water while mixing on medium speed, followed by egg. Cover dough with plastic wrap and refrigerate for 30 minutes.

Roll out dough on a floured surface to a ¼-inch thickness and into a rectangular shape. Cut the rectangle in half to form two equal pieces. Spread butter over the surface of each piece. Set one piece on top of the other, buttered side facing up. Starting from the nearest end, roll to form a log. Wrap dough in plastic wrap and refrigerate for 1 hour.

Preheat oven to 300 degrees. Remove dough from plastic wrap, stand it on one end, and press it downward to form a ½-inch thick circle about 6-8 inches in diameter. Prick the dough with the tines of a fork and sprinkle with sesame seeds (if using). Place fatir on greased baking sheet and bake for 35 minutes. Allow to cool completely on wire rack.

To serve, shred fatir into medium-sized pieces and add to qurutob. Divide between four large serving bowls and garnish with parsley and basil.

Per serving: 441 calories, 30 g fat, 11 g saturated fat, 351 mg sodium, 20 g carbohydrates, 23 g protein.

VARIATIONS:

Lamb is optional in qurutob; for a vegetarian version, omit the second step and add tomatoes directly to pot after sautéing onions. For more heat, add 1 tsp. chili powder to other spices.

TIP:

While not traditional, you can reduce cooking time by heating the yogurt in a saucepan on the stovetop instead of baking it in the oven. Cook until reduced by at least one-third before straining.

TURKMENISTAN IÇLEKLI

2 / 1 / 1
COOK TIME: 30 MINUTES
ACTIVE PREP TIME: 25 MINUTES
INACTIVE PREP TIME: 5 MINUTES
MAKES 4 SERVINGS

THE MAIN DIFFERENCE BETWEEN THE CUISINE OF TURKMENISTAN AND THE other Central Asian nations that surround it is that fish and seafood are staples, owing to the country's large coastline on the Caspian Sea. But the national dish of Turkemistan, içlekli, features lamb instead. Resembling a stuffed flatbread, içlekli is the Turkmen rendition of the shepherd's pie, traditionally baked in an underground oven with embers and hot sand.

1 lb. ground lamb
2 c. all-purpose flour
1-½ c. water, plus more for brushing, divided
¼ c. butter, melted
2 tsp. salt, divided
1 medium tomato, seeded and chopped
1 small onion, finely chopped
1 small bell pepper, seeded and finely chopped
4 cloves garlic, minced
1 tsp. ground black pepper
½ tsp. smoked paprika

In a large bowl, combine flour, 1-¼ c. water, butter, and 1 tsp. salt. Knead until a soft dough is formed. Divide dough into two balls, cover with a damp towel, and allow to rest for 5 minutes.

Heat a large skillet over medium-high heat. Cook lamb until completely browned, about 5 minutes, and drain any fat. Combine meat with tomato, onion, bell pepper, garlic, remaining water and salt, pepper, and paprika. Set aside.

Preheat oven to 475 degrees. On a floured surface, roll one ball of dough into a circle 12 inches in diameter. Place dough circle on a large baking sheet lined with parchment paper and spread meat mixture over surface, leaving a ½-inch border around the edge.

Roll the second ball of dough into a circle the same size as the first. Lay the second circle on top of the first and press the edges to seal.

With a fork, poke holes in the top of the pie and flute the edges. Brush the top of the pie with water. Cook for 25 minutes or until top of pie is brown. Cut into four slices and serve immediately.

Per serving: 569 calories, 21 g fat, 10 g saturated fat, 1337 mg sodium, 54 g carbohydrates, 40 g protein.

VARIATIONS:

Use ground beef in place of lamb, or an equal amount of cooked lentils in place of meat for a vegetarian version.

UZBEKISTAN
SAMARKAND DIMLAMA

1 / 1 / 1
COOK TIME: 1 HOUR, 45 MINUTES
ACTIVE PREP TIME: 15 MINUTES
MAKES 8 SERVINGS

THE NATION OF UZBEKISTAN OCCUPIES AN IMPORTANT PLACE ON THE FORMER Silk Road, and its second largest city, Samarkand, is dripping with history. One of the world's oldest continuously inhabited cities, Samarkand has been an important point not only on the Silk Road but also in the empires of the Achaemenids, Alexander the Great, and Genghis Khan. This recipe for dimlama, a traditional layered Uzbek stew, is unique to Samarkand.

2 lbs. lamb shoulder, cut into medium pieces
2 Tbsp. butter, melted
2 Tbsp. paprika
2 tsp. salt
2 tsp. ground cumin

1 tsp. ground white pepper
2 onions, thinly sliced
3 tomatoes, seeded and quartered
4 carrots, sliced crosswise
2 green bell peppers, sliced
1 red chili pepper (optional)
2 heads garlic, peeled
4 potatoes, peeled and chopped
1 bunch fresh dill
5-6 cabbage leaves

Pour butter into an unheated stockpot, covering the bottom. Add lamb meat and season with half of the paprika, salt, cumin seed, and pepper.

Layer the meat with other ingredients, in this order: sliced onions, tomatoes, carrots, bell peppers, chili pepper (if using), whole garlic heads, and potatoes. Season with remaining paprika, salt, cumin, and pepper. Top with dill.

Use the cabbage leaves to form a "dome" over the stew. Cover pot with lid and turn heat to medium-high under pot. Cook for 15 minutes, reduce heat to low, and cook for 1-½ hours longer. Remove lid and cabbage leaves and stir stew. Stew is ready to serve when meat is fully cooked. Serve dimlama on large plates.

Per serving: 400 calories, 12 g fat, 5 g saturated fat, 734 mg sodium, 37 g carbo-hydrates, 38 g protein.

SERVING SUGGESTION:

Serve with naan bread.

VARIATIONS:

Use pork or beef in place of lamb. Add other vegetables such as beetroot and eggplant after potatoes. For a vegan version, replace meat with an equal amount of extra vegetables. In addition to dill, other herbs such as cilantro or basil may be added.

EAST ASIA

BHUTAN
EMA DATSHI

1 / 2 / 2
COOK TIME: 15 MINUTES
ACTIVE PREP TIME: 5 MINUTES
INACTIVE PREP TIME: 10 MINUTES
MAKES 4 SERVINGS

AGRICULTURE IS NOT EASY IN THE TINY HIMALAYAN KINGDOM OF BHUTAN, where less than 3 percent of the land is arable. But one crop that thrives in this environment is the chili, by far Bhutan's most important vegetable. Nearly every Bhutanese dish contains some type of chili. Its national dish, ema datshi, is traditionally made from *sha ema* peppers and local cheese (made from the curd of yak milk).

1 poblano pepper, peeled and cut into strips
6 Thai chili peppers, cut into strips
1 medium sweet onion, such as Vidalia, finely chopped
1-½ cups water
½ lb. soft cheese, such as farmer's cheese or mild Cheddar
5 cloves garlic, minced
¼ c. fresh cilantro, minced

Place the poblano pepper, chilies, onion, and water in a large saucepan. Bring to a boil, reduce heat to medium, and boil uncovered for 10 minutes. Add tomato and garlic and boil for 2 minutes longer.

Add cheese to the pan and cook an additional 2-3 minutes or until cheese is completely melted and smooth. Remove from heat and stir in cilantro. Cover and allow to stand for 10 minutes before serving.

Per serving: 244 calories, 18 g fat, 12 g saturated fat, 369 mg sodium, 7 g carbohydrates, 15 g protein.

SERVING SUGGESTIONS:

In Bhutan, ema datshi is almost invariably served with Bhutanese red rice. Short-grain brown rice or Arborio rice can be substituted. While more American than Bhutanese, ema datshi can also be eaten with tortilla chips.

The Thai chili peppers in this recipe can be substituted with any spicy green chili, such as Serrano or jalapeno, or with a second poblano pepper.

BRUNEI
BEEF RENDANG

2 / 2 / 2
COOK TIME: 1 HOUR, 15 MINUTES
ACTIVE PREP TIME: 10 MINUTES
MAKES 4 SERVINGS

A MINISCULE COUNTRY, BRUNEI'S CULTURE IS HEAVILY INFLUENCED BY its neighbors, including Indonesia, Malaysia, and Singapore. As a result, few of Brunei's dishes are completely endemic to the nation. Beef rendang made its way to Brunei from Indonesia. Since beef is expensive and uncommon in Brunei, rendang is typically reserved for wedding feasts and other special occasions.

¾ lb. beef stew meat, cut into small pieces
⅔ c. shredded coconut
⅔ c. finely ground almonds
2 shallots, coarsely chopped
2 cloves garlic
10 red chili peppers
One 3-inch piece ginger, peeled and coarsely chopped
One 3-inch piece lemongrass, coarsely chopped
1-¼ tsp. coriander seed
1-¼ tsp. cumin seed
1-¼ tsp. fennel seed
Vegetable oil, for frying
1 dash ground nutmeg
1 Tbsp. sugar
4 whole cloves

½ cinnamon stick, broken into pieces

1-¼ c. coconut milk

½ c. water

Toast the coconut and almonds in a dry pan over high heat until brown, about 2 minutes. Remove from pan and set aside.

Blend shallots, garlic, chili peppers, ginger, and lemongrass in a food processor to make a thick paste. With a mortar and pestle, grind the coriander, cumin, and fennel seeds to a fine powder.

Heat oil in a large frying pan or wok over medium heat. Add shallot mixture to the pan and fry for 3 minutes. Add ground seeds and nutmeg, and continue to cook 3 minutes longer.

Add beef to the pan, and stir to coat. Cook for about 5 more minutes or until meat is browned.

Stir in sugar, coconut mixture, coconut milk, water, cinnamon, and cloves. Bring to a boil. Reduce heat to low and simmer for about 1 hour, or until most of the liquid has evaporated and meat is very tender.

Per serving: 490 calories, 36 g fat, 20 g saturated fat, 72 mg sodium, 15 g carbo-hydrates, 32 g protein.

SERVING SUGGESTION:

Beef rendang is traditionally served with ketupat (rice dumplings), but steamed basmati rice is a good accompaniment as well.

VARIATION:

Cooking the meat for less time than specified (before the liquid evaporates) will yield a significantly different result.

CAMBODIA
AMOK TREY

3 / 3 / 3
COOK TIME: 20 MINUTES
ACTIVE PREP TIME: 20 MINUTES
MAKES 4 SERVINGS

AMOK TREY, THE NATIONAL DISH OF CAMBODIA, IS TRADITIONALLY MADE WITH fish (along coastal areas), as included here, or rice paddy snails (further inland). Both versions are made with a lemongrass-heavy curry and steamed in banana leaves. The steaming process locks in the flavor and the moisture of the curry and fish.

2 lbs. cod filets (or other firm white fish), cut into large pieces
6 stalks lemongrass, thinly sliced (bottom of stalks only)
3 Tbsp. galangal root, finely grated
1 Tbsp. ground turmeric
16 kaffir lime leaves, thinly sliced, plus more for serving
2 heads garlic, peeled
Oil, for sautéing
One 15-oz. can full-fat coconut milk
2 Tbsp. brown sugar
2 Tbsp. fish sauce
2 eggs, beaten
4 large banana leaves
Red chili, finely chopped, for serving

Begin by making the kroeung curry paste: Grind together lemongrass, galangal root, turmeric, kaffir lime leaves, and garlic in a food processor or with a mortar and pestle until thoroughly mixed.

Heat oil in a large frying pan over medium heat. Add the kroeung curry paste and sauté for about 2 minutes. Add coconut milk, sugar, and fish sauce and stir. Simmer curry sauce for about 5 minutes or until warm and fragrant. Allow the sauce to cool, then slowly fold in the eggs. Add the fish, coating completely with curry sauce.

Fold each banana leaf into a square shape. Lift the edges and fold to form a "container" for the curry; you may need to use toothpicks to secure the corners. Place the banana leaf "containers" in a steamer and steam for 7-10 minutes. Garnish with shredded kaffir lime leaves and red chili before serving.

Per serving: 459 calories, 25 g fat, 17 g saturated fat, 905 mg sodium, 8 g carbohydrates, 46 g protein.

TIPS:

Foil can be used in place of banana leaves for steaming this dish; simply fold pieces of foil as instructed in Step 4. If you do not have a steamer, amok trey can also be prepared in the oven. Using baking dishes instead of banana leaves, cover with foil and cook at 350 degrees for 25-35 minutes.

CHINA
PEKING DUCK

3 / 2 / 3
COOK TIME: 50 MINUTES
ACTIVE PREP TIME: 25 MINUTES
INACTIVE PREP TIME: 3 HOURS
MAKES 4 SERVINGS

CHINESE FOOD HAS A STORIED HISTORY IN THE UNITED STATES THAT begins with the first immigrants in the nineteenth century. But many Americans are unfamiliar with China's national dish, Peking duck. Eaten in China since the fifth century CE, Peking duck is traditionally served as three separate courses. First, the skin is fried crisp in the duck's fat and served with a sweet sauce. Second, the duck meat is served wrapped in thin pancakes. And third, a broth made from the duck's bones and remaining fat is served. While traditional Peking duck is air-dried before roasting whole, this recipe uses duck breasts only and refrigeration to dry the skin.

For duck:
4 boneless duck breasts (about 6 oz. each), with skin
2 Tbsp. molasses
1 Tbsp. dark soy sauce
1 tsp. Chinese five-spice powder

¼ tsp. salt
¼ tsp. ground black pepper
Peanut oil, for frying

Combine molasses, soy sauce, five-spice powder, salt, and pepper. Brush duck breasts with molasses mixture and place in refrigerator, skin side up. Refrigerate for at least 2 hours (preferably overnight).

Heat peanut oil a large skillet or wok over high heat. Cut slits in the skin of the duck to expose fat beneath. Sear duck breasts, skin side down, in hot oil for about 5-7 minutes or until skin is crisp (be careful not to burn).

Preheat oven to 350 degrees. Roast duck breasts for 30 minutes or until an internal temperature of 170 degrees is reached.

Per serving: 397 calories, 22 g fat, 7 g saturated fat, 1767 mg sodium, 14 g carbohydrates, 33 g protein.

For pancakes:
1-½ c. all-purpose flour
¼ tsp. salt
⅔ c. hot water
Oil, for brushing

Combine flour and salt. Gradually stir in hot water until a dough forms, then knead dough until pliable. Cover dough with plastic wrap and allow to rest for 1 hour.

Pinch dough into 12 portions, and form each portion into a round disc. Brush six of the discs on one side with oil. Top each oiled portion with one of the other six portions. With a rolling pin, flatten each pair into a round pancake about 6 inches in diameter.

Heat a nonstick skillet over medium heat. Fry each pancake approximately 30 seconds on each side or until small air bubbles begin to form between the pancakes. Remove from pan and allow to cool slightly, and then peel the top pancake from the bottom one. Repeat until all pancakes are fried.

Per pancake: 67 calories, 1 g fat, 0 g saturated fat, 51 mg sodium, 12 g carbohydrates, 2 g protein.

For sauce:
Sesame oil, for frying
3 cloves garlic, finely minced
3 Tbsp. hoisin sauce
1 Tbsp. white wine vinegar

Heat sesame oil in a small saucepan over medium-high heat. Fry garlic until brown and fragrant. Add hoisin sauce and vinegar, stirring with a fork or small whisk.

To serve, spread a small amount of sauce on each pancake. Slice duck breasts into thin strips, including skin. Serve duck wrapped in pancakes with sauce.

Per serving: 61 calories, 4 g fat,1 g saturated fat, 194 mg sodium, 6 g carbohydrates, 1 g protein.

SERVING SUGGESTIONS:

Serve with sliced cucumbers, cantaloupe, oranges, scallions, and cilantro.

VARIATION:

Add chili flakes to the sauce or marinade for more heat.

TIP:

To further simplify this recipe, use pre-packaged Mandarin pancakes (available at Asian food stores) and bottled duck sauce.

HONG KONG WIND SAND CHICKEN

2 / 1 / 2
COOK TIME: 1 HOUR, 10 MINUTES
ACTIVE PREP TIME: 15 MINUTES
INACTIVE PREP TIME: 20 MINUTES
MAKES 4 SERVINGS

ONE OF THE WORLD'S LARGEST AND MOST COSMOPOLITAN PORTS OF commerce, the former British territory of Hong Kong has seen its culture impacted by those of many others. But its cuisine, while showing a fair amount of global influence, remains largely Cantonese in its character. Hong Kong has placed its unique stamp on many dishes that originated in Guangdong. In one example, wind sand chicken, a whole chicken is roasted at a high temperature until its skin is crisp and golden and its meat is juicy and tender; it is then dusted with fried garlic and shallot pieces that resemble wind-blown "sand" and add a superlative level of flavor and texture.

One whole chicken (about 3-4 pounds)
4 large shallots, minced
8 cloves garlic, minced
1 c. vegetable oil
1 small onion, quartered
1 tsp. sea salt
1 tsp. ground white pepper
2 Tbsp. ground cumin
1 tsp. red pepper flakes (optional)
¼ c. honey, warmed

Heat oil in a small saucepan over high heat. Add shallots and sauté for 5 minutes on high heat, and then reduce heat to medium-low and continue cooking for another 5 minutes. Add garlic and sauté for 10 minutes longer. Transfer shallots and garlic to a paper towel to drain, reserving oil.

Preheat oven to 450 degrees. Place chicken in a baking dish, tie legs together with twine, and pull on the skin to loosen it and to separate it from the meat. Use a sharp knife to score the surface of the chicken skin. Place onion quarters in cavity, and season generously with salt and pepper. Combine cumin, red pepper flakes (if using), and reserved vegetable oil and spread over entire surface of chicken. Insert a meat thermometer in the thickest part of the thigh.

Roast chicken with breast side down in oven for 25 minutes, and then turn chicken so that the breast side is up and roast for 15 minutes longer or until meat thermometer registers 135 degrees. Raise oven temperature to 500 degrees, drizzle chicken with honey, and continue roasting for 10 minutes or until meat thermometer registers 175 degrees. Remove from oven and allow to rest for 20 minutes. Dust chicken with shallots and garlic before serving.

Per serving: 860 calories, 65 g fat, 13 g saturated fat, 599 mg sodium, 27 g car-

bohydrates, 42 g protein.

SERVING SUGGESTION:

Serve with chili sauce and white rice.

TIP:

For crispier skin and a more intense cumin flavor, cover chicken with plastic wrap and refrigerate for at least 2 hours (preferably overnight) after seasoning.

INDONESIA
SATE AYAM

1 / 3 / 3
COOK TIME: 25 MINUTES
ACTIVE PREP TIME: 20 MINUTES
INACTIVE PREP TIME: 9 HOURS, 10 MINUTES
MAKES 5-6 SERVINGS

STREET FOOD IS A STAPLE FOR LOCALS AND TOURISTS ALIKE THROUGHOUT Southeast Asia, but possibly nowhere more than Indonesia, where the traveling food and drink vendor is a tradition dating back over one thousand years. Indonesia is a country that has become increasingly urban, with 14 cities boasting populations of one million or more and a population density as high as 40,000 per square mile in the capital of Jakarta. Sate ayam, or chicken satay, is enjoyed in Jakarta's fine restaurants as well as from the carts of many of its 53,000 street vendors.

2 lbs. boneless chicken thighs, cut into strips with excess fat trimmed
5 stalks lemongrass, chopped
1 red onion, chopped
½ c. sugar or agave nectar
¼ c. kecap manis or soy sauce
One 1-inch piece fresh ginger, peeled and grated
2 tsp. fennel seed
2 tsp. cumin seed
1 tsp. ground turmeric

1 tsp. salt
Oil, for brushing and sautéing

Place lemongrass and onion in a blender or food processor with sugar, kecap manis, ginger, fennel and cumin seeds, turmeric, and salt. Pulse until a thick paste is formed. Coat chicken with paste, place in a shallow dish, and cover with plastic wrap. Marinate for 8-12 hours.

Soak about 30 bamboo skewers in cold water for 30 minutes. Thread chicken strips onto bamboo skewers.

Preheat oven to 375 degrees. Place the skewers about 1 inch apart on baking sheets and brush with oil. Bake for 20 minutes or until browned, turning and brushing with more oil once.

Per serving: 339 calories, 18 g fat, 5 g saturated fat, 1090 mg sodium, 21 g carbohydrates, 27 g protein.

For sauce:
2 cloves garlic, quartered
3-4 dried bird's eye chilies (optional)
2 Tbsp. tamarind paste
½ c. dry roasted peanuts
¼ c. water, plus more for soaking
2 Tbsp. sugar or agave nectar
1 Tbsp. kecap manis or soy sauce
1 tsp. salt

Soak garlic and chilies (if using) in a small amount of hot water for 10 minutes. Drain.

Place garlic, chilies, tamarind paste, peanuts, water, sugar, kecap manis, and salt in a blender or food processor and blend until very smooth, adding more water if needed. Serve sauce with sate.

Per serving: 93 calories, 6 g fat, 1 g saturated fat, 541 mg sodium, 8 g carbohydrates, 3 g protein.

VARIATIONS:

Sate can be made with any type of meat, as well as tofu or tempeh (the latter of which originated in Indonesia).

JAPAN
NIKUJAGA

2 / 3 / 2
COOK TIME: 1 HOUR, 45 MINUTES
ACTIVE PREP TIME: 10 MINUTES
INACTIVE PREP TIME: 40 MINUTES
MAKES 4 SERVINGS

SUSHI, RAMEN NOODLES, MISO SOUP, AND TENDER, RARE-COOKED WAGYU beef come to mind when many people think of Japanese food. A recipe such as nikujaga (whose name means "meat and potatoes") may not. But in this beloved dish, soy sauce, sake, mirin, and the umami-rich broth called dashi combine with the familiar beef and potatoes to create Japanese comfort food at its finest.

1 lb. lean beef, cubed
One 5-inch piece kombu (dried kelp)
3 c. katsuobushi (dried bonito flakes)
1 qt. water, plus more for soaking
1 large onion, sliced
Olive oil, for frying
½ c. sake
¼ c. soy sauce
2 Tbsp. mirin (rice wine)
1 Tbsp. sugar
3-4 Yukon Gold potatoes, cubed
Chopped green onions, for serving

First, make the dashi. Cut kombu into 3-4 pieces and soak in water for at least 30 minutes (3 hours or longer is preferable).

Bring kombu and water to a boil in a large saucepan over medium-low heat. Remove kombu just before water boils. Remove pot from heat and allow to cool, skimming any foam that rises to the surface.

Add the katsuobushi to the pot and bring to a boil. Once boiling, turn off heat and allow the katsuobushi to sink to the bottom (this will take about 10 minutes). Pour mixture through a very fine sieve (line with a paper towel if necessary).

Heat olive oil in a Dutch oven over medium-high heat. Add beef and cook over medium-high heat until brown, about 7-8 minutes. Remove meat from pan. Add onions and sauté until translucent, about 5 minutes.

Return meat to pot and add dashi, sake, soy sauce, mirin, sugar, and potatoes. Reduce heat to medium-low, cover, and simmer until potatoes are fully cooked, about 30 minutes. Garnish with green onions and serve.

Per serving: 463 calories, 11 g fat, 3 g saturated fat, 1127 mg sodium, 36 g carbohydrates, 49 g protein.

SERVING SUGGESTIONS:

Nikujaga can be served by itself or with rice or noodles.

VARIATION:

Use lean pork in place of beef.

TIP:

If time is a constraint, dashi can be substituted with fish broth.

KOREA
BULGOGI STEW

2 / 3 / 2
COOK TIME: 20 MINUTES
ACTIVE PREP TIME: 15 MINUTES
INACTIVE PREP TIME: 8 HOURS, 30 MINUTES
MAKES 4 SERVINGS

BULGOGI, A DISH SERVED IN KOREA SINCE THE GOGURYEO ERA (37 BCE –668 CE), has become a cultural phenomenon. It can be found everywhere in South

Korea from fine restaurants to small barbecue joints; some fast-food restaurants even sell bulgogi-flavored hamburgers. The word *bulgogi* literally means "fire meat," a reference to its traditional preparation, but it can be pan-fried or stewed.

1 lb. beef tenderloin or skirt steak, sliced in thin strips
2 cloves garlic, minced
2 Tbsp. soy sauce
2 Tbsp. honey
2 tsp. sesame oil, plus extra for frying
½ tsp. ground black pepper
2 oz. glass noodles (dangmyeon)
1 qt. water, plus more for soaking
1 tsp. fish sauce
1 tsp. salt
1 small onion, sliced in thin strips, plus more for serving
4 green onions, sliced, plus more for serving
6 oz. mushrooms (preferably enoki)
1 c. fresh basil leaves

Combine garlic, soy sauce, honey, sesame oil, and black pepper. Place meat in a shallow dish and coat with soy sauce mixture. Cover with plastic wrap and marinate in refrigerator for 8 hours or overnight.

Place noodles in a large bowl of water. Allow to soak for at least 30 minutes or up to 1 hour.

Heat sesame oil in a heavy Dutch oven over medium-high heat. Add marinated meat and sear until browned, about 5 minutes. Add water, fish sauce, and salt and bring to a boil. Add onion and green onions and reduce heat to medium-low. Cook for about 10 minutes uncovered, stirring occasionally and skimming off any foam that rises to the top. Add noodles and mushrooms to pot and stir. Cook for about 3 minutes longer. Stir in basil leaves.

Divide stew among four bowls. Top with onion and green onions, and serve.

Per serving: 365 calories, 13 g fat, 4 g saturated fat, 1222 mg sodium, 26 g carbohydrates, 36 g protein.

LAOS
LARB GAI WITH
STICKY RICE

3 / 2 / 3
COOK TIME: 45 MINUTES
ACTIVE PREP TIME: 20 MINUTES
INACTIVE PREP TIME: 2 HOURS
MAKES 4 SERVINGS

GLUTINOUS RICE, THE LOW-AMYLOSE VARIETY CHARACTERIZED BY ITS STICKY, glue-like texture, is the key staple of Lao cuisine. Considered a lower-quality product in most Southeast Asian countries, Laotians prefer it over other types. Sticky rice is eaten by hand in Laos, and in its most popular dish, larb gai, it is used as a utensil of sorts for eating the spicy chicken salad. While larb gai is also served in Thailand, the lime juice and fresh mint in this recipe make it distinctly Lao.

1 lb. ground chicken, or finely chopped chicken thighs
1 c. plus 1 Tbsp. short-grain glutinous rice, divided
Water, for soaking and boiling
Oil, for frying
2 Tbsp. lime juice
1 Tbsp. fish sauce
¼ tsp. sugar
3 shallots, peeled and thinly sliced
3 green onions, sliced diagonally (white parts only)
1 Thai red chili, sliced diagonally
½ c. fresh mint, finely chopped
¼ c. fresh cilantro, finely chopped

Rinse rice in a sieve until all white residue is washed away. Cover with cold water and allow to soak for at least 2 hours (overnight is preferable). Drain and rinse rice once again, reserving 1 Tbsp.

Bring a large pot of water to a boil. Place the rice (in the sieve) inside over the pot without allowing it to touch the water. Cover and simmer for 15 minutes. Uncover, place rice in pot with boiling water, and cook uncovered for 10 minutes longer or until rice is fully cooked.

Heat reserved 1 Tbsp. of glutinous rice in a small, dry skillet over medium heat. Toast until golden and fragrant, about 10 minutes. Grind the rice grains to a fine powder using a spice grinder or mortar and pestle.

Heat oil in a large skillet over medium-high heat. Add chicken and fry until brown, about 5-6 minutes. Add rice powder, lime juice, fish sauce, and sugar and mix well. Add shallots, green onions, chili, mint, and cilantro to pan and stir-fry for 1 minute longer.

Per serving: 433 calories, 12 g fat, 3 g saturated fat, 455 mg sodium, 41 g carbohydrates, 37 g protein.

SERVING SUGGESTIONS:

Serve with cucumber and cabbage or lettuce leaves, or topped with chopped peanuts.

MACAU MINCHI

1 / 1 / 2
COOK TIME: 30 MINUTES
ACTIVE PREP TIME: 10 MINUTES
INACTIVE PREP TIME: 5 MINUTES
MAKES 4 SERVINGS

OF ALL THE CUISINES THAT CAN BE "FUSED," CHINESE AND PORTUGUESE seem among the least likely. But in the tiny semi-autonomous region of Macau, located on the southern Chinese coast, the Sino-Portuguese culinary tradition is one that extends all the way back to the mid-sixteenth century. Macau was a Portuguese colony for over four hundred years before returning to Chinese control in 1999, and its unofficial national dish, minchi, combines Portuguese staples such as olive oil and bay leaf with Chinese soy sauce. But that's not all; the conspicuously British Worcestershire sauce also makes an appearance, and the dish's name is a corruption of the word "mince" (or "ground beef" in British English).

1 lb. ground beef
1 lb. Russet potatoes, cut into small cubes
Cold water, for parboiling
Olive oil, for frying and sautéing
1 bay leaf
1 onion, finely chopped
3 cloves garlic, minced
1 tsp. curry powder
3 Tbsp. soy sauce
1 Tbsp. Worcestershire sauce
1 tsp. brown sugar
4 eggs

Place potatoes in a large saucepan and cover with enough cold water to cover. Bring to a boil, turn off heat, and allow saucepan to stand for 5 minutes. Drain water from potatoes and pat dry with paper towels.

Heat olive oil in a heavy skillet over medium-high heat. Add potatoes and bay leaf and sauté until golden brown and cooked throughout, about 4-5 minutes. Remove from heat and set potatoes on paper towels to drain.

Return pan to heat, add a small amount of additional olive oil, and add onion. Sauté onion until translucent, about 3-4 minutes. Add garlic and curry powder and sauté for 1 minute longer. Remove onion and garlic from pan and set aside.

Add ground beef to pan. Sauté beef until brown, about 5 minutes. Add onion and garlic back to pan and sauté for 3 minutes longer. Combine soy sauce, Worcester sauce, and brown sugar, stir until brown sugar is dissolved, and add to pan with beef. Continue to cook for about 3-5 minutes or until meat is completely cooked. Add potatoes and remove from heat.

Heat additional olive oil in a second skillet over medium-high heat. Once skillet is hot, crack eggs into skillet and reduce heat to low. Fry eggs over low heat until desired level of doneness is reached. (In Macau, sunny-side-up eggs are usually served with minchi.)

Divide beef and potato mixture between four plates. Top each with a fried egg and serve.

Per serving: 411 calories, 15 g fat, 5 g saturated fat, 863 mg sodium, 24 g carbohydrates, 43 g protein.

SERVING SUGGESTION:

Serve with white rice and sliced green onions.

VARIATIONS:

Ground pork may be used in place of some or all of the beef in this recipe. For extra heat, add ¼ tsp. of cayenne pepper with garlic and curry powder.

TIP:

Instead of parboiling, cubed potatoes can be cooked in the microwave for 4 minutes to soften before sautéing.

MALAYSIA
NASI LEMAK

2 / 3 / 3
COOK TIME: 30 MINUTES
ACTIVE PREP TIME: 15 MINUTES
INACTIVE PREP TIME: 30 MINUTES
MAKES 4 SERVINGS

THE IMPACT OF MALAYSIA'S CENTRAL LOCATION IN THE DUTCH EAST INDIES on its cuisine cannot be overstated. Malay cuisine is characterized by lots of spices and dozens of international influences. Many types of regional cuisines can be found within the geographically small nation. Regional variations abound in Malaysia's national dish, nasi lemak ("creamy rice"), which is eaten throughout the country. Traditionally a breakfast food, some Malay people eat nasi lemak throughout the day at every meal.

1 c. dried anchovies (*ikan bilis*)
1 c. tamarind paste
3-¼ c. water, plus more for soaking
1-½ c. jasmine rice
One 15-oz. can full-fat coconut milk
One 2-inch piece ginger, peeled and grated
1 stalk lemongrass, chopped
½ tsp. salt
1 onion, chopped
1 clove garlic, minced
Oil, for sautéing
2 tsp. fish sauce
2 tsp. Sriracha sauce
1 c. roasted peanuts

Place anchovies in enough water to cover and soak for at least 30 minutes, and then drain. Combine tamarind paste with 1-½ c. water and stir until dissolved. Set aside.

Add rice, remaining water, coconut milk, ginger, lemongrass, and salt to a large saucepan and bring to a boil. Reduce heat to medium and simmer for 15 minutes or until all liquid is absorbed.

As rice cooks, heat oil in a large skillet over medium-high heat. Sauté onion and garlic until onion is translucent, about 5 minutes. Add anchovies, fish sauce, and Sriracha sauce and stir until combined. Reduce heat to medium-low, add sugar and tamarind paste water, and simmer until sauce is reduced by at least half, about 10 minutes.

Remove lemongrass from rice. Divide rice between 4 small bowls. Press rice into bowls until compressed, and then invert each rice bowl onto a plate (the rice should take the shape of the bowl when it is released). Spoon anchovy and tamarind sauce over rice. Serve with peanuts.

Per serving: 623 calories, 33 g fat, 8 g saturated fat, 1001 mg sodium, 66 g carbohydrates, 20 g protein.

Serve with hard-boiled eggs and sliced cucumber.

MONGOLIA
BUUZ

2 / 1 / 2
COOK TIME: 15 MINUTES
ACTIVE PREP TIME: 30 MINUTES
INACTIVE PREP TIME: 1 HOUR, 20 MINUTES
MAKES 18 BUUZ

NEARLY EVERY EAST ASIAN COUNTRY HAS SOME VARIATION ON THE STEAMED dumpling. Mongolia's version, buuz, is characterized by the way it is folded: a ball of meat is placed in the dough's center and the edges are gathered around it, leaving an opening at the top. Buuz is one of the few dishes that is eaten year-round in a country where the hottest and coldest temperatures of the year are often 150 degrees apart, though it is most recognizable as a chief part of the Tsagaan Sar (Mongolian Lunar New Year) feast in late January or February.

1-½ lb. lean ground beef or lamb
3-½ c. all-purpose flour
1 Tbsp. plus 1 tsp. salt, divided
1-½ c. water, at room temperature
1 small onion, finely chopped
3 scallions (white part only), minced
4 cloves garlic, minced
1 Tbsp. ground coriander
1 tsp. ground black pepper
Oil, for brushing
Water, for boiling

Blend flour and 2 tsp. salt in a bowl and make a well in the center. Pour the water into the well a little at a time, stopping to mix flour and water from the outsides of the bowl inward, until a dough is formed. Place dough on a floured surface and knead until smooth and pliable. Return to bowl, cover with plastic wrap, and refrigerate for 1 hour.

Combine meat, onion, scallions, garlic, coriander, pepper, and remaining 2 tsp. salt and mix thoroughly. Refrigerate for about 20-30 minutes.

Remove dough from refrigerator, knead briefly, and roll into a log about 18 inches long. Use a serrated knife to slice the log into 1-inch pieces. Roll each piece into a ball, and then flatten into a 4-inch circle.

Divide meat mixture into 18 portions, and roll each into a ball. Place a meatball in the center of each dough circle. Hold the dough and meatball in one hand, use the other to fold the edge of the dough circle over the meatball, pinching the edges as you go. When you are finished, there should be a small opening in the top of the dumpling.

Brush each dumpling with oil and place in a bamboo steamer or steamer basket. Boil 2 inches of water in a deep pan or wok and set steamer above the pan. Cover steamer and steam for 15 minutes.

Per buuz: 169 calories, 3 g fat, 1 g saturated fat, 112 mg sodium, 19 g carbohydrates, 14 g protein.

SERVING SUGGESTIONS:

Serve with ketchup (as the Mongolians do) or soy sauce.

VARIATION:

Grated spinach, cabbage, carrots, potato, or other vegetables may be added to substitute for part of the meat in the filling.

MYANMAR MOHINGA

2 / 2 / 3
COOK TIME: 40 MINUTES
ACTIVE PREP TIME: 10 MINUTES
MAKES 4 SERVINGS

FISH IS THE CHIEF PROTEIN USED IN BURMESE CUISINE, AND IT MAKES ITS way into nearly every dish—either fresh, salted, or dried, or in the form of fish sauce or a fermented paste called ngapi. It is difficult to visit Myanmar without sampling mohinga, a noodle soup sold in both restaurants and from street vendors who carry around large cauldrons of the soup and ladle it into bowls for passers-by. Some versions include fresh fish, while others incorporate other fish products. This version uses both filets and prepared fish sauce.

1 lb. catfish, tilapia, or seabass filets, cut into chunks
3 small onions, divided
4 cloves garlic, crushed
One 1-inch piece ginger, peeled and grated
1 stalk lemongrass, chopped
1 tsp. ground turmeric
1 tsp. Sriracha sauce
1 qt. water, plus more for boiling
½ c. fish sauce
¼ c. rice flour
1 lb. rice noodles
2 eggs, hard-boiled and halved, for serving
Chopped fresh cilantro, for serving

Heat oil in a Dutch oven over medium heat. Grate one of the onions and sauté along with garlic, ginger, lemongrass, Sriracha sauce, and turmeric for 3-4 minutes or until onion is soft.

Quarter remaining two onions and add to pot with water, fish sauce, and rice flour. Bring to a boil, stirring vigorously to dissolve any lumps in flour. Reduce heat to low and simmer for 20 minutes. Add fish filets to pot and cook for 10 minutes longer.

Bring a large saucepan of water to a boil. Add noodles, reduce heat to medium, and simmer for 5 minutes. Drain and rinse noodles.

Divide noodles between 4 bowls. Ladle soup on top of noodles and serve topped with egg and cilantro.

Per serving: 692 calories, 29 g fat, 6 g saturated fat, 3015 mg sodium, 44 g carbohydrates, 60 g protein.

VARIATION:

Use a few Tbsp. of ngapi or shrimp paste in place of fresh fish.

NEPAL
DAL BHAT

1 / 1 / 1
COOK TIME: 35 MINUTES TO 1 HOUR
ACTIVE PREP TIME: 10 MINUTES
INACTIVE PREP TIME: 20 MINUTES TO 2 HOURS, 20 MINUTES
MAKES 4 SERVINGS

LIKE ITS MUCH LARGER NEIGHBOR, INDIA, NEPAL HAS NO SINGLE CUISINE but rather many based on region and ethnicity. Only in the 1950s did Nepal open its borders, allowing outside cultures to influence the diets of its people. Having the second highest average elevation in the world and several of the planet's highest peaks, Nepal's topography makes agriculture difficult, especially where growing rice is concerned. Nonetheless, steamed rice is as much a staple food in Nepal as it is in most of Asia, and along with lentils it forms the cornerstone of its most popular dish. Many Nepalese enjoy dal bhat at more than one meal per day.

2 c. red, brown, or green lentils
1-½ c. basmati rice
1 large onion, finely chopped
4 cloves garlic, crushed
One 1-inch piece ginger, peeled and minced
Oil, for sautéing

1-½ tsp. sea salt

1 tsp. cumin seed

1 tsp. ground turmeric

1 tsp. black mustard seed

1 tsp. ground coriander

½ tsp. ground black pepper

2 tomatoes, seeded and chopped

1 Tbsp. ghee or coconut oil

2 qt. water, divided, plus more for soaking

Chopped fresh cilantro, for serving

Wash and rinse lentils. If using green lentils, soak for 2 hours. Rinse basmati rice, cover with water, and soak for 20 minutes. Drain lentils and rice.

Heat oil in a Dutch oven over medium-high heat. Add onion, garlic, and ginger and sauté until onion is translucent, about 5 minutes. Add salt, cumin seed, turmeric, mustard seed, coriander, and pepper. Reduce heat to medium, stir, and cook for 2 minutes longer. Add tomatoes and ghee or coconut oil and stir until ghee or oil melts. Add lentils, reduce heat to medium-low, cover, and simmer for 5 minutes.

Add 1-¼ qt. water and continue to simmer until lentils are done, checking often and adding more water if needed. (Brown lentils generally take about 20 minutes; red lentils, about 30 minutes; and green lentils, 45 minutes.)

Bring remaining 3 c. of water to a boil in a medium saucepan. Add rice, cover, reduce heat to medium, and simmer for 10 minutes or until all liquid is absorbed. Remove lid and allow to stand for 5 minutes, then fluff rice with a fork. Divide rice between four bowls and top with dal bhat. Garnish with cilantro and serve.

Per serving: 605 calories, 9 g fat, 3 g saturated fat, 482 mg sodium, 103 g carbohydrates, 30 g protein.

SERVING SUGGESTIONS:

Top with yogurt and serve with naan bread, chutney, and pickled vegetables.

PHILIPPINES
CHICKEN ADOBO

1 / 1 / 2
COOK TIME: 45 MINUTES
ACTIVE PREP TIME: 10 MINUTES
INACTIVE PREP TIME: 18 HOURS
MAKES 6-8 SERVINGS

BEFORE THE SPANISH FIRST INVADED THE PHILIPPINES IN THE SIXTEENTH century, its indigenous people discovered a method of preparing food that would keep it from spoiling in their immensely hot climate while also preserving its flavor. This method involved using vinegar and soy sauce to create a brine that was both highly acidic and very salty. The term *adobo*, which is Spanish for "marinade," should not be confused with the adobo seasoning used in Latin American cooking.

3 lbs. skin-on, bone-in chicken pieces (preferably thighs and legs)
One 15-oz. can stewed tomatoes, chopped, with 1 c. juice reserved
½ c. cider vinegar
¼ c. soy sauce
8 cloves garlic, crushed
2 bay leaves
1 tsp. black peppercorns, crushed
1 large onion, sliced
Oil, for frying
Green onions, diagonally sliced, for serving

Combine tomatoes and juice, vinegar, soy sauce, garlic, bay leaves, and peppercorns. Pour over chicken and marinate for at least 18 hours.

Place chicken and marinade in a large, heavy lidded skillet. Bring marinade to a boil, reduce heat to medium, and simmer for 10 minutes uncovered. Cover and simmer for 15 minutes longer. Remove chicken and garlic, reserve marinade, and wipe out pan.

Heat oil in skillet over medium-high heat. Add garlic from pan and onions and cook for 3 minutes or until fragrant. Add chicken and cook until brown, about 8-10 minutes. Add marinade and continue to cook until meat is done, about 5 minutes longer. Garnish with green onions and serve.

Per serving: 240 calories, 9 g fat, 2 g saturated fat, 668 mg sodium, 7 g carbohydrates, 30 g protein.

SERVING SUGGESTIONS:

Serve with rice and steamed vegetables.

VARIATIONS:

Use pork instead of chicken; pork adobo often includes pineapple. In some parts of the Philippines, a can of coconut milk is used in lieu of the tomatoes and juice.

SINGAPORE CHILI CRAB WITH MANTOU

3 / 3 / 3
COOK TIME: 35 MINUTES
ACTIVE PREP TIME: 25 MINUTES
INACTIVE PREP TIME: 1 HOUR, 40 MINUTES
MAKES 4 SERVINGS

IN 1956, A SINGAPOREAN WOMAN NAMED CHER YAM TIAN AND HER HUSBAND had a business selling steamed crabs from a pushcart on the streets of the city. One day, she tried stir-frying the crabs in a tomato and chili sauce, and one of Asia's most iconic dishes was born. In Singapore today, you're more likely to eat chili crab served in a fine restaurant than from a pushcart. Mantou (steamed buns) are served with chili crab and dipped in the sweet and savory (but not too spicy) sauce.

4 lbs. Dungeness or mud crabs, cleaned and cut into quarters
½ c. chili sauce
One 1-inch piece ginger, peeled and minced
4 shallots, chopped
1 head garlic, peeled and cloves separated
Sesame oil, for sautéing

2 Tbsp. fermented bean paste
1-½ c. water
¼ c. sugar
½ c. tomato sauce or ketchup
2 tsp. salt
¼ c. cornstarch
4 eggs, beaten

Place chili sauce, ginger, shallots, and garlic in a blender and process until a paste is formed.

Heat oil in a heavy skillet over medium heat. Add chili sauce mixture and sauté until fragrant, about 2-3 minutes. Add crab (except for hard outer shell) and fermented bean paste, and continue to cook for 3 minutes. Add water, reserving ¼ c., and increase heat to high until boiling. Add sugar, tomato sauce, and salt. Stir, reduce heat to medium-low, cover, and simmer for 10 minutes.

Combine remaining water with cornstarch and mix until a slurry is formed. Add to pan and stir until sauce is thickened. Add eggs and cook for 3 minutes longer.

Per serving: 621 calories, 13 g fat, 3 g saturated fat, 3591 mg sodium, 31 g carbohydrates, 92 g protein.

For mantou:
⅓ c. plus 2 Tbsp. warm water, plus more for steaming
1 tsp. sugar
1 tsp. yeast
1 c. all-purpose flour

Combine water, sugar, and yeast and allow to stand for 5 minutes. Combine with flour and stir until a dough is formed. Knead dough for 5 minutes or until it is smooth. Place dough in a bowl and cover with plastic wrap. Allow to stand in a warm place for 1 hour or until doubled in size. Punch dough to remove any bubbles that may form.

Divide dough into 8 portions. Form each portion into an oval shape. Cover with plastic wrap and allow to stand for 30 minutes longer.

Bring about 1 inch of water to a boil in a large pot. Coat the bottom of a steamer basket with oil and place buns in basket. Lower basket into pot, cover, and steam over high heat for 15 minutes. Remove from heat and allow to stand for 5 minutes longer before removing lid.

Per bun: 60 calories, 0 g fat, 0 g saturated fat, 1 mg sodium, 13 g carbohydrates, 2 g protein.

VARIATIONS:

Increase or decrease the number of eggs based on personal preference. Use broth in place of water for added flavor.

TAIWAN
BEEF NOODLE SOUP

3 / 3 / 2
COOK TIME: 2 HOURS, 20 MINUTES
ACTIVE PREP TIME: 25 MINUTES
MAKES 6 SERVINGS

THE ISLAND OF TAIWAN HAS BEEN HOME TO THE GOVERNMENT OF THE

Republic of China since the end of the Chinese Civil War in 1949. Most of its people are ethnically Chinese, but Taiwan's culture is in many ways its own. Taiwanese cuisine includes dishes such as iron eggs, which are stewed in soy sauce until they develop a chewy texture; stinky tofu, which is fermented in a brine of sour milk; and pig's blood cake, a combination of pork blood and glutinous rice cooked and served on a stick. This recipe, while still distinctively Taiwanese, is more likely to appeal to the American palate.

2 lbs. bone-in beef shanks
Oil, for sautéing
6 cloves garlic, crushed
1 small onion, thinly sliced
One 4-inch piece ginger, peeled and minced
3 pods star anise
1 Tbsp. Sichuan peppercorns

3 Tbsp. chili bean paste
2 Tbsp. tomato paste
2 Tbsp. brown sugar
3 Sichuan red chili peppers, crushed, or ¼ tsp. red pepper flakes (optional)
2-½ qt. water, plus more for boiling
½ c. soy sauce
½ c. sake or mirin
1 lb. baby bok choy cabbage, coarsely chopped
2 Tbsp. kosher salt
8 oz. fresh Chinese wheat noodles
Chopped fresh cilantro, for serving
Sliced onions, for serving
Lime slices, for serving

Heat oil in a large Dutch oven over medium heat. Sauté garlic, onion, and ginger for 3 minutes. Add star anise and Sichuan peppercorns and cook for 1 minute longer. Add chili bean paste, tomato paste, brown sugar, and chili peppers or flakes (if using) and stir until onion mixture is coated. Add water, soy sauce, and sake and bring to a boil.

Heat more oil in a heavy skillet over high heat. Cook beef shanks just until brown on all sides, about 2-3 minutes per side. Add beef to pot and reduce heat to low. Cover and simmer for 2 hours or until beef is completely cooked and very tender.

Remove beef from pot and set aside. Strain the broth through a fine sieve. Skim fat from the surface of the broth and return to pot. Discard all remaining solids. Trim fat and gristle from meat, remove bones, and shred into bite-size pieces. Return to pot and bring to a low boil. Reduce heat to low and cover.

Bring a second pot of water to a boil. Add bok choy cabbage and salt and boil until bok choy is tender but still crisp, about 3 minutes. Remove bok choy from pot and set aside. Reduce heat to low. Add noodles, cook for 5-7 minutes or until done, and drain and rinse with cold water.

Divide noodles, bok choy, beef, and broth (in that order) between 6 bowls. Garnish with cilantro and onions and serve with lime wedges.

Per serving: 413 calories, 18 g fat, 3 g saturated fat, 3834 mg sodium, 33 g car-

bohydrates, 26 g protein.

VARIATIONS:

Other vegetables may be used, such as tomatoes and bell peppers. Blanch and serve along with bok choy cabbage. For an additional pungent flavor, add a spoonful of black vinegar to broth before serving.

THAILAND
PAD THAI

2 / 2 / 2
COOK TIME: 15 MINUTES
ACTIVE PREP TIME: 15 MINUTES
INACTIVE PREP TIME: 5 MINUTES
MAKES 6 SERVINGS

IN RECENT YEARS, THAILAND'S ONCE OBSCURE CUISINE HAS BECOME extremely popular throughout the world. Thai cuisine focuses on spices and richly-flavored ingredients that combine sweet, sour, salty, bitter, and spicy flavors, but not so much on preparation. When preparing dishes such as the well-known pad Thai (stir-fried noodles), it's important not to omit any ingredients. Doing so will remove flavor profiles from the dish.

½ lb. small- to medium-sized shrimp, peeled and deveined
½ lb. tofu, drained and cut into small pieces
8 oz. rice stick noodles
Water, for boiling
¼ c. peanut oil
¼ c. fish sauce
¼ c. brown sugar
¼ c. tamarind paste
2 Tbsp. rice vinegar
1 dried Thai chili, crushed, or 1 tsp. red pepper flakes
6 green onions, finely chopped
2 cloves garlic, peeled and minced

3 eggs, beaten
1 small head Napa cabbage, chopped
1 c. mung bean sprouts
½ c. roasted peanuts, chopped
1 bunch fresh cilantro, chopped
2 limes, cut into wedges

Bring a large pot of water to a boil. Remove from heat and add noodles. Allow to stand for 5 minutes or until tender. Drain noodles, toss with a small amount of peanut oil, and set aside.

In a medium saucepan, combine fish sauce, brown sugar, tamarind paste, and vinegar. Heat over medium-low heat until warm. Add chili or red pepper and set aside.

Heat remaining oil in a large skillet or Dutch oven over medium-high heat. Add green onions and garlic and sauté for 1 minute. Add eggs and scramble for 3-4 minutes or until fully cooked. Add cabbage, bean sprouts, shrimp, and tofu and continue to cook until cabbage is wilted and shrimp is opaque, about 5-6 minutes. Add drained noodles and sauce to pot and stir thoroughly.

Divide between 6 bowls and garnish with peanuts, cilantro, and lime wedges to serve.

Per serving: 463 calories, 20 g fat, 4 g saturated fat, 1224 mg sodium, 50 g carbohydrates, 23 g protein.

VARIATIONS:

Pad Thai can be made with shrimp or tofu alone or with chicken, beef, or pork.

TIBET
MOMO

2 / 2 / 2
COOK TIME: 45 MINUTES
ACTIVE PREP TIME: 45 MINUTES
INACTIVE PREP TIME: 40 MINUTES
MAKES 30 MOMO

Unlike much of China, of which it is an autonomous region, Tibet is rural, sparsely populated, and relatively isolated. Sometimes called the "Roof of the World," Tibet also has the planet's highest elevation. Although Buddhist tradition mandates vegetarianism, the difficulties involved in growing crops at such high altitudes have made plant-based diets difficult to follow for Tibet's people. Momo, an indigenous Tibetan dumpling dish that has made its way across the Himalayans, can be made with either meat or with vegetables only (as included here).

2 c. all-purpose flour, plus more for flouring surface
2 tsp. salt, divided
¾ c. water
1 Tbsp. plus 2 tsp. ghee, divided
¼ head green cabbage, finely shredded
2 carrots, finely grated
2 scallions, finely chopped
½ c. extra-firm tofu, drained and chopped
¼ c. fresh cilantro, finely chopped
4 cloves garlic, minced
One ½-inch piece fresh ginger, peeled and grated
½ tsp. garam masala
¼ tsp. ground turmeric
¼ tsp. chili powder
Water, for boiling
Cabbage leaves, for lining steamer
Tomato chutney (recipe below)

Sift together flour and ½ tsp. salt. Add water and 1 Tbsp. ghee and mix to form a firm dough. Turn dough onto a floured surface and knead until pliable and smooth. Cover with a damp towel and allow to stand for 30 minutes.

Combine cabbage, carrot, and scallions in a large bowl and sprinkle with remaining salt. Toss cabbage mixture so that salt is evenly distributed. Allow to stand for 10 minutes, and then use a dry towel to squeeze extra water from cabbage mixture.

Combine tofu, cilantro, garlic, ginger, garam masala, turmeric, and chili powder in a small bowl. In a larger bowl, add tofu mixture to cabbage mixture and mix to combine.

Roll out dough onto a floured surface as thinly as possible. (It may help to divide the dough in half and to roll each half separately.) Use a large, round cookie cutter to cut circles from the dough. To assemble the momo, place 1 Tbsp. of filling in the center of each dough circle, pull edges of dough over filling, and pinch to close. Repeat until all of the dough and filling has been used.

Bring a large pot of water to a boil over high heat. Line a bamboo steamer with cabbage leaves and fill with as many momo as it will hold (they may touch, but they should not be too crowded; work in batches if necessary). Place steamer basket over boiling water and steam for 10-15 minutes or until slightly translucent. Serve immediately with chutney.

Per momo: 44 calories, 1 g fat, 1 g saturated fat, 160 mg sodium, 7 g carbohydrates, 1 g protein.

For tomato chutney:
2 large tomatoes
10 red Thai chilies
1 Tbsp. white vinegar
Water, for boiling
8 cloves garlic, peeled
1 tsp. fresh ginger, grated
½ tsp. salt
1 Tbsp. oil
½ c. hot water

Bring a small pot of water to a boil. Score the surface of the tomatoes with a sharp knife and add to pot along with chilies and vinegar. Boil for 10 minutes or until the tomatoes' skins begin to peel away. Remove tomatoes and chilies from water and allow to cool; peel off tomato skins.

In a blender or food processor, combine tomatoes, chilies, garlic, ginger, and salt, and puree until smooth.

Heat oil in a small skillet over medium heat. Add tomato puree and sauté, stirring constantly, until thickened. Add hot water and continue to cook until a sauce-like consistency is reached. Serve chutney warm or at room temperature.

Per serving: 8 calories, 1 g fat, 0 g saturated fat, 40 mg sodium, 1 g carbohydrates, 0 g protein.

VARIATIONS:

For a non-vegetarian version, replace cabbage and tofu with 1 lb. finely diced, cooked brisket, chicken, or (if available) yak meat.

TIMOR-LESTE BAKSO NOODLE SOUP

3 / 2 / 3
COOK TIME: 50 MINUTES
ACTIVE PREP TIME: 25 MINUTES
INACTIVE PREP TIME: 3 HOURS
MAKES 4 SERVINGS

BAKSO ARE ENJOYED THROUGHOUT SOUTHEAST ASIA. THESE INDONESIAN-style meatballs can be found everywhere from fine restaurants to street food carts. Bakso were introduced to the East Indies by the Dutch, who colonized the region in the nineteenth century. The options for this dish are endless, but this recipe uses beef meatballs and rice noodles.

For meatballs:
½ lb. ground beef, finely minced
3 cloves garlic, finely minced
Oil, for sautéing

½ c. all-purpose flour
¼ tsp. baking powder
½ tsp. salt
¼ tsp. ground black pepper
Water, for boiling

Heat oil in a small skillet over medium-high heat. Sauté garlic until fragrant, about 2-3 minutes. Combine sautéed garlic, meat, flour, baking powder, salt, and pepper. Chill mixture in refrigerator for 30 minutes.

Bring large pot of water to a boil. Form meat mixture into 1-inch balls. Reduce heat to medium and lower meatballs into water one by one with a slotted spoon. Meatballs are fully cooked when they begin to float on the water's surface.

For soup:
1-½ qt. beef broth (or water with 1 Tbsp. beef bouillon dissolved)
2 cloves garlic, crushed
1 stalk celery, chopped
1 small onion, chopped
½ tsp. sugar
½ tsp. ground black pepper
Salt, to taste
8 oz. vermicelli rice noodles
2 heads baby bok choy cabbage
Water, for boiling

Combine broth, garlic, celery, onion, sugar, and pepper in a large stockpot. Bring to a boil, reduce heat to medium, and simmer uncovered until reduced by one-third, about 15-20 minutes. Remove celery, onion, and garlic and discard.

In a separate pot, boil water and cook noodles according to package directions, about 3-4 minutes. Drain noodles, reserving water.

Return water used to boil noodles to pot and bring to a boil. Cook baby bok choy until just tender, about 1-2 minutes. (Leaves should remain a bright green color.) Remove bok choy from pot and coarsely chop.

To serve, divide noodles, bok choy, and meatballs between four bowls. Ladle an equal amount of broth into each bowl over noodles.

Per serving: 672 calories, 9 g fat, 2 g saturated fat, 1179 mg sodium, 116 g carbohydrates, 34 g protein.

VARIATIONS:

Chicken or fish may be used in place of beef. Add hard-boiled eggs, fried tofu, fried onions, scallions, celery, ginger, soy sauce, chili, or tomato sauce to soup.

VIETNAM
PHO

2 / 2 / 2
COOK TIME: 7 HOURS, 5 MINUTES
ACTIVE PREP TIME: 20 MINUTES
INACTIVE PREP TIME: 1 HOUR
MAKES 4 SERVINGS

ONE OF THE MOST QUINTESSENTIALLY ASIAN DISHES OF ALL, THE ORIGINS OF the Vietnamese noodle soup known as pho are somewhat surprising. The soup and its name are believed to be adaptations of the French pot-au-feu (p. 32), which was introduced to Vietnam by its colonizers in the late nineteenth century. Red meat is not traditionally eaten in Vietnam, but while pho can be made with chicken, pork, shrimp, or only vegetables, it is characterized by a rich and meaty beef broth.

1 lb. beef sirloin, very thinly sliced
5 lbs. beef soup bones
1 onion, halved
Water, for boiling and soaking
2 pods star anise
2 sticks cinnamon
2 Tbsp. whole black peppercorns
One medium-sized hand fresh ginger, peeled and sliced
2 Tbsp. fish sauce
1 Tbsp. salt
8 oz. dried rice noodles

3 green onions, sliced diagonally
½ c. fresh cilantro, chopped
Mung bean sprouts, for serving
Fresh basil leaves, for serving
Lime wedges, for serving
Hoisin sauce, for serving
Sriracha sauce, for serving
Sliced red jalapeno chilies, for serving

Preheat oven to 425 degrees. Place bones and onion halves on a baking sheet and roast for 1 hour or until bones are brown and onion is soft. Meanwhile, toast star anise, cinnamon, and peppercorns in a small, dry skillet until very fragrant.

Place bones and onion in a large stockpot and add enough water to cover. Add ginger, star anise, cinnamon, peppercorns, fish sauce, and salt. Bring to a boil, reduce heat to low, cover, and simmer for at least 6 hours, skimming fat from surface periodically. Remove bones and strain broth to remove solids.

Place rice noodles in a small bowl of water and allow to soak for 1 hour. Boil a small pot of water, add rice noodles, and cook for 1 minute. Drain noodles and divide among four large bowls.

Heat beef stock until warm. Add an equal amount of sirloin slices, green onions, and cilantro to each bowl. Ladle broth over noodles and meat and stir. Soup will be ready to eat when meat is warmed.

Serve with sprouts, basil leaves, lime wedges, hoisin sauce, Sriracha sauce, and jalapeno chilies.

Per serving: 299 calories, 8 g fat, 3 g saturated fat, 2530 mg sodium, 20 g carbohydrates, 36 g protein.

SERVING SUGGESTION:

Serve with a French baguette on the side.

OCEANIA

AUSTRALIA ROAST LAMB

SHEEP HAVE BEEN VERY IMPORTANT TO AUSTRALIA'S CULTURE AND ECONOMY ever since they were brought to the first European settlement in Australia in 1788. Today Australia is the world's largest producer of wool, and sheep outnumber humans by over 12 to 1. While native animals and plants such as kangaroo, emu, and bush berries dominate the traditional diet of the aboriginal people, no trip to modern Australia is complete without a meal of roast lamb or mutton.

1 leg of lamb (about 2 to 2-½ lbs.)
¼ c. olive oil
1 Tbsp. sea salt
6 cloves garlic, sliced
3-4 sprigs fresh rosemary
8 medium red potatoes, sliced
2 large sweet potatoes, sliced
2 onions, halved

Preheat the oven to 300 degrees. Arrange potatoes and onions on baking tray and drizzle with olive oil and salt. Place on bottom rack of oven and roast for 30 minutes.

Coat lamb in olive oil and sprinkle with salt. Make small incisions throughout surface of lamb using the point of a sharp knife and insert garlic slices and rosemary sprigs in holes. Place a meat thermometer in thickest part of lamb.

Place lamb in oven above vegetables. Roast for 1-½ hours or until meat thermometer registers 145 degrees for medium rare, 160 for medium, or 170 for well-done. Remove lamb from oven, transfer to a plate, and cover with aluminum foil. Allow to rest for 10 minutes before slicing.

Per serving: 777 calories, 25 g fat, 7 g saturated fat, 1117 mg sodium, 64 g car-

bohydrates, 74 g protein.

SERVING SUGGESTION:
Roast lamb is often served with mint sauce.

FIJI
KOKODA

1 / 2 / 3
ACTIVE PREP TIME: 15 MINUTES
INACTIVE PREP TIME: 2 HOURS
MAKES 4 SERVINGS

AS ONE WOULD EXPECT OF ANY ARCHIPELAGO COMPOSED OF OVER 300
islands and over two thousand miles from the mainland, fish is the primary staple of
the Melanesian nation of Fiji. While the Fijians are not the only people in the world
who eat their fish raw, they put a South Pacific spin on the citric acid preparation by
using miti, a condiment made from coconut milk, lemon or lime juice, tomato, and
chili. When preparing fish in this manner, it is important to use either "sashimi-
grade" fish or high-quality filets that have been flash-frozen at -4 degrees Fahrenheit
or below for at least one week before preparing.

1 lb. mahi mahi or red snapper filets, cut into small pieces
½ c. lemon juice
½ c. lime juice
1 c. coconut milk
1 small red onion, finely chopped
1 small green bell pepper, finely chopped
1 small English cucumber, peeled and finely chopped
2 Roma tomatoes, seeded and finely chopped
3 fresh red chilies, thinly sliced
2 Tbsp. fresh cilantro, finely chopped

Combine fish with lemon and lime juices in a nonreactive bowl. Make sure that
fish is completely submerged in juice. Cover with plastic wrap and refrigerate for at

least 2 hours or overnight. Remove from refrigerator when fish has become opaque.

Drain fish and combine with coconut milk. Add onion, bell pepper, cucumber, tomatoes, chilies, and cilantro and stir well. Serve cold.

Per serving: 321 calories, 16 g fat, 13 g saturated fat, 151 mg sodium, 17 g carbohydrates, 30 g protein.

SERVING SUGGESTIONS:

For a nice presentation, serve kokoda in coconut halves or wrapped in lettuce leaves.

VARIATIONS:

Kokoda can be prepared with any firm fish, such as tuna or mackerel, and with any vegetables. One option for serving is to allow guests to prepare their own kokoda with the ingredients of their choice.

KIRIBATI
TE BUA TORO NI BAUKIN

1 / 2 / 3
COOK TIME: 45 MINUTES
ACTIVE PREP TIME: 10 MINUTES
MAKES 4 SERVINGS

THE MICRONESIAN NATION OF KIRIBATI CONSISTS OF 33 ISLANDS, INCLUDING twelve that are uninhabited, and has the distinction of being the only country in the world to fall within all four hemispheres. Thousands of miles separate the I-Kiribati people from the continental world, yet many American food products have gained great followings. The canned meat product SPAM® was introduced to the Pacific world during World War II.

One 12-oz. can processed meat or cooked corned beef, cut into small cubes
1 small sugar pumpkin, peeled, seeded, and grated
1 medium green cabbage, shredded
1 c. all-purpose flour
¼ c. plus 2 Tbsp. powdered milk

2 Tbsp. lemon juice
1 tsp. baking powder
Salt and pepper, to taste
Butter, for coating pan

Preheat oven to 350 degrees. Place pumpkin in a paper towel and squeeze to remove any excess water. Combine with cabbage in a bowl. Add meat, flour, and baking powder and stir to combine. Season with lemon juice, salt, and pepper and spread mixture into a medium baking dish. Bake for 45 minutes or until brown.

Per serving: 742 calories, 28 g fat, 14 g saturated fat, 1931 mg sodium, 63 g carbohydrates, 66 g protein.

VARIATION:

One-half cup of dairy or soy milk may be used in place of the powdered milk in this recipe.

MARSHALL ISLANDS TAITUUJ

2 / 1 / 1
COOK TIME: 20 MINUTES
ACTIVE PREP TIME: 10 MINUTES
MAKES 4 SERVINGS

IN THE MARSHALL ISLANDS, THE EXPRESSION "KAN DIKDIK KAN IN IOKWE" ("LITTLE food with lots of love") indicates the importance of sharing food with strangers. Marshallese meals are shared by many family members and guests and are cooked over open fires. A dish such as taituuj (banana pancakes), which may seem like an indulgent breakfast or dessert to an American, would be eaten as a main course at a Marshallese dinner.

1 c. all-purpose flour
1 Tbsp. white sugar
2 tsp. baking powder

¼ tsp. salt
1 egg, beaten
1 c. whole milk
2 Tbsp. oil, plus more for frying
2 ripe bananas, mashed
½ tsp. vanilla extract

In one bowl, combine flour, sugar, baking powder, and salt and sift all ingredients together. In another, combine egg, milk, oil, bananas, and vanilla and stir vigorously. Slowly add flour mixture to egg mixture, stirring to combine.

Heat oil in a large non-stick skillet. In ¼-cup measures, spoon batter onto skillet. Cook for 30 seconds on each side until golden brown.

Per serving: 294 calories, 10 g fat, 3 g saturated fat, 191 mg sodium, 44 g carbohydrates, 7 g protein.

For macadamia syrup:
1 c. macadamia nuts, plus more for serving
1 Tbsp. butter
2 Tbsp. all-purpose flour
1 c. whole milk
1 c. light cream
3 Tbsp. honey
2 tsp. vanilla extract

Place nuts in a blender or food processor and pulse until finely ground. Toast ground nuts in a dry skillet over high heat for about 5 minutes or until lightly brown. Remove from pan.

Add butter to pan and reduce temperature to medium-low. When butter has melted, add flour and cook for 1 minute, whisking constantly, until a thick sauce forms and butter has begun to brown. While still whisking, add milk and cream to pan, followed by honey and vanilla extract. Continue to cook for 5 minutes longer. Pour sauce over pancakes and dust with macadamia nuts before serving.

Per serving: 458 calories, 40 g fat, 13 g saturated fat, 58 mg sodium, 25 g carbohydrates, 6 g protein.

SERVING SUGGESTIONS:

If serving as a dessert, add a scoop of vanilla ice cream. These pancakes are also very good American-style, with maple syrup.

MICRONESIA SUNDAY SOUP

1 / 1 / 2
COOK TIME: 10 MINUTES
ACTIVE PREP TIME: 20 MINUTES
INACTIVE PREP TIME: 30 MINUTES
MAKES 6 SERVINGS

IN THE WESTERN PACIFIC OCEAN, THE FEDERATED STATES OF MICRONESIA covers an area the size of Argentina, but only 270 square miles is above water. Kosrae, the second-largest of its 607 islands, is well-known for its soup, which is traditionally eaten on Sundays after attending church services. Kosraean cooks typically prepare the creamy porridge-like dish on Saturday evening, as cooking and other laborious tasks are eschewed on Sundays.

One large yellowfin tuna filet (about 1 lb.), skin removed
2 qt. water
3 Tbsp. fish stock base
1 onion, finely chopped
1 small carrot, finely chopped
1 c. short-grain white rice
¾ c. full-fat coconut milk
1 tsp. salt
Chopped parsley, for garnish

Bring water to a boil in a medium-sized stockpot or large saucepan over high heat. Add tuna filet and cook for 2 minutes or until mostly done and remove from pot. Break tuna filet into small pieces and set aside.

Add fish stock base to pot and stir until dissolved. Reduce heat to low and add tuna, onion, carrot, and rice to pot. Cover and simmer for 30 minutes.

Slowly stir coconut milk into soup. Remove from heat and add salt, stirring to dissolve. Garnish soup with parsley and serve.

Per serving: 320 calories, 10 g fat, 7 g saturated fat, 789 mg sodium, 28 g carbohydrates, 28 g protein.

VARIATION:

Other types of seafood, such as crab, can be used in place of yellowfin tuna.

TIP:

Many Micronesian cooks prefer to use bone-in fish rather than filets, which add extra flavor to the broth. If using fish with bones, be careful to strain any large pieces from broth before serving.

NAURU COCONUT-CRUSTED FISH

2 / 1 / 1
COOK TIME: 10 MINUTES
ACTIVE PREP TIME: 20 MINUTES
INACTIVE PREP TIME: 30 MINUTES
MAKES 6 SERVINGS

NAURU HAS EVEN LESS ARABLE LAND THAN MOST SMALL PACIFIC ISLANDS, largely owing to environmental devastation caused by decades of phosphate mining. Accordingly, its people import most of the food they eat, and canned and refined foods are the most popular. But two fresh ingredients are still plentiful in Nauru: fish and coconuts.

6 tilapia or mahi-mahi filets
2 Tbsp. lime juice
1 fresh coconut
½ c. panko bread crumbs
Salt and pepper, to taste

1 egg, beaten
Oil, for frying
Lime wedges, for serving

Coat fish filets with lime juice and allow to marinate for 30 minutes.

Use a screwdriver to make three holes in the coconut's shell. Drain liquid and reserve for another use. With a hammer, tap the coconut around its circumference until it cracks in half. Scrape the inside of the coconut and grate flesh until you have ½ c. of fresh coconut.

Combine coconut and bread crumbs. Season fish filets with salt and pepper and dredge each filet first in egg, and then in coconut mixture.

Heat oil in a heavy skillet over medium-high heat. Fry fish filets for about 3 minutes on each side or until completely cooked and golden brown. Serve fish with lime wedges.

Per serving: 873 calories, 49 g fat, 25 g saturated fat, 321 mg sodium, 17 g carbohydrates, 94 g protein.

SERVING SUGGESTION:

Serve with French fries.

VARIATION:

One-half cup of pre-shredded, unsweetened coconut can be used in place of fresh coconut.

NEW ZEALAND MEAT PIE

3 / 1 / 1
COOK TIME: 1 HOUR, 45 MINUTES
ACTIVE PREP TIME: 45 MINUTES
INACTIVE PREP TIME: 2 HOURS
MAKES 12 PIES

EVER SINCE THE MEAT PIE WAS INTRODUCED TO THE MAORI PEOPLE BY BRITISH settlers in the nineteenth century, it has been an integral part of the New Zealand diet. Today, the popular handheld snack food can be purchased at bakeries, rugby matches, convenience stores, and even fast food restaurants. While the average New Zealand meat pie is far from a delicacy, this recipe is truly indulgent–and worth the effort.

1-¾ lb. ground beef, divided
½ lb. bacon, chopped
2 onions, chopped, divided
7 cloves garlic, chopped, divided
2 Tbsp. fresh thyme
3 bay leaves
1 tsp. black peppercorns
Oil, for sautéing
¼ c. brandy
¼ c. Worcestershire sauce
1-½ qt. chicken stock, divided
1-½ tsp. sea salt
3 Tbsp. cornstarch
2 Tbsp. water
Puff pastry (recipe below)
½ c. Cheddar cheese, coarsely grated
1 egg, beaten

Heat oil in a large stockpot over medium-high heat. Add ¾ lb. beef and bacon and cook for 8-10 minutes or until very brown and crispy, stirring frequently and scraping bottom of pan. Reduce heat to medium and add 1 onion, 5 cloves garlic, thyme, bay leaves, and peppercorns and cook until onion is translucent, about 5-6 minutes.

Add brandy and Worcestershire sauce and continue to cook over medium heat for about 5 minutes or until most of the liquid has evaporated. Add 1 c. of chicken stock and cook for 10 minutes until stock has almost evaporated. Repeat with another 1 c. of chicken stock.

Add remaining 4 c. of chicken stock to pot, reduce heat to low, and simmer for about 45 minutes. Strain stock and transfer to saucepan. Simmer over medium heat until all but about 1-¼ c. of stock has evaporated, about 10 more minutes.

In a large, heavy skillet or Dutch oven, heat oil over medium-high heat. Brown remaining 1 lb. of beef for about 8 minutes or until fully cooked. Remove meat from pan and drain, reserving a small amount of fat.

Heat reserved fat in the same pan. Add remaining onion and 2 cloves garlic and sauté until onion is translucent, about 5 minutes. Add stock, cooked beef, and sea salt and raise heat to bring to a boil.

In a small bowl, combine cornstarch and water to make a thin slurry. Add to pan and whisk together until sauce thickens, about 3-4 minutes. Remove from heat and allow to cool.

Preheat oven to 350 degrees. Roll out pastry and use a round cookie cutter or knife to make 24 equal circles, each about 3-4 inches wide. Press 12 of the dough circles into the cups of a 12-cup muffin tin and divide half of the Cheddar cheese between the 12 cups. Spoon beef mixture in the cups (you may not need it all) and top with remaining cheese.

Place the 12 remaining dough circles on top of the filled cups and press the edges to seal with a fork. Brush tops of pies with egg and bake for 25-30 minutes or until golden.

For puff pastry:
3-¾ c. all-purpose flour
1-¼ c. cold water
1 tsp. salt
2 c. butter

Mix flour, water, and salt using a pastry blender or food processor until a ball is formed.

Place butter between two pieces of plastic wrap and use a rolling pin to flatten to a 1-inch thick square. Roll dough into a square about 1 inch wider than the square of butter on each side. Place the butter square on top of dough (at a 45-degree angle) and fold corners over butter. Roll dough into a rectangle about 2 feet long and fold into thirds. Roll out again to same length and fold into thirds once more.

Place dough in refrigerator and chill for 30 minutes. Remove from refrigerator and roll out dough once again. Fold and chill for 30 more minutes, and then roll out one more time. Chill for a least 1 hour before using.

Per pie: 702 calories, 46 g fat, 25 g saturated fat, 1096 mg sodium, 35 g carbo-hydrates, 34 g protein.

VARIATIONS:

Lamb or chicken may be used in place of beef. Potatoes, carrots, or any other vegetables may be added or used in place of meat.

TIP:

Pre-made puff pastry can be used in this recipe.

PALAU
UKOY

2 / 2 / 3
COOK TIME: 25 MINUTES
ACTIVE PREP TIME: 15 MINUTES
MAKES 12 UKOY

PALAU LIES ABOUT 400 MILES EAST OF THE PHILIPPINES, ITS CLOSEST

neighbor and the homeland of its first residents. Ever since the earliest settlers arrived in Palau from the Philippines three thousand years ago, Filipino culture has impacted the Pacific archipelago nation. Many of Palau's most popular dishes, such as the shrimp and vegetable fritters known as ukoy, originated in the Philippines.

1 lb. small to medium shrimp, peeled and deveined
1-½ c. water
1 c. cornstarch
1 c. all-purpose flour
1 Tbsp. baking powder
2 tsp. salt
2 tsp. fish sauce
1 tsp. annatto powder (optional; mainly for color)

5 c. mung bean sprouts
2 c. firm tofu, drained and cubed
4 green onions, sliced diagonally
Oil, for frying

Combine water, cornstarch, flour, baking powder, salt, fish sauce, and annatto powder (if using) and mix until smooth. Gradually stir in shrimp, bean sprouts, tofu, and green onions.

Heat oil to a depth of ½-inch in a large frying pan. Divide mixture into 12 portions and fry three at a time for 3 minutes on each side until brown and crispy. Drain on paper towels.

Per ukoy: 251 calories, 12 g fat, 2 g saturated fat, 563 mg sodium, 23 g carbohydrates, 16 g protein.

SERVING SUGGESTION:

Serve with garlic dipping sauce: Combine ½ c. white vinegar with 2 or more cloves minced garlic and season generously with salt and pepper.

VARIATION:

Use grated carrots or sweet potatoes in place of some or all of the bean sprouts.

PAPUA NEW GUINEA MUMU

1 / 1 / 3
COOK TIME: 6 HOURS
ACTIVE PREP TIME: 10 MINUTES
MAKES 6 SERVINGS

A COUNTRY WHERE OVER 80 PERCENT OF THE POPULATION IS RURAL AND largely relies on subsistence agriculture, Papua New Guinea is one place where globalization has had a very minimal impact. Most common ingredients are native to the island, including pork, leafy greens, pineapple, coconut, taro, kaukau, and yams. Traditionally, the layered dish mumu is prepared in an earth oven in which heated stones are arranged around the pot in which it is prepared.

1-½ lb. pork loin, fat trimmed and sliced
Oil, for coating dish
1 lb. sweet potatoes, sliced
¾ lb. pineapple, peeled and chopped
¾ lb. spinach, stems removed
1 onion, sliced
2 cloves garlic, chopped
One 15-oz. can coconut milk

Coat the inside of a heavy metal casserole dish or Dutch oven with oil. Line with spinach leaves. Arrange sweet potatoes in a layer at bottom. Top with a layer of pork, followed by a layer of pineapple and a layer of onion and garlic. Pour coconut milk over the top and cover with one more layer of spinach leaves.

Place pot on stove and cook over medium heat for 15 minutes. Reduce heat to low and cook 45 minutes longer. Do not remove lid or stir at any point.

Preheat oven to 275 degrees. Place pot in oven and cook slowly for 5 hours. Serve immediately; make sure that pork is completely cooked before serving.

Per serving: 402 calories, 19 g fat, 8 g saturated fat, 108 mg sodium, 33 g carbohydrates, 24 g protein.

VARIATIONS:

Use chicken in place of pork in this recipe. Use fruits and vegetables such as mango, papaya, banana, carrots, parsnips, kale, cabbage, broccoli, or green beans in place of some or all of the sweet potatoes, pineapple, and spinach.

SAMOA
TAISI MOA

1 / 1 / 2
COOK TIME: 1 HOUR
ACTIVE PREP TIME: 15 MINUTES
INACTIVE PREP TIME: 30 MINUTES
MAKES 4 SERVINGS

SAMOAN FOOD IS CHARACTERIZED BY ITS FRESHNESS. MOST SAMOAN families still cook their food the traditional way, using a umu (an outdoor oven covered in hot stones). Poultry, fish, and fresh fruits are wrapped in banana leaves, often along with coconut cream, and cooked over the umu's stones. Taisi moa would be prepared this way in Samoa, but this recipe uses aluminum foil and a conventional oven instead.

4 bone-in chicken breasts or leg quarters
One 15-oz. can full-fat coconut milk
One 2-inch piece fresh ginger, peeled and minced
2 tsp. soy sauce
2 tsp. tomato paste
1 Tbsp. molasses
1-½ tsp. apple cider vinegar
1 tsp. garlic powder
½ tsp. liquid smoke
4 plantains, peeled and sliced
2 large sweet potatoes, peeled and sliced

Whisk together coconut milk, ginger, molasses, soy sauce, tomato paste, apple cider vinegar, garlic powder, and liquid smoke. Place chicken, plantains, and sweet potatoes in a shallow dish and pour coconut milk mixture on top. Cover with plastic wrap and marinate in refrigerator for 30 minutes.

Preheat oven to 350 degrees. Place one piece of chicken and an equal amount of plantain and sweet potato on each of four squares of aluminum foil and spoon remaining marinade over contents. Fold foil and seal edges to form a packet. Set packets on a baking sheet and cook for 1 hour or until chicken is completely cooked and plantains and sweet potatoes are tender.

Per serving: 599 calories, 11 g fat, 7 g saturated fat, 269 mg sodium, 84 g carbo-hydrates, 45 g protein.

VARIATIONS:

Banana leaves may be used in place of foil to make packets, which can also be cooked over an open grill. Add a dash of cayenne pepper to marinade for extra heat.

SOLOMON ISLANDS FISH CURRY WITH TOMATOES AND SWEET POTATO PUREE

2 / 2 / 2
COOK TIME: 30 MINUTES
ACTIVE PREP TIME: 15 MINUTES
MAKES 4 SERVINGS

A CHAIN OF HUNDREDS OF ISLANDS JUST EAST OF PAPUA NEW GUINEA, THE Solomon Islands are probably best known for their role in the Pacific Theater during World War II. But these islands are home to over five thousand years of history, as well as many cultures that have left their mark on the people and their food. Native ingredients, and especially fish, still remain the cornerstone of the Solomon Islands' cuisine.

4 medium-sized red snapper or yellowfin filets
1 Tbsp. coconut oil
1 Tbsp. sesame oil
1 small onion, finely chopped
4 tomatoes, peeled, seeded, and chopped
3 Tbsp. yellow curry powder

1 lime, sliced

Heat oils in a large skillet over medium-high heat. Add onion and sauté until soft, about 3 minutes. Add tomatoes and curry powder and cook for 3 minutes longer.

Add fish filets to skillet. Reduce heat to medium and cook for 2-3 minutes on each side or until fish flakes with a fork.

Per serving: 311 calories, 10 g fat, 4 g saturated fat, 104 mg sodium, 8 g carbohydrates, 46 g protein.

For sweet potato puree:
2 lbs. sweet potatoes, peeled and cut into chunks
1 tsp. salt
Water, for boiling
¾ c. plain Greek-style yogurt
½ c. whole milk
Juice of 1 lime
Sliced scallions, for serving

Bring a large pot of water to a boil. Add sweet potato and salt and cook for 15-20 minutes or until sweet potatoes are tender. Drain and allow to cool.

Place sweet potato in a blender with yogurt, milk, and lime juice and process until smooth. Garnish puree with scallions and serve curry with lime slices.

Per serving: 514 calories, 7 g fat, 5 g saturated fat, 713 mg sodium, 77 g carbohydrates, 35 g protein.

VARIATION:

Any type of fish can be used for this recipe.

TIP:

While a blend of coconut and sesame oils give this dish a distinctive flavor, regular vegetable or olive oil can be used as well.

TONGA
'OTA 'IKA

FOOD IS OF GREAT IMPORTANCE TO THE PEOPLE OF TONGA, WHO UNTIL recently practiced a feudal-like system in which farmers were allowed to pay taxes to the king with bananas, coconuts, and yams. 'Ota 'ika, one of many Polynesian dishes that incorporate raw seafood, and its coconut milk broth should be eaten as a soup.

1 lb. sashimi-grade lump crab or lobster meat, uncooked
Juice of 2 lemons
Juice of 2 limes
5 scallions, chopped
4 tomatoes, peeled, seeded, and chopped
2 mild red chilies (preferably Hawaiian peppers), chopped
1 English cucumber, peeled and chopped
1 green bell pepper, seeded and chopped
2 c. coconut milk
¼ c. fresh cilantro, finely chopped

Place crab or lobster meat in lemon and lime juice and marinate until meat becomes opaque, about 15 minutes. Drain meat from juice.

Combine meat with scallions, tomatoes, chilies, cucumber, and bell pepper. Stir in coconut milk and chill for at least 2 hours. Serve topped with cilantro.

Per serving: 427 calories, 30 g fat, 26 g saturated fat, 581 mg sodium, 18 g carbohydrates, 27 g protein.

SERVING SUGGESTIONS:
Serve with taro, yams, or sweet potatoes.

VARIATIONS:
Use sashimi-grade fish, mussels, or shrimp in place of crab or lobster.

TUVALU COCONUT FISH WITH TARO

2 / 3 / 3
COOK TIME: 50 MINUTES
ACTIVE PREP TIME: 15 MINUTES
MAKES 4 SERVINGS

AS IS TRUE WITH MOST PACIFIC ISLANDS, TUVALU'S CUISINE LEANS heavily on local ingredients such as coconut, fresh fish, and a starchy tuber called pulaku. Pulaku is similar to taro, which is easier to find in the United States and to cook. If taro cannot be found, large white potatoes can be used in their place in this dish.

1 lb. tuna or mahi mahi filets, cut into large pieces
1-½ lb. taro roots
One 15-oz. can coconut cream
½ c. water, plus more for boiling
1 onion, chopped
2 Tbsp. butter, divided
1 c. taro leaves, chopped

Bring a large pot of water to a boil over high heat. Boil taro roots until fork-tender but not mushy, about 15-20 minutes. Remove from water and allow to cool before peeling and slicing.

Heat 1 Tbsp. butter in a heavy skillet over medium-high heat. Sauté onion until softened and browned, about 4 minutes. Add coconut cream and water to skillet and stir until smooth and heated throughout.

Heat remaining 1 Tbsp. butter in a separate skillet over medium-high heat. Add fish and cook until seared on both sides, about 2-3 minutes per side. Add fish to coconut milk mixture, reduce heat to medium-low, and cook gently for 5 minutes longer, stirring occasionally.

Add taro leaves and sliced taro. Continue to cook until taro leaves are wilted, about 5-10 minutes longer. Serve immediately.

Per serving: 928 calories, 39 g fat, 29 g saturated fat, 256 mg sodium, 113 g carbohydrates, 35 g protein.

VARIATIONS:

Use swiss chard or beet greens in place of taro leaves. Shrimp or tofu can be substituted for fish in this recipe.

VANUATU CHICKEN AND PUMPKIN SOUP

2 / 2 / 2
COOK TIME: 1 HOUR, 35 MINUTES
ACTIVE PREP TIME: 15 MINUTES
MAKES 4-6 SERVINGS

THE PEOPLE OF VANUATU, A MELANESIAN ISLAND NATION EAST OF AUSTRALIA and north of New Zealand, have more contact with the mainland than those of many other Pacific islands. But when it comes to food they tend to prefer local; the majority still grow most of their own food in their gardens. Native foods such as chicken, pumpkin, and coconut products form the backbone of Vanuatuan cuisine.

1 lb. chicken breast, cut into small pieces
One 2-lb. sugar pumpkin
1 small onion, chopped
Oil, for sautéing
2 c. chicken broth or water
1 Tbsp. plus 1-½ tsp. lemon juice
½ tsp. salt
1 tomato, peeled and chopped
1 small green chili, finely chopped
½ c. coconut cream

Preheat oven to 325 degrees. Halve pumpkin, remove seeds, and wrap cut sides in foil. Bake for 1 hour with foil sides facing up. Remove pumpkin flesh with a large spoon and puree in blender or food processor until smooth. Set aside.

Heat oil in a medium stockpot over medium-high heat. Add onion and sauté until translucent, about 5 minutes. Add chicken pieces and cook for 10 minutes longer. Add broth or water, lemon juice, and salt to pot. Cover, reduce heat to medium-low, and simmer for 15 minutes. Add pumpkin, tomato, and green chili and cook for 5 minutes longer. Stir in coconut cream, remove from heat, and serve.

Per serving: 519 calories, 38 g fat, 27 g saturated fat, 614 mg sodium, 21 g carbohydrates, 26 g protein.

TIP:

One 15-oz. can of pumpkin puree (not pumpkin pie filling) can be used in place of fresh roasted pumpkin.

THE AMERICAS

ANTIGUA AND BARBUDA FUNGEE AND PEPPERPOT

2 / 1 / 2
COOK TIME: 2 HOURS, 15 MINUTES
ACTIVE PREP TIME: 10 MINUTES
MAKES 6-8 SERVINGS

PEPPERPOT, A DISH ORIGINATING WITH THE NATIVE PEOPLE OF GUYANA, is ubiquitous throughout the Caribbean. In Antigua and Barbuda, pepperpot is distinguished by its inclusion of spinach. Antiguans and Barbudians serve pepperpot with fungee, a cornmeal porridge containing okra.

1 lb. corned beef brisket, cut into 1-inch pieces

1 smoked ham hock

2 qt. water

Vegetable oil, for sautéing

4 scallions, minced

3 garlic cloves, minced

1 large onion, chopped

1 habanero pepper, minced

One 15-oz. can whole tomatoes, drained

¼ c. tomato paste

1 tsp. dried chives

½ tsp. dried thyme

1 medium eggplant, chopped

1 lb. summer squash or zucchini, chopped

1 medium sweet potato, chopped

One 15-oz. can black-eyed peas, drained and rinsed

4 oz. fresh spinach

In a large pot, bring corned beef brisket, ham hock, and water to a boil. Cook for 1-½ hours or until tender. Drain the meat, reserving liquid, and remove meat from ham hock.

Heat vegetable oil in another large pot over medium-high heat. Add scallions, garlic, onion, and habanero pepper. Sauté until the onion is translucent, about 5 minutes. Stir in tomatoes, tomato paste, chives, and thyme. Bring to a boil, reduce heat to low, and simmer for 10 minutes.

Stir in eggplant, squash, and potato, and cook for 5 minutes longer, stirring frequently. Add the meat and reserved liquid. Simmer for 20 minutes or until vegetables are tender. Stir in black-eyed peas and spinach, and cook until the spinach is wilted, about 5 minutes. Season with salt and pepper and serve with fungee.

Per serving: 348 calories, 18 g fat, 7 g saturated fat, 722 mg sodium, 22 g carbohydrates, 29 g protein.

For fungee:
2 c. corn meal
1 qt. water, divided
6 small okras, thinly sliced
1 tsp. salt
Salt and pepper, to taste

Combine corn meal with 2 c. water, stir, and set aside. Bring water to a boil. Add okra and salt and continue to boil until okra is cooked, about 5 minutes.

Add wet cornmeal to boiling water. Reduce heat to low and stir constantly until the mixture is stiff and cake-like, about 5 minutes. Serve immediately.

Per serving: 140 calories, 1 g fat, 0 g saturated fat, 334 mg sodium, 31 g carbohydrates, 4 g protein.

ARGENTINA EMPANADAS

3 / 1 / 1
COOK TIME: 45 MINUTES
ACTIVE PREP TIME: 35 MINUTES
INACTIVE PREP TIME: 1 HOUR
MAKES 24 EMPANADAS

THE EMPANADA WAS FIRST CREATED IN SPAIN. BUT NOWHERE ARE THEY more integral to the culture of cuisine than in Argentina, where every province boasts its own varieties of the stuffed, fried pastry. The northern Argentine town of Famaillá even hosts an annual National Empanada Festival every September. While beef is the most common filling, many others are popular as well, and patterns are often added to the pastry seam after folding to indicate the type. The recipe included here reflects one of many variations, known in Argentina as empanadas mendocinos.

For dough:
2-¼ c. all-purpose flour, plus more for flouring surface
1-½ tsp. salt
½ c. unsalted butter, cold, cut into small pieces
1 egg
⅓ c. ice water
1 tsp. distilled white vinegar

For filling:
½ lb. lean ground beef
Olive oil, for sautéing
1 small red bell pepper, seeded and diced
1 small onion, minced
1 egg, hard-boiled, chopped
8 oz. canned tomatoes
1 Tbsp. capers
1 Tbsp. paprika
1 Tbsp. ground cumin
1 Tbsp. fresh parsley, finely chopped
1 egg, beaten, for brushing
Salt and pepper, to taste

Begin the dough by blending together flour, salt, and butter. Mix egg, water, and vinegar in a separate bowl, and then stir into the dry ingredients. With floured hands, knead the dough into a flat ball. Wrap the dough in plastic wrap and refrigerate for 1 hour.

Heat olive oil in a heavy skillet over medium-high heat. Sauté onion and pepper until tender, about 5 minutes. Add tomatoes and simmer for 3 minutes longer. Add the beef to the pan along with the capers, paprika, cumin, and parsley and season with salt and pepper. Cook until beef is browned, about 5-7 minutes. Stir in the hard-boiled egg and reduce heat to low.

Preheat oven to 400 degrees. Remove dough from refrigerator and roll to a ¼-inch thickness on a floured surface. Cut dough into 4-inch circles. Place 2 Tbsp. filling in the center of each circle, fold in half, and pinch edges to close. Place empanadas on a baking sheet and brush with beaten egg. Bake empanadas in the oven for 25 minutes, or until browned.

Per empanada: 115 calories, 6 g fat, 3 g saturated fat, 151 mg sodium, 10 g carbohydrates, 5 g protein.

VARIATIONS:

A few variations include mushroom empanadas, with portobello mushrooms, shallots, balsamic vinegar, raisins, and fontina cheese; choriqueso empanadas, with chorizo sausage and cheese; turkey empanadas, with ground turkey, onions, garlic, peppers, tomatoes, cumin, and oregano; and cheese and poblano empanadas, with roasted poblano peppers, queso fresco, Oaxaca, and goat cheese. Dessert empanadas can be made with fruit, caramel, or dulce de leche fillings and chocolate or gingerbread dough.

TIP:

Uncooked empanadas can be stored in the freezer for future use. After filling and closing empanadas, place in freezer bags before freezing. When ready to eat, thaw in refrigerator, brush with egg, and bake as directed.

THE BAHAMAS
CONCH CHOWDER

1 / 3 / 3
COOK TIME: 2 HOURS, 40 MINUTES
ACTIVE PREP TIME: 10 MINUTES
MAKES 8 SERVINGS

MANY AMERICANS VISITING THE BAHAMAS ARE SOMEWHAT SURPRISED TO see the influence of the American South on its cuisine, as apparent in the prevalence of cooked peas, fried fish, and the use of ham and bacon for seasoning. However, it is not surprising at all that local seafood is its cornerstone, especially the island's most distinctive staple, conch. In the Bahamas, conch is served fried, grilled, raw, or stewed, as it is in this island chowder.

1 lb. conch meat, diced

6 oz. ham or bacon, cut into cubes

2 qt. water

2 Tbsp. butter

2 onions, chopped

1 green bell pepper, chopped

2 stalks celery, sliced

One 15-oz. can stewed tomatoes

One 6-oz. can tomato paste

6 large potatoes, peeled and chopped

2 carrots, sliced

2 bay leaves

2 Tbsp. fresh thyme

Salt and pepper, to taste

Hot sauce, for serving

Chopped fresh parsley, for serving

Place ham or bacon in a pot with water and bring to a boil. Add conch meat, reduce heat to low, cover, and simmer for 2 hours.

Melt butter in a large saucepan over medium heat. Add onion, green pepper, and celery and sauté for 5 minutes or until lightly browned. Add tomatoes and tomato paste and continue to cook for 2-3 minutes.

Add vegetable and tomato mixture to pot along with potatoes, carrots, bay leaves, and thyme. Simmer until potatoes are fully cooked, about 30 minutes. Season with salt and pepper. Serve with hot sauce and garnish with chopped parsley.

Per serving: 352 calories, 5 g fat, 3 g saturated fat, 645 mg sodium, 58 g carbohydrates, 20 g protein.

BARBADOS COU-COU AND FLYING FISH

3 / 3 / 3
COOK TIME: 2 HOURS, 10 MINUTES
ACTIVE PREP TIME: 10 MINUTES
INACTIVE PREP TIME: 1 HOUR, 10 MINUTES
MAKES 6-8 SERVINGS

BARBADOS IS SOMETIMES CALLED "THE LAND OF THE FLYING FISH." THESE wide-finned fish are seen gliding across the surface of the warm waters surrounding the island and are eaten fried, steamed, or in sandwiches (which the Bajans call "cutters"). A national symbol, the flying fish has a prominent place not only in Barbados's official dish, but also on its one-dollar coin.

For cou-cou:
2 c. finely ground cornmeal
1-½ qt. water, divided
1 Tbsp. oil
1 small onion, finely chopped
1 red bell pepper, finely chopped
3 cloves garlic, minced
1 tsp. dried thyme
1 c. okra, thinly sliced

1 Tbsp. butter, plus more for greasing bowl
1 tsp. salt

Soak the cornmeal in 2 c. of the water. In the meantime, heat oil in a large pot over medium-high heat. Sauté onion, bell pepper, garlic, and thyme until onion is translucent, about 5 minutes. Add okra and sauté 1 minute longer. Add the remaining 4 c. of water to the pot and bring to a boil. Allow to boil for 10 minutes. Remove 2 c. of water from the pot and set aside.

Add cornmeal, butter, and salt to the pot and reduce heat to low and stir with a whisk. Simmer for 1 ½ hours or until cornmeal is completely cooked. When cornmeal begins to become dry, add reserved water, stir well, and remove from heat. Transfer cornmeal to a greased bowl, allow to cool slightly, and invert onto a flat plate. Serve cou-cou with flying fish and sauce.

Per serving: 175 calories, 5 g fat, 2 g saturated fat, 359 mg sodium, 31 g carbohydrates, 4 g protein.

For flying fish:
8 flying fish filets
Juice of 3 limes
1 Tbsp. sea salt
3 Tbsp. Bajan (or green) seasoning
Butter, for sautéing
6 cloves garlic, minced
1 large onion, diced
1 green bell pepper, diced
1 large tomato, peeled, seeded, and chopped
1 Tbsp. fresh parsley, finely chopped
2 c. fish broth or water
1 dash hot sauce

Combine lime juice and salt in a shallow dish. Add flying fish filets and marinate for at least 10 minutes. Rinse the fish, coat with Bajan seasoning, and continue to marinate for at least 1 hour.

Heat butter in a heavy skillet. Sauté the garlic, onion, and bell pepper in butter until onion is translucent and pepper is soft, about 5 minutes. Add tomato and parsley to the pan and cook for 2 minutes longer. Add broth or water and hot sauce to the pan, raise heat to high, and bring just to a boil. Add flying fish filets to the pan. Reduce heat to medium-low, cover, and simmer for 10 minutes or until fish is fully cooked. Reserve sauce from pan for serving.

Per serving: 293 calories, 6 g fat, 3 g saturated fat, 251 mg sodium, 7 g carbohydrates, 52 g protein.

VARIATIONS:

Tilapia, mahi mahi, and cod are all acceptable substitutes for flying fish. You will need about 1-½ lb. of fish for this recipe.

TIP:

If you cannot find pre-made Bajan seasoning, also called green seasoning, you can make your own: Combine 1 medium chopped white onion, 3 cloves garlic, and 1 habanero pepper in a food processor and process until coarse. Then, process ½ c. of white wine vinegar with 1 Tbsp. each of fresh thyme, parsley, and marjoram. Blend onion mixture with vinegar mixture and add 1-½ tsp. of Worcestershire sauce, 1 Tbsp. salt, and a dash each of ground cloves and pepper. Bajan seasoning is best refrigerated for one week before using.

BELIZE BOIL-UP

2 / 1 / 2
COOK TIME: 45 MINUTES
ACTIVE PREP TIME: 20 MINUTES
MAKES 4 SERVINGS

THE ONLY FORMER BRITISH COLONY IN CENTRAL AMERICA, BELIZE HAS ONE of the most ethnically diverse populations of any Western Hemisphere country. Kriols, the descendants of Belize's indigenous people and the enslaved Africans brought to the colony, make up about one-quarter of Belize's population. Boil-Up (or "bile up") is a dish specific to this ethnic group.

2 lbs. red snapper filets

2 oz. salt pork, diced

2-¼ c. water, plus more for boiling

4 green bananas or plantains, cut into large pieces

1 large sweet potato, cut into large pieces

1 large white potato, cut into large pieces

1 c. self-rising flour

½ c. evaporated milk

1 Tbsp. butter

1 small onion, sliced

1 tomato, peeled, seeded, and chopped

1 small sweet pepper, minced

1 Tbsp. tomato paste

2 tsp. sugar

4 eggs, hard-boiled and cut into quarters

Boil salt pork and 2 c. of water in a large saucepan. Place a steamer basket in saucepan and add bananas, sweet potato, and white potato to basket. Reduce heat to medium-low, cover, and simmer for 15-20 minutes or until all vegetables are fully cooked, adding more water to pan if necessary. Remove vegetables from basket and add red snapper fillets. Steam fish for 10-15 minutes or until fully cooked, adding more water to pan if necessary.

Bring a separate pot of water to a boil. Combine flour, evaporated milk, and remaining ¼ c. water to make a dough. Drop dough in water 1 large spoonful at a time and boil until dumplings are fully cooked, about 3-4 minutes. Remove from water with a slotted spoon and set aside.

Melt butter in a small saucepan over medium-high heat. Add onion, tomato, and sweet pepper and sauté until onion is translucent, about 5 minutes. Add tomato sauce and sugar, reduce heat to medium-low, and cook until smooth, about 2-3 minutes. To serve, divide fish, eggs, and vegetables between four plates and pour sauce on top.

Per serving: 754 calories, 22 g fat, 8 g saturated fat, 147 mg sodium, 80 g carbohydrates, 59 g protein.

VARIATIONS:

Boil-Up is a very adaptable, use-what-you-like recipe. Vegetables such as cabbage, yam, cassava, carrots, celery, and tomato can be used in place of or in addition to the bananas and potatoes. It can also be eaten without sauce if desired.

BOLIVIA
AJÍ DE CARNE

1 / 2 / 2
COOK TIME: 1 HOUR, 35 MINUTES
ACTIVE PREP TIME: 10 MINUTES
MAKES 8 SERVINGS

THE AJÍ PEPPER IS NATIVE TO WEST-CENTRAL SOUTH AMERICA, WHERE IT is a staple in many local cuisines. Unlike in other countries, in Bolivia *ají* is usually used in powdered rather than fresh form. A heavy meal such as ají de carne would be most likely served at lunch, the main meal of the day in Bolivian culture.

1 lb. boneless pork loin, cut into small cubes
Olive oil, for sautéing
4-6 green onions (white parts only), finely chopped
1 large sweet onion (such as Vidalia), chopped
6 cloves garlic, minced
One 28-oz. can chopped tomatoes
1-½ c. chicken broth
2 Tbsp. chili powder (preferably *ají* or New Mexico chili)
½ tsp. saffron powder
½ tsp. ground black pepper
¼ tsp. ground cinnamon
6-8 small potatoes, cut into pieces
3 slightly unripe bananas, cut into large pieces
1 c. coconut milk
2 Tbsp. molasses

2 Tbsp. smooth peanut butter

Heat olive oil in a large Dutch oven over medium-high heat. Sauté the green and sweet onions and garlic until translucent, about 5 minutes. Add the pork to the pot and cook until well browned, about 5-10 minutes.

Add the tomatoes, broth, chili powder, saffron, pepper, and cinnamon and bring to a boil. Reduce heat, cover, and simmer for 45 minutes.

Add potatoes to the pot and cook 30 minutes longer. Add bananas and cook 10 more minutes.

Drain liquid from Dutch oven into a smaller saucepan. Add coconut milk, molasses, and peanut butter. Simmer sauce over low heat until smooth, about 2-3 minutes. Serve meat and vegetables with sauce on the side.

Per serving: 380 calories, 14 g fat, 8 g saturated fat, 284 mg sodium, 46 g carbohydrates, 22 g protein.

SERVING SUGGESTIONS:

Aji de carne is traditionally served wrapped in tortillas with cabbage.

VARIATION:

If additional heat is desired, add 1-2 minced habanero peppers to the pot with the spices.

BRAZIL
FEIJOADA

1 / 1 / 1
COOK TIME: 5 HOURS
ACTIVE PREP TIME: 10 MINUTES
INACTIVE PREP TIME: 8 HOURS
MAKES 10-12 SERVINGS

LIKE THE UNITED STATES, BRAZIL IS A CULTURAL MELTING POT, WHERE immigrants from dozens of countries around the world have settled over the course of centuries. The influence of many European and African cultures can be seen in Brazilian cuisine. But Brazil's national dish, feijoada, has its origins in Portugal, the country that began colonizing Brazil in the early sixteenth century.

1 lb. pork shoulder or loin, cut into small pieces
1 lb. ground beef
1 lb. smoked sausage, sliced
Olive oil, for frying
2 onions, finely chopped
8 cloves garlic, minced
1 smoked ham hock
3 bay leaves
Water, to cover
1 lb. dried black beans, soaked at least 8 hours
One 15-oz. can crushed tomatoes
Salt and pepper, to taste

Heat olive oil in a large Dutch oven or stockpot over medium-high heat. Fry pork in oil until browned, about 5-10 minutes, and remove from pan. Sauté onions and garlic in the same oil until onion is translucent, about 5 minutes, and remove from pan. Fry ground beef until brown, about 5 minutes, and drain fat. Fry sausage until browned, about 5-10 minutes.

Return pork, beef, onions, and garlic to pot along with sausage and add ham hock and bay leaves. Add enough water to the pot to cover contents. Bring to a boil, reduce heat to low, cover, and simmer 1 hour.

Drain and rinse black beans and add to the pot. Continue to simmer about 1-½ hours, or until beans are cooked thoroughly.

Add tomatoes and season with salt and pepper. Continue to cook for 2 hours or until the meat from the ham hock has fallen from the bone.

Per serving: 540 calories, 27 g fat, 9 g saturated fat, 419 mg sodium, 30 g carbohydrates, 44 g protein.

SERVING SUGGESTIONS:
Serve with white rice, collard greens, and fresh orange slices.

VARIATIONS:
Bacon can be substituted for part of the sausage, and chorizo may be used for a spicier stew.

CANADA
TOURTIÈRE

2 / 1 / 2
COOK TIME: 1 HOUR, 40 MINUTES
ACTIVE PREP TIME: 20 MINUTES
INACTIVE PREP TIME: 1 HOUR
MAKES 8 SERVINGS

THE REGION OF CANADA, FORMERLY KNOWN AS NEW FRANCE, IS HOME to a vibrant and distinctive culinary culture. Local ingredients like wild game (particularly caribou), salmon, maple syrup, and foraged berries and mushrooms make Quebeçois cuisine very distinct from its French counterpart. Tourtière, also popular among French-Canadian communities in New England, originated with French trappers and traders who explored the New World in the seventeenth century, making it as old as Quebec itself.

For crust:
2-½ c. all-purpose flour
½ tsp. salt
1 c. cold butter, cut into cubes
1 c. ice water

Blend flour, salt, and butter together (or use a food processor) until the mixture is fine and crumbly. Add ice water a little at a time until a dough is formed. Divide dough into two equal portions and refrigerate for 1 hour.

For filling:
1 lb. lean ground beef
1 lb. lean ground pork
Olive oil, for sautéing

1 onion, finely chopped

2 large potatoes, peeled, cooked, and mashed

¾ c. beef broth

1 tsp. salt

½ tsp. ground cinnamon

½ tsp. ground nutmeg

½ tsp. ground cloves

¼ tsp. ground black pepper

1 egg, beaten

Heat olive oil a large frying pan or Dutch oven over medium heat. Sauté onion until very soft and golden, about 10 minutes. Add beef and pork to the pan and cook another 10 minutes. Drain fat from browned meat and return to pot.

Add potatoes, broth, salt, cinnamon, nutmeg, cloves, and pepper. Simmer over medium-low heat for 20-30 minutes or until liquid is absorbed. Cool filling completely (refrigerate if necessary) before assembling.

To assemble pie, roll each ball of dough into a circle approximately ¼-inch thick. Line a 9-inch pie plate with one crust, and then spoon meat mixture into crust. Top with second crust and press edges together to seal. Trim excess crust from edges and vent top crust with a fork.

Preheat oven to 375 degrees. Evenly brush the top crust and edges of the pie with beaten egg. Bake for 50 minutes or until top crust is golden.

Per serving: 655 calories, 38 g fat, 17 g saturated fat, 726 mg sodium, 46 g carbohydrates, 32 g protein.

SERVING SUGGESTIONS:

Ketchup, cranberry sauce, and maple syrup are usually served with tourtière.

VARIATIONS:

In more rural areas, chicken and game such as rabbit are used in place of beef and pork. In other parts of Canada, different spice combinations are used such as mustard, celery salt, and herbs.

CHILE
CAZUELA DE POLLO

THE WORD CAZUELA, WHICH MEANS "COOKING POT" IN SPANISH, IS A NAME given to many South American soups and stews. Nearly every region has its own version. While the cazuelas served in the northern Andes Mountains incorporate pasta and cream, the cazuela typical of Chile is much lighter, with a savory, complex stock built around many fresh local vegetables and spices.

1 lb. chicken thighs or legs
2 Tbsp. olive oil
Salt and pepper, to taste
1-½ qt. water or chicken broth
1 onion, coarsely chopped
1 tsp. dried oregano
1 tsp. ground cumin
3 c. butternut squash, peeled and cut into cubes
6 medium red potatoes, peeled and quartered
3 ears fresh corn, cut into thirds
2 carrots, chopped
1 large sweet potato, cubed
1 stalk celery, chopped
Chopped fresh cilantro, for serving

Preheat oven to 425 degrees. Place chicken in a shallow baking dish, drizzle with olive oil, and season with salt and pepper. Bake for 20 minutes or until fully cooked. Allow to rest for 10 minutes after removing from oven.

Place chicken, water or broth, onion, oregano, and cumin in a large stockpot. Bring to a boil and reduce heat to medium-low. Add squash, potatoes, corn, carrots, sweet potato, and celery to the pot. Simmer for 20-30 minutes or until potatoes are completely cooked.

Divide soup between 6 bowls. Sprinkle with chopped cilantro before serving.

Per serving: 357 calories, 9 g fat, 2 g saturated fat, 91 mg sodium, 50 g carbohydrates, 23 g protein.

SERVING SUGGESTIONS:

Serve over rice or noodles.

VARIATION:

One lb. brisket may be substituted for chicken. Chop brisket into large pieces and brown in vegetable oil before serving.

COLOMBIA
AJIACO DE BOGOTANO

1 / 1 / 2
COOK TIME: 1 HOUR, 45 MINUTES
ACTIVE PREP TIME: 10 MINUTES
INACTIVE PREP TIME: 4 HOURS
MAKES 10-12 SERVINGS

AJIACO IS A POTATO STEW EATEN THROUGHOUT COLOMBIA AND PERU THAT has many regional variations. The version associated with Bogotá, Colombia's capital city, is made with chicken, corn, and a native herb known as "gallant weed." This recipe substitutes the hard-to-find herb with oregano. Unlike many other versions, ajiaco Bogotano does not incorporate the hot peppers that its name ("*aji*") implies.

1-½ lb. chicken, cut into pieces
1 c. heavy cream
¼ c. sour cream
Olive oil, for frying
1 lb. red potatoes, peeled and cut into chunks
1 lb. Yukon Gold potatoes, peeled and cut into chunks
1 large carrot, cut into chunks
1-¼ qt. chicken stock

1 onion, chopped
3 cloves garlic, minced
2 ears corn, cut into pieces
1 Tbsp. dried oregano
2 Tbsp. capers (optional)
Chopped cilantro, for serving

In a small saucepan, heat heavy cream over medium heat just until warmed. Whisk in sour cream. Allow to stand for at least 4 hours at room temperature.

Heat olive oil in a large stockpot over medium-high heat. Fry chicken until browned, about 5-7 minutes. Add potatoes, carrot, and 4 c. of chicken stock. Reduce heat to low, cover, and simmer for 1 hour.

Heat more olive oil in a separate skillet over high heat. Sauté onion and garlic until brown, about 5-7 minutes. Once browned, pour remaining cup of stock in skillet to loosen bits from pan and add to stockpot along with corn and oregano. Simmer, covered, for an additional 30 minutes.

Remove from heat and stir in cream mixture. Add capers, if using. Garnish bowls with cilantro and serve.

Per serving: 238 calories, 9 g fat, 4 g saturated fat, 384 mg sodium, 18 g carbohydrates, 23 g protein.

SERVING SUGGESTIONS:
Serve with cornbread (traditional) or white rice, with sliced avocados on the side.

COSTA RICA GALLO PINTO

1 / 1 / 1
COOK TIME: 2 HOURS, 10 MINUTES
ACTIVE PREP TIME: 10 MINUTES
INACTIVE PREP TIME: 8 HOURS
MAKES 6 SERVINGS

BEAN AND RICE DISHES ARE POPULAR THROUGHOUT LATIN AMERICA, AND IN
Costa Rica gallo pinto (whose name means "spotted rooster") can be found at nearly

every meal—even at breakfast, where it is served with fried eggs. Made with black beans and colorful vegetables that give the rice a "spotted" appearance, gallo pinto can be served as either a side dish or as a filling vegetarian main course.

1 c. black beans, dried
Water, for soaking and boiling
1 tsp. salt
2 c. white rice
Olive oil, for sautéing
2 cloves garlic, minced
1 small purple onion, chopped
1 small red bell pepper, chopped
1 bunch cilantro, finely chopped
3 c. vegetable broth or water
Chopped fresh cilantro, for serving
Chopped green onions, for serving

Place beans in water and allow to soak for 8 hours or overnight. Drain and rinse beans. Bring a large pot of water to a boil. Add beans and salt. Return to a boil, reduce heat to low, cover, and simmer for 2 hours or until beans are fully cooked.

In the last hour of cooking time, prepare the rice. Heat olive oil in a large skillet over medium-high heat. Sauté the rice for 2 minutes or until lightly toasted. Add garlic, onion, red bell pepper, and cilantro to the pan and cook until onion is translucent, about 5 minutes. Add broth or water, cover, and simmer for 25-30 minutes or until liquid is absorbed and rice is tender.

Drain the beans, reserving cooking water. Add beans to the pan and mix together with rice. Sauté briefly until warmed, adding a little of the cooking water if mixture becomes dry. Garnish with cilantro and green onions and serve.

Per serving: 387 calories, 4 g fat, 1 g saturated fat, 775 mg sodium, 73 g carbohydrates, 14 g protein.

SERVING SUGGESTION:
Serve topped with a fried egg if desired.

VARIATIONS:

Chopped zucchini, tomatoes, eggplant, sweet potatoes, and most other vegetables can be used to make gallo pinto. For extra heat, peppers or canned salsa may be added with the beans.

CUBA
ROPA VIEJA

1 / 1 / 2
COOK TIME: 2 HOURS, 45 MINUTES
ACTIVE PREP TIME: 10 MINUTES
MAKES 6 SERVINGS

ROPA VIEJA IS SPANISH FOR "OLD CLOTHES." THIS DISH OF SHREDDED MEAT, onions, and peppers resembles a pile of torn rags of many different colors. According to legend, a poor man who could not afford to feed his family shredded and boiled his own clothing, and after praying over the meal saw the pieces of fabric turn into strips of seasoned meat. What is certain is that ropa vieja has its roots in the Canary Islands, where many Spanish conquistadores called home. It is enjoyed throughout the Spanish Caribbean, but it was Cuba that made ropa vieja its national dish.

2 lbs. flank steak, cut into 2-inch pieces
Salt and pepper, for seasoning
Oil, for sautéing
1 yellow onion, sliced
1 green bell pepper, sliced
1 red bell pepper, sliced
6 cloves garlic, finely minced
One 6-oz. can tomato paste
1 Tbsp. ground cumin
1 Tbsp. dried oregano
1 tsp. sugar
1 c. white wine

2 c. chicken broth
1 15-oz. can tomato puree
1 carrot, peeled
1 stalk celery
2 bay leaves
½ c. Spanish green olives (optional)
¼ c. pimientos (optional)
3 Tbsp. capers (optional)
¼ c. fresh cilantro, chopped, for serving

Season steak with salt and pepper. Heat oil in a Dutch oven over medium-high heat. Fry meat until browned on all sides, about 5-6 minutes, and remove from pot. Add onions and peppers to pot and sauté until soft, about 5 minutes. Add garlic and sauté for 1 minute longer.

Add tomato paste, cumin powder, oregano, and sugar and cook for another 3 minutes or until fragrant. Add wine and cook for another 1-2 minutes, constantly stirring and scraping bottom of pot.

Return steak to pot and add broth, tomato puree, carrot, celery, and bay leaves. Bring to a boil, reduce heat to medium low, cover, and simmer for 2 hours.

Remove carrot, celery, and bay leaves from pot. Shred meat into smaller strips and add olives and capers to the pot (if using). Remove lid and continue cooking until sauce thickens, about 30 minutes. Garnish with cilantro and serve.

Per serving: 437 calories, 16 g fat, 6 g saturated fat, 529 mg sodium, 19 g carbohydrates, 47 g protein.

SERVING SUGGESTIONS:

Serve with rice, black beans, or fried plantains.

VARIATION:

A slow cooker can be used to make ropa vieja. Before returning to pot, add all ingredients to slow cooker and cook on the Low setting for 8 hours.

DOMINICA
LE RÔTI

2 / 2 / 2
COOK TIME: 1 HOUR, 45 MINUTES
ACTIVE PREP TIME: 20 MINUTES
INACTIVE PREP TIME: 6 HOURS, 30 MINUTES
MAKES 6 SERVINGS

DOMINICA IS A FORMER FRENCH COLONY, AND ITS CUISINE IS VERY colonial in nature—but not exactly how you would expect. The word *roti* means "roast" in French, but the name of this Caribbean dish has its origins in the Sanskrit word *rotikā*, meaning "bread." Le rôti, which resembles a burrito, can refer to either the dish or the type of bread used to make it. The combination of East Indian and Caribbean flavors and ingredients in this dish suggest the island of Dominica's rich heritage and prominent place in the commerce of the colonial era.

2 lbs. chicken thighs, cut into pieces
9 cloves garlic, minced, divided
¼ c. plus 1 Tbsp. curry powder, divided
1 Tbsp. lemon juice
1 tsp. salt
Oil, for sautéing
2 onions, minced
3 green onions, finely chopped
1 Scotch bonnet pepper, finely minced (optional)
2 tsp. fresh thyme
2 large potatoes, skinned and cubed
Water, to cover

Combine 4 cloves garlic, 1 Tbsp. curry powder, lemon juice, and salt. Pour over chicken and marinate in refrigerator for at least 6 hours or overnight.

Heat oil in a Dutch oven over medium-high heat. Sauté onions until translucent, about 5 minutes. Add chicken and sauté until brown, about 5 minutes longer. Add remaining curry powder and garlic, green onions, Scotch bonnet pepper (if using), and thyme. Reduce heat to medium-low and cook for 10 minutes longer.

Add potatoes and water to cover meat and vegetables. Reduce heat to low, cover, and simmer for 1 hour or until sauce has thickened and meat is cooked.

For flatbread:
4 c. all-purpose flour, plus more for flouring surface
1 tsp. yeast
½ tsp. salt
3 Tbsp. baking powder
1-½ c. water
¼ c. vegetable oil

Sift together flour, salt, yeast, and baking powder. Add water and mix until a dough is formed. Cover and allow to rest in a cool, dry place for 30 minutes.

Gently knead dough until pliable and divide into 6 portions. With a rolling pin on a floured surface, flatten each portion to form a circle 12 inches wide and ¼-inch thick.

Brush dough circles with oil and cook on a hot skillet for 2 minutes on each side, or until bubbles begin to rise to surface of dough.

To serve, place one-sixth of the filling in the center of each flatbread. Fold each side towards the middle to form a wrap.

Per serving: 827 calories, 24 g fat, 5 g saturated fat, 735 mg sodium, 96 g carbohydrates, 56 g protein.

VARIATIONS:

Grilled tofu may be used in place of chicken for a vegetarian option. Carrots, bell peppers, celery, or other vegetables may be used in place of some or all of the potatoes and meat.

DOMINICAN REPUBLIC LA BANDERA

2 / 1 / 1
COOK TIME: 2 HOURS, 30 MINUTES
ACTIVE PREP TIME: 10 MINUTES
INACTIVE PREP TIME: 8 HOURS, 30 MINUTES
MAKES 6 SERVINGS

IN THE DOMINICAN REPUBLIC, A TYPICAL MEAL CONSISTS OF A COMBINATION OF meat (usually beef or chicken), rice, and beans. The national dish's name, La Bandera, comes from the Spanish word for "flag" and from the flag of the Dominican Republic. In this recipe, the three main ingredients represent the flag's three colors: red (pinto beans), white (rice), and blue (chicken).

For chicken:
2 lbs. chicken (any type), cut into pieces
2 limes, sliced
1 red onion, sliced
1 stalk celery, chopped
1 tsp. salt
1 clove garlic, crushed
¼ tsp. dried oregano
Oil, for sautéing
1 tsp. sugar
½ c. plus 2 Tbsp. water, plus more if needed
4 Roma tomatoes, seeded and quartered
2 green bell peppers, chopped
¼ c. green olives, halved (optional)
One 8-oz. can tomato sauce
¼ c. fresh cilantro
Salt and pepper, to taste

Rub the entire surface of the chicken with lime slices. Combine onion, celery, salt, garlic, and oregano and marinate with chicken for at least 30 minutes.

Heat oil in a Dutch oven over medium-high heat and add sugar. Once sugar has caramelized, add chicken, onion, and celery and sauté until the chicken is brown, about 5-10 minutes. Add 2 Tbsp. of water to pot. Reduce heat to low, cover, and simmer for 15 minutes, adding water as necessary.

Add tomato sauce and ½ c. of water and stir to make a sauce. Continue to simmer until sauce is slightly thickened, about 5-10 minutes. Add cilantro and salt and pepper to taste.

Per serving: 298 calories, 7 g fat, 2 g saturated fat, 841 mg sodium, 12 g carbohydrates, 46 g protein.

For rice:
2 c. long-grain rice
2 Tbsp. olive oil, divided
½ tsp. salt
3 c. water

Heat 1 Tbsp. of oil and salt in a large non-reactive pot. Add water and bring to a boil. Add rice to pot and reduce heat to medium.

Cook rice, stirring frequently, until most water has evaporated or been absorbed, about 10 minutes. Reduce heat to low, cover, and simmer for 15 minutes. Stir in remaining olive oil, recover, and simmer for 5 minutes longer or until rice is tender and fluffy.

Per serving: 265 calories, 5 g fat, 1 g saturated fat, 197 mg sodium, 49 g carbohydrates, 4 g protein.

For beans:
2 c. pinto beans, dried
Water, for soaking and boiling
Oil, for sautéing
2 cloves garlic, minced
1 green bell pepper, chopped
1 red onion, chopped
1 c. butternut squash, diced
One 8-oz. can tomato sauce
1 Tbsp. fresh cilantro, minced

¼ tsp. dried oregano
Salt, to taste

Soak the beans in water for 8 hours or overnight. Drain and rinse beans.

Bring a large pot of water to a boil. Add beans and boil until soft, about 1 hour. Drain beans again, this time reserving water.

Heat oil in a Dutch oven over medium-high heat. Sauté garlic, bell pepper, onion, and squash until onion begins to soften and garlic is fragrant, about 3-4 minutes. Add tomato sauce, cilantro, and oregano and cook for about 1 minute longer. Add beans and simmer for 5 minutes longer.

Add 1-½ qt. of the water in which the beans were boiled, adding fresh water to make up the balance if necessary. Mash beans slightly with a potato masher (do not completely break the beans). Cook for 20 minutes longer or until the beans begin to reach a creamy consistency.

Per serving: 282 calories, 3 g fat, 1 g saturated fat, 497 mg sodium, 49 g carbohydrates, 15 g protein.

SERVING SUGGESTION:

Serve with a simple green salad (ensalada verde), with lettuce, tomato, cucumber, onion, and an oil-vinegar dressing.

ECUADOR CHURRASCO

2 / 1 / 2
COOK TIME: 15 MINUTES
ACTIVE PREP TIME: 15 MINUTES
INACTIVE PREP TIME: 2 HOURS, 35 MINUTES
MAKES 4 SERVINGS

THE WORD CHURRASCO COMES FROM A PORTUGUESE TERM FOR GRILLED or barbecued meat, particularly beef. Churrasco is eaten throughout Latin America, where steakhouses are referred to as churrascarias. In South America each country has its own version of this dish, which is especially popular in the beef-producing countries of the Southern Cone. The fried eggs and green chimichurri sauce in this recipe make it distinctly Ecuadorian.

2 lbs. skirt or flank steak
4 large eggs
2 Tbsp. olive oil, plus more for frying
6 cloves garlic, minced
2 tsp. ground cumin
½ tsp. salt
½ tsp. black pepper

Combine olive oil, garlic, cumin, salt, and pepper and coat surface of meat. Cover with plastic wrap and marinate in refrigerator for at least 2 hours. Allow meat to sit at room temperature for about 30 minutes before cooking.

Heat oil in a heavy skillet over high heat. Fry the meat for 5 minutes on each side or until desired doneness is reached. Transfer to a cutting board and allow to rest for 5 minutes longer.

While meat is resting, cook the eggs. Heat additional oil in skillet used to cook meat and crack eggs into skillet. Cook eggs for 1-2 minutes on each side or until desired doneness is reached.

Slice meat and divide into 4 portions. Top each serving with a fried egg and serve with chimichurri sauce.

Per serving: 613 calories, 35 g fat, 11 g saturated fat, 490 mg sodium, 3 g carbohydrates, 70 g protein.

For chimichurri sauce:
1-½ c. fresh parsley or cilantro
¼ c. fresh oregano
1 small white onion, coarsely chopped
3 cloves garlic
3 Tbsp. red wine vinegar
1 Tbsp. lemon juice
1 small chili pepper, diced, or 1 tsp. chili flakes (optional)
¼ tsp. salt

¼ c. olive oil

Combine all ingredients except olive oil in a food processor and blend until smooth. Refrigerate until chilled. Stir in olive oil just before serving.

Per serving: 148 calories, 13 g fat, 2 g saturated fat, 164 mg sodium, 8 g carbohydrates, 2 g protein.

SERVING SUGGESTIONS:

Serve with French fries, fried plantains, white rice, pickled onions, hot sauce, cucumber slices, and a slice of fresh avocado.

EL SALVADOR PUPUSAS DE CHICHARRÓN

2 / 2 / 3
COOK TIME: 1 HOUR, 45 MINUTES
ACTIVE PREP TIME: 30 MINUTES
MAKES 5 SERVINGS

IN ANY CENTRAL AMERICAN COUNTRY, WHAT AMERICANS CALL A "SANDWICH" places meat, cheese, and other fillings between two tortillas. El Salvador's classic dish, the pupusa, is like a stuffed sandwich—a thick homemade tortilla with meat, beans, cheese, or a combination of the three enclosed on the inside. This version uses seasoned pork as its filling.

1 lb. pork (any cut), shredded or cut into chunks
Olive oil, for frying
2 tsp. ground cumin
2 tsp. garlic powder
¼ tsp. salt
¼ tsp. ground black pepper
2-¼ c. water

3 Roma tomatoes, seeded and chopped
1 white onion, chopped
1 green bell pepper, chopped
2 c. masa (corn flour)
Salt and pepper, to taste
Salsa, for serving

Heat oil in heavy skillet over medium-high heat. Season pork with cumin, garlic powder, salt, and pepper and sauté over medium heat until brown, about 5-10 minutes. Add 1 c. water to skillet. Reduce heat to low, cover, and cook until liquid is completely evaporated and pork is cooked throughout, about 1 hour.

Place meat, tomatoes, onion, and bell pepper in a blender or food processor and pulse until finely ground. This will have to be done in several batches.

Combine masa and 1-¼ c. water in a bowl. Season with salt and pepper. Knead until a soft dough is formed (more water may be needed). Divide masa into 10 portions and flatten each portion into a circle. Place a spoonful of filling in the center of each circle. Pinch the edges of the circle towards the middle to make a closed ball with the meat mixture in its center. Flatten the ball between your hands.

Heat a small amount of oil in a heavy skillet over medium heat. Fry each pupusa for 5-6 minutes on each side or until brown and crispy. Drain on paper towels and serve with salsa.

Per serving: 381 calories, 11 g fat, 2 g saturated fat, 180 mg sodium, 43 g carbohydrates, 30 g protein.

VARIATIONS:

Other options for pupusa filings include beef, chicken, shrimp, shredded cheese, refried beans, potatoes, peppers, or a combination of any of these. You will need about 1 c. of filling for each batch of pupusas.

GRENADA OIL DOWN

GRENADA, A SMALL ISLAND IN THE SOUTHERN CARIBBEAN SEA, WAS ONCE known as the "Spice Isle" because of its nutmeg plantations. Nutmeg is not an ingredient in Grenada's national dish, although Oil Down features several other native products such as breadfruit and callaloo leaves. In this recipe, those difficult-to-find ingredients are replaced with potatoes and spinach. Oil Down receives its peculiar name from the layer of coconut oil and meat fat left at the bottom of the pot after cooking.

2 lbs. beef brisket
2-½ qt. water, plus more to cover
1-½ c. salt
¾ c. sugar
2 bay leaves
2 tsp. black peppercorns
1 tsp. whole cloves
1 onion, chopped
1 clove garlic, crushed
Oil, for sautéing
2 lbs. potatoes, cut into ½-inch slices
1 qt. coconut milk
½ c. fresh chives, finely chopped
2 Tbsp. fresh thyme
2 tsp. ground turmeric
1 Scotch bonnet pepper
2 c. fresh spinach, chopped

Bring water, salt, sugar, bay leaves, peppercorns, and cloves to a boil in a large non-reactive pot. Remove from heat and allow to completely cool.

Place brisket in a large non-reactive dish and cover with brine. Cover dish with plastic wrap and refrigerate 8 hours or overnight.

Rinse meat thoroughly to remove any residual salt. Place in a large pot and add enough cold water to cover. Bring to a boil, reduce heat to low, and simmer for about 4 hours or until beef is very tender. Slice meat into 2-inch pieces.

Heat oil in a Dutch oven over medium-high heat. Add onions and garlic and cook until soft, about 3 minutes. Add meat, potatoes, coconut milk, chives, thyme, turmeric, and Scotch bonnet pepper. Bring to a boil.

Reduce heat to medium-low, cover, and simmer for 30 minutes or until potatoes are fully cooked. Add spinach and cook until wilted, about 10 minutes. Remove Scotch bonnet pepper before serving.

Per serving: 523 calories, 12 g fat, 4 g saturated fat, 1283 mg sodium, 54 g carbohydrates, 50 g protein.

VARIATIONS:

Use pork, ham, or cod in place of brisket. Use an equal amount of breadfruit and/or callaloo leaves, if available, in place of potatoes and spinach.

GUATEMALA PEPIÁN

2 / 2 / 2
COOK TIME: 1 HOUR
ACTIVE PREP TIME: 20 MINUTES
INACTIVE PREP TIME: 30 MINUTES
MAKES 6 SERVINGS

To THE PEOPLE OF GUATEMALA, PEPIÁN IS MORE THAN JUST THEIR country's national dish. It is also a record of its history. Pepián blends both Spanish and Mayan influences by combining European elements (onion, cilantro, and cinnamon) with native ingredients like tomatoes, chilies, and pepitoria, a spice made from the roasted and ground seeds of an indigenous squash. This recipe replaces pepitoria with pumpkin seeds.

2 lbs. boneless chicken (breasts or thighs)

1 dried guajillo pepper

Hot water, for soaking

1 poblano pepper

5 tomatoes, halved

3 tomatillos, halved

2 small onions, halved

1 head garlic, peeled and halved crosswise

¼ c. sesame seeds

¼ c. pumpkin seeds

1 Tbsp. black peppercorns

1 tsp. cloves

One 3-inch cinnamon stick

Oil, for sautéing

1 qt. chicken broth

1 lb. potatoes, peeled and sliced (optional)

Place guajillo pepper in a cup of hot water and allow to soak for 20-30 minutes. Meanwhile, roast poblano over an open flame until skin blackens and begins to peel. Place poblano pepper in a brown paper bag until it begins to sweat, and then peel, seed, and chop both peppers. Set aside.

Preheat oven to 450 degrees. Place tomatoes, tomatillos, onions, and garlic in a deep baking dish, cut sides down. Roast for 15-20 minutes or until vegetables are soft and tomato skins begin to blacken and peel. Set aside to cool.

Heat a small amount of oil in a small skillet over medium heat. Add sesame and pumpkin seeds, peppercorns, cloves, and cinnamon stick to pan and toast until fragrant, about 5 minutes. Shake pan constantly and do not allow the ingredients to burn. Set aside and allow to cool completely.

Place roasted vegetables in a blender or food processor with a small amount of chicken broth. Working in batches, pulse until mixture is a smooth paste. Strain and remove any large solids.

Heat oil in a Dutch oven over high heat. Add chicken pieces and fry until seared on all sides, about 5 minutes. Add roasted vegetable puree, peppers, toasted seeds and spices, remaining broth, and potatoes (if using) to pot. Bring to a boil, reduce heat to medium, and cook uncovered for 30 minutes or until sauce has thickened and chicken is fully cooked. Shred chicken with two forks and serve.

Per serving: 440 calories, 20 g fat, 4 g saturated fat, 144 mg sodium, 17 g carbohydrates, 49 g protein.

VARIATIONS:

Substitute beef or pork for chicken. For a vegan version, replace meat with additional potatoes or squash and use vegetable broth.

GUYANA
GUYANESE PEPPERPOT

1 / 3 / 3
COOK TIME: 3 HOURS, 20 MINUTES
ACTIVE PREP TIME: 10 MINUTES
MAKES 10 SERVINGS

IN GUYANA, CHRISTMAS IS SELDOM CELEBRATED WITHOUT PEPPERPOT, A dish served mainly on special occasions due to its lengthy preparation time. The indigenous people of Guyana used it as a method for preserving meat. The key ingredient, cassareep, is a syrup made by boiling and grating the root of the cassava. Cassareep contains preservative agents that will protect the meat's freshness for days or even weeks without refrigeration. The bird cherry, or wiri-wiri, pepper is another key ingredient that is native to Guyana and extremely hot.

3 lbs. stew beef or brisket, all fat removed and cut into 2-inch pieces
Oil, for frying
1 c. cassareep
4 cinnamon sticks
One 2-inch strip orange peel
2 tsp. whole cloves
2 bird cherry (wiri-wiri) peppers

¾ c. brown sugar
1 tsp. salt
4 qt. water

Heat oil in large Dutch oven. Cook meat pieces, in batches if necessary, until brown on all sides. Add cassareep, cinnamon sticks, orange peel, cloves, peppers, brown sugar, and salt. Add water and bring to a boil. Reduce heat to medium and simmer, uncovered, until liquid is reduced by three-quarters, about 3 hours. Meat should be extremely tender when cooking is complete.

Per serving: 332 calories, 10 g fat, 1 g saturated fat, 1020 mg sodium, 30 g carbohydrates, 32 g protein.

VARIATIONS:

Use goat, pork, mutton, lamb, or chicken in place of beef. Remove all fat from the meat before cooking. Habanero or Scotch bonnet peppers can be used in place of bird cherry peppers.

TIPS:

Leftovers do not have to be refrigerated. In Guyana, pepperpot is typically left in its pot on the stove and eaten over the course of several days. Cassareep should be used to make pepperpot if at all possible, but if it cannot be obtained it can be substituted with ½ c. molasses, ¼ c. plus 2 Tbsp. fresh lime juice, and 2 Tbsp. balsamic vinegar.

HAITI
PORK GRIOTS

3 / 2 / 2
COOK TIME: 1 HOUR, 50 MINUTES
ACTIVE PREP TIME: 15 MINUTES
INACTIVE PREP TIME: 8 HOURS
MAKES 4 SERVINGS

HAITI HAS MANY REGIONS WITH DISTINCT CULINARY TRADITIONS, ESPECIALLY for its being a geographically small area. Much like Louisiana, Haiti's cooking style bears characteristics of French, Spanish, African, and indigenous cuisine. The name of this recipe, griots, is a Creole word derived from the French *grillades*, or "grilled"; this griots, however, is braised in the oven.

2 lbs. pork shoulder, cut into 2-inch pieces
1 small onion, chopped
1 red bell pepper, chopped
5 scallions, sliced
4 cloves garlic, crushed
1 Scotch bonnet pepper, chopped
¼ c. plus 2 Tbsp. freshly squeezed lime juice
¼ c. freshly squeezed orange juice
2 tsp. fresh thyme
1 tsp. ground black pepper
1-½ c. water
Salt and pepper, to taste
Oil, for frying

Combine onion, bell pepper, scallions, garlic, Scotch bonnet pepper, lime and orange juices, thyme, and black pepper in a blender. Pulse until smooth.

Place pork in a deep, non-reactive dish and cover with onion and bell pepper puree. Cover dish with plastic wrap and allow to marinate in refrigerator 8 hours or overnight.

Preheat oven to 325 degrees. Place pork in a Dutch oven, reserving marinade, and add water. Bring water to a boil, remove from heat, and transfer to oven. Braise pork for 1-½ hours, stirring frequently, until tender.

Remove pork from braising liquid. Transfer liquid to a small saucepan and boil for 10 minutes or until reduced by two-thirds (you should have about ½ c. of liquid). Strain liquid to remove solids, add marinade to pan, and bring to a boil.

Season pork with salt and pepper. Heat oil in a large skillet over medium-high heat. Add pork with sauce and cook until pork is browned on both sides, about 3 minutes per side.

Per serving: 757 calories, 56 g fat, 19 g saturated fat, 162 mg sodium, 8 g carbohydrates, 54 g protein.

Serve with red kidney beans and rice.

HONDURAS BALEADA

2 / 2 / 1
COOK TIME: 25 MINUTES
ACTIVE PREP TIME: 20 MINUTES
INACTIVE PREP TIME: 20 MINUTES
MAKES 6 SERVINGS

THE HONDURAN BALEADA COULD EASILY BE CONFUSED WITH THE Mexican taco but is much bigger and usually includes a wider range of contents (even though these can be very simple as well). The word *baleada* is Spanish for "the shot woman," a name that has many possible sources. According to one story, the dish was invented by a woman who sold wrapped tortillas and continued to do so even after recovering from a shooting injury. Another story claims that the name comes from the dish's ingredients: "Beans are bullets, cheese is gunpowder and the tortilla is the gun."

2 c. all-purpose flour, plus more for flouring surface
½ c. water
3 Tbsp. oil, plus more for frying
1 tsp. baking powder
1 dash salt
One 15-oz. can red beans
2 Tbsp. red onion, finely chopped
2 cloves garlic, minced
6 eggs, beaten
¼ c. whole milk
1 Tbsp. butter
½ c. queso fresco, crumbled
¼ c. plus 2 Tbsp. sour cream

Salt and pepper, to taste

Sift together flour, salt, and baking powder. Add water and oil and mix to form a dough. Knead dough on a floured surface until pliable, about 5 minutes. Place dough in a bowl, cover with plastic wrap, and allow to rest in a warm, dry place for 20 minutes.

Divide dough into six equal portions and roll each portion into a 9-inch circle. Heat oil in a large skillet and cook each tortilla until brown and puffy, about 1 minute per side.

Place beans in a blender (with liquid) and pulse until smooth. Heat oil in a skillet. Fry onion and garlic until soft, about 2-3 minutes. Add beans to skillet and cook until warm, about 1-2 minutes longer. Season with salt and pepper.

Heat butter in a separate skillet over medium heat. Combine eggs and milk and add to skillet. With a small spatula, stir eggs occasionally (but not constantly) until fully cooked, about 5 minutes. Season with salt and pepper.

To serve baleadas, spread an equal amount of bean mixture on each tortilla. Follow with scrambled eggs, queso fresco, and sour cream.

Per serving: 384 calories, 18 g fat, 6 g saturated fat, 352 mg sodium, 41 g carbohydrates, 15 g protein.

VARIATIONS:

This recipe describes a special baleada. To make a simple baleada, omit scrambled eggs. To make a super-special baleada, add meat (pork or beef), avocado, plantain, bell pepper, and hot sauce.

JAMAICA JERK CHICKEN AND PEAS

THE "JERK" METHOD OF COOKING MEAT IS INTEGRAL TO JAMAICAN COOKING. Pioneered by the indigenous Taino people and later adapted by enslaved Africans, it involves marinating chicken, pork, goat, seafood, or vegetables in a spicy onion-based marinade and then slow-cooking over wood and coals. This recipe uses the oven instead and pairs jerk chicken with rice and peas (beans).

2 lbs. bone-in, skin-on chicken thighs and/or drumsticks
6 green onions, chopped
1 small onion, chopped, divided
One 2-inch piece ginger, peeled and chopped
5 cloves garlic, chopped
1 Scotch bonnet chili, seeded (more if desired)
3 Tbsp. dark brown sugar
2 Tbsp. lime juice
2 Tbsp. soy sauce
2 Tbsp. olive oil
3 Tbsp. fresh thyme, divided
1 Tbsp. ground allspice
1 tsp. salt
Oil, for frying
1 c. basmati rice
One 15-oz. can red kidney beans, drained and rinsed
1 c. unsweetened coconut milk
1 c. chicken broth

1 bay leaf
Lime slices, for serving

Combine spring onions, one-half of onion, ginger, 3 cloves garlic, chili, brown sugar, lime juice, soy sauce, olive oil, 1 Tbsp. thyme, allspice, and salt in a blender or food processor. Pulse until very smooth.

Score the surface of the chicken and rub onion mixture into surface. Place in a dish, cover, and marinate in the refrigerator for 8 hours or overnight.

Preheat oven to 350 degrees. Heat oil in a heavy, oven-proof skillet over medium-high heat. Remove chicken from marinade and cook skin-side down for about 5-6 minutes or until skin is crisp. Turn and continue to cook for 3-5 minutes or until other side is brown. Remove chicken from skillet.

Sauté remaining onion until softened, about 3 minutes. Add rice and beans and cook for 2 minutes longer. Stir in coconut milk, broth, and bay leaf and bring to a boil. Remove from heat, return chicken to pan (skin-side up) and sprinkle with remaining thyme. Bake in oven until rice is thoroughly cooked, about 25-30 minutes. Serve with lime slices.

Per serving: 616 calories, 33 g fat, 14 g saturated fat, 764 mg sodium, 50 g carbohydrates, 35 g protein.

SERVING SUGGESTIONS:
Serve with grilled pineapple, sweet potatoes, or corn fritters.

MEXICO
ENMOLADAS

3 / 2 / 2
COOK TIME: 1 HOUR, 5 MINUTES
ACTIVE PREP TIME: 20 MINUTES
INACTIVE PREP TIME: 30 MINUTES
MAKES 4-6 SERVINGS

IN MOST PARTS OF THE UNITED STATES, MEXICAN FOOD IS BY FAR THE MOST popular ethnic cuisine, as Mexican restaurants can be found in even the smallest American towns. While enchiladas are one of the most familiar Mexican dishes to most Americans, enmoladas are less so. Several legends have been told about how mole sauce originated; the most popular centers around a group of nuns in a poor, rural convent who had to prepare for an unannounced visit from the archbishop by making a sauce from what they had on hand at the time. This included an odd array of fruit, nuts, spices, and chilies with some chocolate and day-old bread mixed in. In reality, mole's origins are indigenous. But with African, European, and North American ingredients, the modern version of the sauce (listed here) is regarded as the first truly international dish of the New World. If you want to make your own mole sauce, you'll need plenty of time and a well-stocked spice cabinet.

1-2 chicken breasts (about ¾ lb.)
Water, for poaching
Salt and pepper, to taste
3 c. mole sauce (recipe below)
Twelve 6-inch flour tortillas
Oil, for frying
1-½ c. queso fresco, for serving
1 small white onion, sliced, for serving
Sesame seeds, for serving

Place chicken breasts in a medium saucepan and season with salt and pepper. Cover with 1 inch of water. Bring water to a boil, reduce heat, and simmer gently for about 10-15 minutes. Remove chicken from pot, allow to cool completely, and shred with two forks. Set aside.

In one skillet, warm mole sauce over medium-low heat. Heat oil in another skillet over high heat. Once the oil is very hot, reduce heat to medium and add one tortilla at a time to pan. Fry each tortilla for about 30 seconds on each side or until brown and place on a paper towel-lined plate.

After all tortillas are fried, dip each tortilla in mole sauce. Hold each tortilla using tongs to ensure that its entire surface is submerged. Remove from mole sauce, set on a plate, and fill with shredded chicken. Fold both sides over and place on a serving plate. Repeat with remaining tortillas. Spoon remaining mole sauce over enmoladas. Garnish with queso fresco, onion, and sesame seeds and serve.

For mole sauce:
5 ancho chilies
5 guajillo chilies
5 chipotle chilies
½ c. raisins
Hot water, for soaking
¼ c. sesame seeds
¼ c. pumpkin seeds
¼ c. peanuts
¼ c. almonds
4 whole cloves
1 pod star anise
One 1-inch cinnamon stick
3 whole allspice berries
1 Tbsp. cumin seed
1 Tbsp. coriander seed
1 Tbsp. peppercorns
1 lb. Roma tomatoes, halved and seeded
1 large onion, quartered
1 head garlic, peeled and cut in half crosswise
Oil, for sautéing
1 ripe banana, peeled and sliced diagonally
1 tsp. dried oregano
1 slice white bread or 1 tortilla (preferably stale), torn into pieces
2 oz. Mexican chocolate, chopped
¼ c. brown sugar
1 tsp. salt

Remove stems and seeds from chilies. Heat a dry skillet and toast chilies over high heat until very fragrant, about 2-3 minutes.

Place chilies and raisins in a bowl and cover with hot water. Cover bowl with a plate to ensure that the chilies remain completely submerged and soak for 30 minutes. Drain, reserving soaking water.

Toast sesame seeds, pumpkin seeds, peanuts, and almonds in a dry skillet over high heat for about 2-3 minutes or until fragrant. Remove from pan and set aside.

Toast cloves, star anise, cinnamon, allspice, cumin and coriander seeds, and peppercorns for about 2-3 minutes or until fragrant. Remove from pan and set aside.

Preheat broiler to High. Place tomatoes, onion, and garlic in a deep baking dish and broil on top rack of oven until charred, about 5-10 minutes. Remove from oven and set aside to cool.

Heat oil in a large skillet. Add banana slices and cook over medium-high heat for about 6 minutes or until brown on both sides. Remove from pan and set aside.

Place chilies, raisins, sesame seeds, pumpkin seeds, peanuts, almonds, tomatoes, onion, garlic, and banana in a blender or food processor and pulse until smooth. (This will probably have to be done in several batches.)

Using a spice grinder or mortar and pestle, grind the cloves, star anise, cinnamon, allspice, cumin and coriander seeds, and peppercorns until reduced to a fine powder.

In a large saucepan, combine tomato mixture, ground spices, oregano, bread, chocolate, brown sugar, and salt. Bring to a boil, reduce heat to medium-low, and simmer until the bread has completely disintegrated into the sauce, about 10 minutes.

Per serving: 897 calories, 37 g fat, 11 g saturated fat, 1742 mg sodium, 115 g carbohydrates, 33 g protein.

SERVING SUGGESTION:

Serve with a lettuce and tomato salad.

NICARAGUA
INDIO VIEJO

1 / 2 / 2
COOK TIME: 35 MINUTES
ACTIVE PREP TIME: 15 MINUTES
MAKES 5 SERVINGS

INDIGENOUS TRADITIONS ARE IMPORTANT IN NICARAGUA'S CUISINE, AND THIS importance is observed nowhere better than in indio viejo (which is Spanish for "old

Indian"). This savory stew has been eaten in Nicaragua since pre-Columbian times, and with the exception of onion (a later addition) includes only native ingredients—most notably Nicaragua's staple crop, corn.

1 lb. chicken breasts
¼ c. butter
1 large onion, chopped
4 cloves garlic, minced
5 tomatoes, seeded and chopped
3 green bell peppers, seeded and chopped
½ c. fresh cilantro, chopped
2 c. corn flour or masa
2 c. chicken broth
1 c. water
1 Tbsp. paprika
Juice of 2 sour oranges
Salt and pepper to taste

Melt butter in a large Dutch oven over medium-high heat. Sauté onion and garlic until onion is brown and translucent, about 5 minutes. Add chicken to pot and cook for about 8-10 minutes or until chicken is brown on both sides. Add tomatoes, bell peppers, and cilantro; stir and continue to cook for 10 minutes. Remove chicken from pot, shred with two forks, and return to pot.

In a medium bowl, combine corn flour or masa, broth, and water. Mix thoroughly with a fork until all lumps are broken. Add corn flour mixture and paprika to pot and cook for 10 minutes longer. Stir in sour orange juice and season with salt and pepper.

Per serving: 503 calories, 19 g fat, 8 g saturated fat, 463 mg sodium, 51 g carbohydrates, 34 g protein.

SERVING SUGGESTIONS:

Serve with rice or tortillas and topped with avocado, cheese, and pickled jalapenos.

TIP:

The juice of one lemon and one lime can be used in place of sour orange juice.

PANAMA
ARROZ CON POLLO

NEARLY EVERY COUNTRY IN CENTRAL AMERICA HAS ITS OWN VERSION OF arroz con pollo (rice with chicken), the regional spin on the Spanish paella (p. 77). In the Panama canal zone this luxe one-pot dish is made with annatto (never saffron), green olives, and capers.

4 chicken leg quarters
1 large onion, chopped
1 red bell pepper, seeded and chopped
1 green bell pepper, seeded and chopped
2 cloves garlic, crushed
1 tsp. annatto powder
Olive oil, for frying and sautéing
One 15-oz. can crushed tomatoes
One 6-oz can tomato paste
1 qt. chicken broth
3 c. white rice
One 8-oz. jar pimientos, drained and sliced
One 8-oz. jar green olives, drained
½ c. capers, drained
½ c. fresh parsley, chopped
2 bay leaves
Chopped cilantro, for serving
Salt and pepper, to taste

Heat oil a large oven-safe Dutch oven over medium-high heat. Add chicken and cook until brown on all sides, about 7-8 minutes. Remove chicken and add onions, bell peppers, garlic, and annatto. Sauté until onion is translucent, about 5 minutes.

Add tomatoes, tomato paste, broth, pimientos, olives, capers, parsley, and bay leaves to pot and bring to a boil. Remove from heat and stir in rice.

Preheat oven to 350 degrees. Cover pot, place in oven, and cook for 30 minutes. Garnish with cilantro, season with salt and pepper, and serve.

Per serving: 808 calories, 38 g fat, 8 g saturated fat, 2224 mg sodium, 70 g carbohydrates, 48 g protein.

SERVING SUGGESTION:

Serve with cooked asparagus.

VARIATIONS:

Add carrots, green peas, or celery along with tomatoes.

PARAGUAY
PIRA CALDO

2 / 2 / 2
COOK TIME: 30 MINUTES
ACTIVE PREP TIME: 10 MINUTES
MAKES 4-6 SERVINGS

BETWEEN 1864 AND 1870, PARAGUAY FOUGHT A VIOLENT WAR AGAINST THE Triple Alliance of Brazil, Argentina, and Uruguay. In the end, Paraguay was devastated by its better-equipped rivals, losing over half its population as a result. The war also made food scarce, and necessity brokered the creation of pira caldo (*pira* meaning "fish" in the native Guarani language, and *caldo* meaning "broth" in Spanish). This simple but nutritious protein- and calorie-rich soup became the cornerstone of Paraguayan cuisine during and after the war.

1 lb. whole cod, flounder, or sea bass, cut into 2-inch pieces
2 poblano peppers, seeded and chopped
1 large onion, chopped
Lard (traditional) or olive oil, for sautéing
5 Roma tomatoes, seeded and chopped

3 carrots, peeled and sliced

5 cloves garlic, minced

2 red chilies, seeded and diced (optional)

1 c. white wine

1 bay leaf

2 c. water, divided

1 c. whole milk

1 Tbsp. dried oregano

1 c. mozzarella or Oaxaca cheese, shredded, for serving

Chopped fresh parsley, for serving

Heat lard or olive oil in a Dutch oven over medium-high heat. Sauté poblano peppers and onion for 5 minutes or until onion is translucent. Add tomatoes, carrots, garlic, and red chilies (if using). Reduce heat to medium and cook 5 minutes longer.

Place fish on top of vegetables at the bottom of the pot. Reduce heat to medium-low, cover, and simmer for another 5 minutes, stirring very occasionally so that the vegetables do not stick to the pot. Add wine and bay leaf to pot and stir, scraping bottom of pot to pick up any brown bits.

Add 1 c. water to the pot and simmer over medium-low heat for about 2 minutes. Add remaining water and simmer for 2 minutes longer. Add milk and oregano and simmer for 5 minutes, stirring frequently, until soup has thickened.

Divide soup between 4-6 bowls and garnish with cheese and parsley, stirring so that cheese melts evenly into the soup.

Per serving: 296 calories, 10 g fat, 5 g saturated fat, 257 mg sodium, 19 g carbohydrates, 25 g protein.

VARIATION:

Pira caldo is traditionally cooked and served with bones and fins. If you prefer, use filets instead of whole fish.

PERU
CEVICHE

1 / 2 / 3
ACTIVE PREP TIME: 15 MINUTES
INACTIVE PREP TIME: 25 MINUTES
MAKES 4-6 SERVINGS

CEVICHE HAS BECOME A POPULAR DISH THROUGHOUT SOUTH AND CENTRAL America, as well as in the United States, and each region has its own variation. But nowhere is it more beloved than in Peru, the country where it originated. The Peruvian government has declared the dish a part of Peru's national heritage, celebrated with its own holiday. Since ceviche is essentially raw seafood, it is important to prepare it safely. This includes flash-freezing the fish at -4 degrees Fahrenheit for at least a week before making the dish (or using fresh fish labeled "sashimi-grade," which has already been flash-frozen). Ceviche should not be eaten by people who are pregnant or in compromised health.

1 lb. sea bass or red snapper filets, sliced into small pieces
½ lb. medium-sized shrimp, sliced into small pieces
Salted water, for soaking
3 cloves garlic, minced
1 stalk celery, finely chopped, divided
1 small red bell pepper, finely chopped, divided
1 manzato, rocoto, or habanero chili, seeded and minced
½ c. fresh cilantro, finely chopped, divided
1 red onion, thinly sliced
2-½ c. fresh lime juice
One 1-inch piece ginger, peeled and minced
2 Tbsp. evaporated milk

Soak seafood in salted water for 15 minutes. Drain fish, reserving water, and combine with garlic, ½ stalk celery, ½ bell pepper, chili pepper, and ¼ c. cilantro. Season with salt and pepper. Place onions in soaking water.

Combine lime juice, a few pieces of fish, ginger, and remaining celery, bell pepper, and cilantro in a blender. Pulse until blended. Pour lime juice mixture over seafood and allow to sit for 10 minutes.

Add evaporated milk and stir. Drain onions from soaking water and serve immediately with ceviche.

Per serving: 437 calories, 8 g fat, 2 g saturated fat, 353 mg sodium, 14 g carbohydrates, 75 g protein.

SERVING SUGGESTIONS:

Serve with cooked sweet potato and corn on the cob. In Peru, a small glass of ceviche marinade is served before the actual dish as an appetizer.

SAINT KITTS AND NEVIS COOK-UP

1 / 2 / 2
COOK TIME: 1 HOUR, 30 MINUTES
ACTIVE PREP TIME: 10 MINUTES
INACTIVE PREP TIME: 8 HOURS
MAKES 6 SERVINGS

IN THE CARIBBEAN, COOK-UP IS A CLASSIC PEASANT DISH, COOKED IN ONE POT at the end of the week when meat and other ingredients are scarce. Anything that is available can be added to this dish, including meat, vegetables, or herbs. Pigeon peas, known in the United States as black-eyed peas, and rice are the only universal ingredients.

3 lbs. chicken (dark meat), shredded
Oil, for frying
1 large onion, chopped, divided
2 Tbsp. fresh thyme, divided
1 c. dried black-eyed peas
2 c. water, plus more for soaking and cooking

One 15-oz. can coconut milk

2 c. long-grain rice

¼ c. fresh basil, coarsely chopped

1 small tomato, peeled, seeded, and chopped

2 green onions, sliced diagonally

1 Scotch bonnet pepper

Salt and pepper, to taste

Place black-eyed peas in enough cold water to cover. Allow to soak for 8 hours or overnight. Drain and rinse peas.

Heat oil in a Dutch oven over medium-high heat. Add chicken and fry until lightly browned but not fully cooked, about 3-4 minutes. Remove from pot and set aside. Add more oil to pot and sauté half of onion and 1 Tbsp. thyme for 5 minutes or until onion is translucent. Add peas and stir. Cook until peas are warmed, about 2 minutes.

Add enough water to cover peas by about 1 inch. Reduce heat and simmer uncovered for about 45 minutes or until peas are mostly cooked (but not completely tender). Add chicken, coconut milk, rice, remaining onion and thyme, basil, tomato, green onions, and Scotch bonnet pepper and season with salt and pepper. Bring to a boil, cover, and cook over high heat for about 5 minutes. Reduce heat to low and simmer for 30 minutes longer or until all liquid has evaporated. Allow to rest for 10 minutes, then fluff and serve.

Per serving: 675 calories, 14 g fat, 6 g saturated fat, 168 mg sodium, 59 g carbohydrates, 73 g protein.

VARIATION:

Use beef brisket in place of some or all of the chicken.

TIP:

One can of cooked black-eyed peas, drained and rinsed, can be used in place of dried peas; adjust cooking time accordingly.

SAINT LUCIA
PETIT PITON

1 / 1 / 2
COOK TIME: 35 MINUTES
ACTIVE PREP TIME: 10 MINUTES
MAKES 4 SERVINGS

TWO MEMORABLE FEATURES OF SAINT LUCIA'S GEOGRAPHY ARE THE volcanic spires Gros Piton and Petit Piton. Together, they have helped make the Caribbean island a sought-after destination for hikers seeking great views. Petit Piton, slightly smaller than its partner, gives its name to Saint Lucia's national dish, a citrus-infused stir-fry made from local ingredients (wherever "local" is to the cook, that is).

1 lb. ground beef
1 onion, chopped
2 Tbsp. butter
Olive oil, for sautéing
1 Tbsp. fresh marjoram
½ tsp. celery salt
½ tsp. fennel seed
5 medium-sized red potatoes, quartered
2 carrots, chopped
½ c. water
2 c. asparagus spears, chopped
½ c. fresh parsley, chopped
Salt and pepper, to taste
2 lemons or limes, halved

Heat butter and olive oil in a Dutch oven over medium-high heat. Add onion and sauté until translucent, about 5 minutes. Add beef and cook until browned, about 6-7 minutes longer. Drain meat and return to pan.

Add marjoram, celery salt, and fennel seed and mix to combine with beef and onion mixture. Add potatoes, carrots and water. Reduce heat to medium, cover, and simmer for about 15 minutes. Add asparagus and parsley and continue to simmer about 5 minutes longer or until asparagus is tender but still crisp and bright green in color. Add water to pot if necessary. Season with salt and pepper, drizzle with fresh lemon or lime juice, and serve.

Per serving: 528 calories, 17 g fat, 7 g saturated fat, 163 mg sodium, 54 g carbohydrates, 42 g protein.

SERVING SUGGESTIONS:

Serve with rice or crusty bread.

VARIATIONS:

Use ground lamb, pork, or turkey in place of beef. Any and all vegetables can be used in this recipe.

SAINT VINCENT AND THE GRENADINES DUCUNA

2 / 1 / 3
COOK TIME: 45 MINUTES
ACTIVE PREP TIME: 20 MINUTES
MAKES 4 SERVINGS

THE NATIONAL FOOD (AND SYMBOL) OF SAINT VINCENT AND THE Grenadines is breadfruit, a crop brought to the islands from Polynesia in the late eighteenth century. But starchy vegetables, and especially sweet potatoes, are also common ingredients in the nation's dishes. Sweet potatoes are served fried, mashed, and baked into breads. Ducuna, a sweet steamed dumpling, blends grated sweet potatoes with flour and spices.

2 large sweet potatoes, finely grated
½ c. sugar
2-½ c. all-purpose flour

½ c. raisins, finely chopped
¼ tsp. salt
¼ tsp. ground allspice
¼ tsp. ground cinnamon
Water, for boiling
4 slices thick-cut bacon (optional)
Oil, for frying (optional)

Combine sweet potato and sugar in a small bowl. Blend in flour, raisins, salt, allspice, and cinnamon to make a dough. Divide dough into 4 portions and place each portion on a square piece of aluminum foil. Fold foil over dough and seal edges to form 4 packets.

Bring water to a boil in a large pot. Place packets in boiling water, reduce heat to medium-high, and cook for 45 minutes.

While ducuna are cooking, heat oil in a skillet over medium-high heat (if using bacon). Fry bacon until crisp, drain on paper towels, and chop into large pieces. Unwrap ducuna and serve with bacon.

Per serving: 462 calories, 1 g fat, 0 g saturated fat, 205 mg sodium, 107 g carbohydrates, 9 g protein.

VARIATIONS:

Ducuna is traditionally wrapped in banana leaves instead of foil and tied with rattan. Add 1 c. of sweetened coconut flakes along with sweet potatoes if desired.

SURINAME
SURINAMESE CHICKEN
AND RICE

1 / 3 / 2
COOK TIME: 1 HOUR, 40 MINUTES
ACTIVE PREP TIME: 15 MINUTES
MAKES 4 SERVINGS

THE ONLY DUTCH COLONY IN SOUTH AMERICA, SURINAME IS OFTEN GROUPED with the nearby Dutch Antilles (Aruba, Curaçao, and the Saint Maarten Islands) rather than with the rest of South America. From the beginning, Suriname's economy was plantation-based, and after the abolition of slavery in 1863 many migrant workers from the Far and Near East were recruited to work there. As a result, while Suriname's population is small it is also among the world's most diverse. Indonesians form one of Suriname's largest ethnic communities, and this spicy national dish includes Indonesian ingredients such as ketjap manis (sweet soy sauce) and sambal oelek (chili paste).

1 lb. bone-in chicken pieces
½ c. all-purpose flour
2 onions, chopped
1 leek, chopped
1 green bell pepper, chopped
Oil, for frying
3 Tbsp. tomato paste
2 Tbsp. ketjap manis
1 Tbsp. sambal oelek
Chicken broth or water, to cover
1 c. basmati rice
1-½ c. water

Place flour in a shallow dish and coat chicken until covered on both sides. Set aside.

Heat a small amount of oil in a heavy skillet. Sauté onions, leek, and bell pepper over medium heat until onions are translucent, about 5-6 minutes. Remove from pan and set aside.

Add more oil to pan and raise heat to medium-high. Add chicken to pan and cook until brown on both sides, about 2-3 minutes per side. Return vegetables to pan and add tomato paste, ketjap manis, sambal oelek, and broth or water. Stir, reduce heat to low, cover, and simmer for 1 to 1-½ hours or until chicken is fully cooked.

While chicken is cooking, boil water in a medium saucepan. Add rice, cover, reduce heat to medium-low, and simmer for 15-20 minutes or until rice is fully cooked. Serve chicken and vegetables over rice.

Per serving: 536 calories, 10 g fat, 2 g saturated fat, 109 mg sodium, 82 g carbohydrates, 30 g protein.

VARIATIONS:

Use sweet potatoes, lentils, or plantains in place of chicken for a vegetarian version.

TIPS:

If you cannot find ketjap manis, combine equal parts soy sauce and brown sugar and simmer over low heat until a thick syrup is formed. If you cannot find sambal oelek, you may substitute regular chili paste, hot sauce (preferably Sriracha), or red pepper flakes.

TRINIDAD AND TOBAGO PHOULOURIE AND CORN SOUP

2 / 2 / 2
COOK TIME: 45 MINUTES
ACTIVE PREP TIME: 20 MINUTES
INACTIVE PREP TIME: 50 MINUTES
MAKES 8 SERVINGS

IF YOU ASK ANYONE WHO'S EVER BEEN TO TRINIDAD AND TOBAGO TO describe the country's cuisine, they will almost certainly mention its street food. Trinidad and Tobago is one place where world-class dishes can be eaten directly from a stand or cart. Two examples are phoulourie, spicy fritters that reflect the influence of Indian migrant workers, and corn soup, a common after-party treat often enjoyed late at night outside the islands' fierce dance clubs.

For phoulourie:
2 tsp. yeast
1 c. warm water
2 c. yellow split pea flour
2 scallions (white parts only), finely chopped
2 cloves garlic, finely minced
1 tsp. ground turmeric
1 tsp. salt
¼ tsp. ground cumin
¼ tsp. cayenne pepper
Vegetable oil, for frying

Combine yeast and warm water. Allow to stand for 10 minutes, and then add flour, scallions, garlic, turmeric, salt, cumin, and cayenne pepper and stir until a dough is formed. Place dough in a large bowl, cover with a damp towel, and allow to rise for 40 minutes.

Heat oil in a heavy skillet over high heat. Add dough in tablespoon-sized amounts to oil and fry in batches for 2-3 minutes or until brown. Remove from oil and drain on paper towels. Serve hot.

Per serving: 102 calories, 7 g fat, 1 g saturated fat, 294 mg sodium, 7 g carbohydrates, 3 g protein.

For corn soup:
1 lb. salt pork, chopped
1 onion, finely chopped
1 sprig fresh thyme
2 scallions, finely chopped
1 carrot, sliced
½ stalk celery, finely chopped
1 jalapeno pepper, finely diced (optional)
4 ears fresh corn, cut into 1-inch pieces
2 sweet potatoes, peeled and chopped
2 c. chicken broth
One 15-oz. can creamed corn
One 15-oz. can coconut milk
Chopped parsley, for serving

In a heavy Dutch oven, fry salt pork over medium-high heat until meat is brown and fat has cooked off, about 5 minutes. Remove pork from pan, leaving fat. Reduce heat to medium. Add onions, garlic, and thyme and sauté until fragrant, about 1 minute. Add scallions, carrot, celery, and jalapeno pepper (if using) and cook for another 5 minutes or until onions are translucent. Add fresh corn and sweet potatoes and cook for 2 minutes longer.

Add broth, creamed corn, and coconut milk and increase heat to high. Stir well and bring to a boil. Reduce heat to medium-low, return salt pork to pot, and simmer for 15 minutes or until sweet potatoes are soft. Garnish with chopped parsley and serve.

Per serving: 530 calories, 42 g fat, 16 g saturated fat, 351 mg sodium, 30 g carbohydrates, 26 g protein.

SERVING SUGGESTION:
Phoulourie is traditionally served with mango or peach chutney.

THE UNITED STATES ROASTED TURKEY AND CORNBREAD DRESSING

3 / 1 / 1
COOK TIME: 3 HOURS, 25 MINUTES
ACTIVE PREP TIME: 20 MINUTES
INACTIVE PREP TIME:
1 DAY, 5 HOURS, 40 MINUTES
MAKES 8-10 SERVINGS

HOW IS IT POSSIBLE TO CHOOSE A SINGLE DISH FOR THE UNITED STATES?

Barbecue, lobster rolls, hamburgers, chili con carne, fried chicken, Coney Island hot dogs, jambalaya, and Cobb salad are all worthy contenders. But the one dish that is truly American—and eaten by 88 percent of all Americans at least once per year—is turkey and dressing. The turkey, a bird native to the Americas, received its name from the country whose ports ships often passed through while transporting the birds to Europe. Whether roasted, smoked, or fried, turkey is traditionally served at Thanksgiving with a breadcrumb-based side dish known as dressing, stuffing, or filling depending on the location. Each part of the United States also has its own dressing variations; cornbread dressing is most popular in the southeastern region.

One 10-lb. turkey
2 Tbsp. kosher salt
1 Tbsp. freshly ground black pepper
1 lemon, quartered, with zest
3 sprigs fresh rosemary

1 bunch fresh sage
1 large head garlic, peeled and cut in half crosswise, divided
2 c. dry white wine or chicken broth (more if needed)
2 small onions, peeled and quartered, divided
3 bay leaves
Melted butter, for basting

Using damp paper towels, clean surface of turkey and remove giblets and neck. Pat surface of turkey dry. Combine salt, pepper, and lemon zest and rub over surface of turkey. Place lemon, rosemary, sage, and half of garlic in the turkey's cavity.

Set turkey in a large roasting pan and cover with plastic wrap. Refrigerate for at least 24 hours. Remove plastic wrap and allow to chill for 4 hours longer. Take turkey from refrigerator and allow to sit at room temperature for 1 hour.

Preheat oven to 450 degrees. In. a separate large roasting pan, add remaining garlic, wine or broth, one onion, and bay leaves. Transfer turkey to second pan, making sure that breast side is facing up. Place second onion in turkey cavity and brush turkey with enough melted butter to coat surface. Cover turkey with aluminum foil.

Roast turkey in oven for 30 minutes. Reduce oven temperature to 350 degrees, remove aluminum foil, and insert meat thermometer in thickest part of the thigh. Continue roasting for 2 hours or until an internal temperature of 165 degrees is reached. Check turkey periodically and add more wine or broth when needed.

Per serving: 492 calories, 21 g fat, 7 g saturated fat, 1703 mg sodium, 3 g carbohydrates, 58 g protein.

For dressing:
1 c. yellow cornmeal
1 c. all-purpose flour
¼ c. plus 2 Tbsp. butter, divided, plus more for greasing skillet and sautéing
¼ c. sugar
1 Tbsp. baking powder
2 tsp. salt
1 c. buttermilk

5 eggs, divided
3 onions, finely chopped
4 stalks celery, finely chopped
1-½ tsp. dried sage
1 tsp. poultry seasoning
½ tsp. pepper
½ c. whole milk
2 c. chicken broth

After removing turkey from refrigerator, preheat oven to 400 degrees. Grease a 9-inch cast iron skillet with butter. Melt ¼ c. of the butter.

Combine cornmeal, flour, sugar, baking powder, and 1 tsp. salt in a medium bowl using a pastry blender. Mix in buttermilk, 2 eggs, and melted butter and stir just until combined. Pour batter into pan and bake for 20-25 minutes or until golden. Remove cornbread from pan after 10 minutes, and set aside to cool while cooking turkey.

Heat butter in a skillet over medium-high heat. Add onions and celery and cook just until soft, about 3-4 minutes. Add sage, poultry seasoning, remaining salt, and pepper.

Break cornbread into crumbs. Whisk together remaining eggs and milk and add to cornbread along with broth. Stir in onion mixture and place in a greased baking dish. Slice remaining 2 Tbsp. butter and place evenly on top of dressing.

Thirty minutes before turkey is finished cooking, place dressing in oven and cook for 30 minutes or until brown on top. Remove turkey and dressing from oven and allow both to rest for 30 minutes before serving.

Per serving: 269 calories, 12 g fat, 6 g saturated fat, 822 mg sodium, 34 g carbohydrates, 9 g protein.

SERVING SUGGESTIONS:

Serve with cranberry sauce, mashed potatoes, roasted vegetables, and pumpkin pie.

TIPS:

Pre-made cornbread can be used in place of freshly baked cornbread; an equal amount of loaf bread can be used as well. To make a gravy for the turkey using the turkey drippings: Simmer giblets and neck over medium-low heat for 1 hour. Remove and set aside, reserving boiling water. Remove drippings from roasting pan and allow fat to separate naturally. Heat about 1 c. of fat in a heavy skillet; add ½ c. flour and stir constantly until a roux is formed. Add remaining drippings, 1 qt. chicken broth, and chopped giblets and neck meat to skillet. Cook for 10 minutes or until reduced by half, adding more broth if needed.

URUGUAY
CHIVITO

2 / 2 / 1
COOK TIME: 30 MINUTES
ACTIVE PREP TIME: 15 MINUTES
MAKES 4 SERVINGS

THE WORD CHIVITO IS SPANISH FOR "LITTLE GOAT," BUT THE URUGUAYAN specialty known as the chivito is made from beef; like their Argentine neighbors, Uruguayans are known for their beef consumption. Now a national dish, the chivito was invented at the El Mejillón restaurant in Punta del Este on New Year's Eve of 1944, when a customer asked for a dish made from goat meat. With no goat meat on hand, the chef invented a new roast beef sandwich on the spot, naming it in honor of the customer's request.

1 lb. beef tenderloin, cut in 4 horizontal slices
2 red bell peppers
1 tsp. kosher salt
Olive oil, for frying
4 thick slices pancetta
4 slices ham, cooked
4 eggs
4 large, soft hamburger buns (seedless)
½ c. mayonnaise or aioli
4 thick slices queso blanco or other white cheese
½ head Boston Bibb lettuce, torn

2 tomatoes, sliced

¼ c. green olives, chopped (optional)

Preheat oven to 400 degrees. Place red bell peppers on a lightly oiled baking sheet and roast for 20 minutes or until blackened, turning once. If desired, toast hamburger buns in oven during last 5 minutes of roasting.

While bell peppers are roasting, pound meat with a mallet until each slice is about ¼-inch thick. Season with salt.

Heat olive oil in a large cast-iron skillet over medium-high heat. Cook pancetta until crisp, about 1 minute on each side; set aside. Add steak to pan and cook to taste, about 2 minutes per side for medium-rare.

Heat more olive oil in a separate skillet over medium-high heat. Fry eggs until cooked to taste (over-medium or -hard).

When bell peppers are finished roasting, remove from oven and remove skins (which should be soft and easy to peel off) as well as stems and seeds. Cut each pepper in half, and pat pepper halves dry with a paper towel.

To assemble sandwiches, spread mayonnaise or aioli on both sides of buns. Place a lettuce leaf and steak slice on each bottom bun, followed by a slice of ham, olives (if using), pancetta, fried egg, roasted bell pepper, and tomato. Top with cheese and top bun. Slice in half to serve.

Per serving: 797 calories, 45 g fat, 14 g saturated fat, 2021 mg sodium, 38 g carbohydrates, 61 g protein.

SERVING SUGGESTION:

Serve with French fries.

VARIATIONS:

Use bacon in place of pancetta and/or ham; use Canadian bacon for a *chivito canadiense.*

VENEZUELA
PABELLÓN CRIOLLO

2 / 1 / 1
COOK TIME: 1 HOUR, 50 MINUTES
ACTIVE PREP TIME: 15 MINUTES
INACTIVE PREP TIME: 8 HOURS
MAKES 4 SERVINGS

WITH A 1,700-MILE COASTLINE, VENEZUELA IS BY FAR THE LARGEST country of Caribbean South America. Like most Caribbean nations, its cuisine combines indigenous, African, and several European influences. Pabellón criollo, the Venezuelan national dish, shares similarities with other Caribbean specialties such as gallo pinto (p. 302) and ropa vieja (p. 304). While usually made with beef, in Venezuela capybara or crocodile meat is occasionally used in pabellón criollo.

2 lbs. flank or skirt steak, cut into four pieces
Olive oil, for sautéing
1 large onion, chopped
4 cloves garlic, finely minced
1 qt. beef broth
One 15-oz. can stewed tomatoes
2 tsp. salt, divided
½ tsp. ground cumin
1 large red bell pepper, seeded and chopped
1 c. white rice
1-¾ c. water

Heat olive oil in a Dutch oven over medium-high heat. Add half of onion and garlic and sauté until onion is transparent, about 5 minutes. Add steak, broth, tomatoes, 1 tsp. salt, and cumin. Reduce heat to low and simmer, uncovered, for at least 1 hour or until meat is thoroughly cooked and very tender. Remove steak from pot and shred with two forks.

Place remaining onion and garlic in a blender or food processor along with red bell pepper. Puree until coarsely ground.

Heat additional olive oil in a heavy skillet over medium-high heat. Add shredded meat and cook until brown on both sides, about 3-4 minutes. Return meat to pot along with onion and red pepper puree. Bring to a boil, reduce heat to medium-low, and simmer until most of the liquid is evaporated, about 20 minutes.

Bring water to a boil in a medium saucepan. Add rice, reduce heat to low, cover, and simmer for 15-20 minutes or until rice is cooked.

Per serving: 738 calories, 28 g fat, 9 g saturated fat, 2496 mg sodium, 47 g carbohydrates, 70 g protein.

SERVING SUGGESTIONS:

Serve with black beans and fried plantains.

VARIATION:

For *pabellón a caballo*, add a fried egg on top.

Made in the USA
Middletown, DE
23 October 2023